DATE DUE

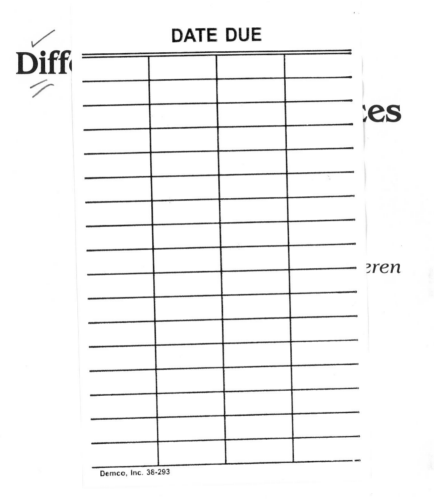

Diff...   ...es

...eren

The works contained herein are, to the best of the publisher's knowledge, original works created solely by the contributors herein. Contributors have represented to the publisher that the stories are true, and publisher disclaims any liability for false or misleading information within the stories.

To all persons with a mental illness who never had a voice

Table of Contents

To perceive, to speak, even on subjects inherently cruel—
To speak boldly even when the facts were, in themselves, painful or dire—
Seemed to introduce among us some new action,
Having to do with human obsession, human compassion . . ."

Louise Gluck

Preface

Outsider Press is a not-for-profit publishing house with the sole mission of publishing and promoting literary works written by persons with a mental illness or by associates of persons with a mental illness. It was first conceived while two siblings, both with a mental illness, were hiking through the hardwood forest of western Michigan. Outsider Press was incorporated in the State of Michigan in September 2004 and was granted tax-exempt status by the Internal Revenue Service in May 2005. We conducted an exhaustive search for funding from private foundations and, partially because of a downturn in the economy, we were not able to secure grant money. We were also confronted with the dilemma that few foundations want to fund organizations that do not have track records, and we discovered that many private foundations specifically do not want to fund publishing endeavors.

Regardless, we persevered, and we went about the work of locating persons with mental illness who wanted to share their story. To do this, we held a national writing contest, conducted writing workshops at Community Mental Health outlets and at Clubhouses, and interviewed homeless veterans suffering from mental illness.

We discovered that there are many people with disabilities trying to gain recognition as artists and as writers. As an individual working diligently toward successfully establishing

Outsider Press, I had to ask myself, "When persons with a mental illness turn to the arts, do they open themselves to a world of false hope?" In trying to come to grips with this question, I realized that there is a class struggle, not only among those who choose to pursue the arts as a career but, more specifically, among artists who have a mental illness. Perhaps what is needed is more outlets for the literature and art of the mentally ill; outlets similar to gay and lesbian bookstores.

Many individuals diagnosed with a severe and persistent mental illness live in poverty (Torrey, 61, 62), and debate continues as to whether poverty causes mental illness or mental illness causes poverty. One recent study claims that poverty can cause mental illness (Hudson, 3–18). As obvious as it may seem, my own experience is that poverty works in both directions. That is, my poverty caused me to be depressed and to have anxiety while my mental illness made it difficult for me to integrate into mainstream American life. After being diagnosed with mental illness, I lived in constant fear of losing all my financial resources. There are many relevant questions relating to impoverishment of the mentally ill: Is it wrong for mentally ill persons to draw disability checks rather than work in fast food restaurants? Should mentally ill people be forced into menial labor rather then receive disability allotments? Is it wrong to accuse mentally ill people on disability of being lazy? As Dream Merchant writes:

> The clouds of poverty are beginning to pour. My dreams of becoming a successful author, a musician and an entrepreneur and of getting off disability permanently and never missing it are all delusions. . . .

Our organization decided to emphasize literature concerned with social justice issues related to mental illness, including poverty, homelessness, unemployment, discrimination in the workforce, and the exorbitant cost of medical care and medications. Some of the stories we chose to include in this anthology highlight the tragedy of once ambitious young men and women whose career plans were never realized after the onset of mental illness.

We include a story about how one mentally ill individual struggled to support himself his entire life by silk-screening and selling T-shirts. His life consisted of sitting in the cold at the farmers' market, braving the elements, while never being guaranteed a paycheck and not being able to afford adequate medical care. His lack of proper medical care eventually led to his demise. He spent his life in fear of losing his freedom to a State hospital.

Although there are mental health workers today who are dedicated to providing quality medical treatment for the mentally ill, the history of conditions in State mental hospitals in America has been one of neglect and abuse by staff members (Whitaker, 4, 35, 69–70). In the past, State mental hospitals made difficult lives even more unbearable with lengthy incarcerations. Today, the fear of permanently losing one's freedom to the State is often unfounded. In present day America, mentally ill patients are often treated and released from State hospitals as quickly as possible to avoid the exorbitant cost of treatment for the uninsured. While it is true that State hospitals were terrible places to be, many mental health patients who were formerly residents of State hospitals are now homeless and unwanted residents of our county jails and State prisons (Torrey, 13–42).

The discovery of Thorazine as a treatment for mental illness is often cited as the stimulus that led to the closing of State psychiatric hospitals. In fact, conservative politicians were in favor of closing State hospitals long before it was discovered that certain forms of mental illness could be treated by antipsychotic medication. The reason that numerous State mental hospitals were closed was because conservative politicians thought State mental hospitals were too expensive to maintain, while liberal politicians wanted to give mental patients more liberty by treating them at Community Mental Health outlets.

Just prior to his assassination, John F. Kennedy passed legislation creating Community Mental Health (CMH) centers throughout the nation; these centers would be responsible for treating the mentally ill. The mentally ill were to be taken out of State mental hospitals and treated as outpatients. When State mental hospitals were closed, medical care for former patients was supposed to be delegated to CMH centers throughout the nation (Grob, 249–278); the CMH centers were to be funded by the Federal government and managed by local governments. However, the initiative for CMH centers was underfunded and adequate treatment for the mentally ill never materialized. With the closing of State hospitals, many of the mentally ill were forsaken and the lack of funding for CMH resulted in a myriad of former State hospital patients becoming homeless.

What happened to CMH? There was little money allocated to CMH during the Johnson years, due to the expense of the Vietnam War (Grob, 262, 279). The Johnson years were followed by many years of Republican administrations that were opposed, for ideological reasons, to the formation of CMH centers (Grob, 279, 280–287). Conservative politicians viewed government-funded CMH centers as socialistic and therefore they were ideologically opposed to them. As a consequence, at many community mental health outlets today, patients are billed for services rendered.

CMH centers were originally intended to treat people with serious and persistent mental illnesses. Instead, many professionals in CMH centers chose to counsel people experiencing difficult life situations, such as divorce, or who were experiencing work-related or other situational types of depression. Organizations such as the National Alliance on Mental Illness (NAMI) have strongly advocated for CMH resources to be used first and foremost for the treatment of persons with chronic mental illness (Torrey, 183–188).

Regarding the homeless mentally ill, the work of liberal politicians has resulted in the mentally ill being given the right to refuse treatment (Torrey, 145–146; Arrigo, 14–17). While involuntary hospitalization is a highly controversial issue among consumers of mental health services and their family members, one solution for the homeless mentally ill is to give mental hospitals the power of recall and the power to deny release to those who refuse treatment. But is such a policy oppressive and prone to abuse? Many people do not understand that it is common for mentally ill people who are on the streets to have no insight into their disease and to believe that their delusions are real (Torrey, 156–157).

In my own life, while I was never truly homeless, I did face financial ruin because of mental illness. I believed my delusions were real. When my illness first set in, I was 23 years old and in graduate school in California. My mother was dying of breast cancer at the time. (My father had passed from cancer when I was a child.) At the time of my mother's funeral, my sister and other siblings noticed that I was acting strangely. My sister told me, years later, that at first she thought I was just exhausted from a difficult schedule and from the intense pressure I was under in a highly competitive chemistry program at the University of California at Santa Barbara. She revealed that my erratic behavior while I was home for the funeral included claims that I was being followed by government officials and by the Mafia. My sister also said that, at that time, my siblings found my delusions to be perplexing. She tells me that she tried to reason with me by pointing out to me that the people I saw at the grocery store or on the street, whom I thought were following me or were prostitutes hired by the Mafia, were only innocent members of the community. She has also divulged to me that her attempts to reason with me were futile and that I became very angry with her for not believing my delusions were real. I even accused her of being involved in some sort of plot against me. At the time of my mother's funeral, a yellow rose arrived at my mother's house from Suzie, a girlfriend of mine. My sister called Suzie, who was in California, and asked her if she had noticed me acting strangely. Suzie told my sister that, indeed, I had been acting strangely and that I had refused to see a psychiatrist. The truth is that I was difficult to deal with because I, like many mentally ill people, had poor insight into my disease and thought my delusions were real—and no one could convince me otherwise. Also at play here was that members of my family and others who were intellectually opposed to psychology for religious reasons had influenced me.

Another issue that the general public does not understand is why so many mentally ill persons are noncompliant when it comes to medication. One reason for noncompliance is that antipsychotic medications cause uncomfortable side effects such as extreme restlessness and fatigue, considerable weight gain, and sexual dysfunction. As patients take the prescribed medication for extended periods, some of the side effects diminish. Consumers under managed care (Health Maintenance Organizations, or HMOs) are often prescribed older medications because these medications are less costly (Torrey, 123). These older medications have more side effects than the newer, more expensive medications. Patients who discontinue taking antipsychotic medication often experience a brief period of well being, during which they think they are well, only to relapse a few weeks later.

Persons with chronic mental illness need much more than medication if they are to experience any sort of meaningful life. Diseases such as schizophrenia and bipolar disorder most often occur during young adulthood and interrupt college educations and career plans. My career as a scientist was virtually ruined by the onset of mental illness. Vocational training for the mentally ill is practically nonexistent and most programs provide services that mentally ill persons can do for themselves (Brooks, 66).

In this anthology, *Different People, Different Voices,* a story appears about a mentally ill mother who lost her children because she was having trouble maintaining her home. Wouldn't it be much more humane and less costly to society in the long run to give her assistance in maintaining her home rather than taking her children from her? I maintain that, with certain supports in place, parents with a mental illness can provide their children with satisfactory care; however, funding to provide for these sorts of programs is not easily obtained.

Independent living is an issue for many people who suffer from mental illness. People with mental illness can feel a loss of autonomy when they are forced to live in a group home. One writer who requested not to be published expressed that he had lost his freedom because his driver's license was revoked. When driving privileges are revoked, one is faced with a choice between a small town, where one can get around because most things are within a short distance, versus a large world, where one lives in a location that has a satisfactory mass transit system. For many, the problem with the second option is that big cities are too expensive to live in while subsisting on a government stipend.

Firsthand experience has shown me that the staff at psychiatric hospitals often treat adult patients like children. From personal experience, I can also state that once a person is committed to a psychiatric hospital the tendency is to overmedicate the patient to avoid a cost-prohibitive, lengthy hospital stay. Also, patients who have been involved in any kind of violence prior to hospitalization are often overmedicated because psychiatrists fear a patient may be released while he or she is dangerous to him or herself or to others (Arrigo, 12). Hospital health care workers can become callused and lack compassion. Often, adversarial relationships between staff members and patients, much like the ones that exist between prison guards and inmates, are put into play.

My own involvement with mental illness has led me to realize that people without prior experience with mental illness often do not know how to navigate through the mental health care system. My sister has relayed to me that she would have acted differently on my behalf with the knowledge she now has regarding mental illness. Mental patients often choose their doctors potluck; they entrust their care and their lives to doctors that they do not know, doctors who may look at the world much differently than they do.

My own belief is that psychiatric patients need to be vested in their treatments. In my opinion, physicians and patients need to communicate with one another before serious interventions are taken. For cases in which electric shock therapy is used, patients need to know exactly what they're getting into before agreeing to treatment. Electric shock therapy is controversial and, although it can be successful in treating severe depression, it also causes memory loss. In my own case, after shock therapy was administered I did not remember my paranoid delusions, and I therefore saw no reason to take anti-psychotic medications that were prescribed to prevent my delusions from returning. Furthermore, as discussed above, my experience with the prescribed medicine was that it caused fatigue and extreme restlessness. So, not remembering my former delusions and experiencing terrible side effects, I was noncompliant with regard to medication. Moreover, there were complications regarding my electric shock therapy that caused me to develop severe pain on the left-hand side of my head. I was afraid of seeking treatment for fear that even more harm would be done. I should have sought the opinion of other doctors before agreeing to my treatment plan but I was under duress in a locked ward when I agreed to shock therapy. It has been said that shock therapy is necessary in medication-resistant patients. Recently, it has been found that medication-resistant depressives may respond to the antiviral drug, Amantadine, which has been used in patients thought to be infected with a virus referred to as Borna (Ferszt et al., 142–147). As a side note, I would like to mention that myself and other siblings of mine may have been exposed to a powerful form of estrogen when my mother was pregnant with us. This estrogen may be a root biological cause of my mental illness (Apfel and Fisher, entire work).

Physicians can misdiagnose because they are not close

enough to the situation. They can downplay real physical problems that are not psychiatric as being due to improper psychiatric medication. Thus, heart or lung failure can instead be diagnosed as anxiety. Head trauma can be misdiagnosed. Furthermore, psychiatrists can dismiss real medical problems as figments of the imagination.

I also believe that alternative medicine can play an important role in recovery. My experience is that nutrition, acupuncture, cardiovascular exercise, yoga, meditation, and certain forms of prayer can all be beneficial for some people suffering from mental illness. In particular, when I engaged in a daily regimen of cardiovascular exercise, I found it to be a safe way to physically treat depression and found that it can improve rather than impair sexual function. However, over-exercising or too much cardiovascular exercise may exacerbate symptoms of mental illness by increasing levels of dopamine in the brain. In my opinion, holistic medicine can be used as an adjunct to Western psychiatric practices.

The stories in this anthology highlight the dire need for improved treatment and services provided by our mental health care system. Our current services and programs fall far short of providing what is needed for individuals living with severe and persistent mental illnesses.

Michael Van Fleteren
Outsider Press

Works Cited

Apfel, Roberta J. and Susan M. Fisher. *To Do No Harm,* New Haven: Yale University Press, 1984.

Arrigo, Bruce A. *Punishing the Mentally Ill.* Albany, NY: State University of New York Press, 2002.

Brooks, Elaine R. "The Decline of Public Health in the United States." *Mental Health, Racism, and Sexism.* Eds. Charles V. Willie, Patricia Perri Ricker, Bernard M. Kramer, and Bertram S. Brown. Pittsburgh: University of Pittsburgh Press, 1995. pp. 51–117.

Ferszt R., K.D. Kuhl, L. Bode, E.W. Serverus, B. Winzer, A. Berghofer,

G. Beelitz, B. Brodhun, B. Muller-Oerlinghausen, and H. Ludwig. "Amantadine Revisited: An Open Trial of Amantadine Treatment in Chronically Depressed Patients with Borna Disease Virus Infection." *Pharmacopsychiatry* 32 (1999):142–147.

Grob, Gerald N. *The Mad Among Us: A History of the Care of America's Mentally Ill.* New York: The Free Press, 1994.

Hudson, Christopher G. "Socioeconomic Status and Mental Illness: Tests of the Social Causation and Selection Hypothesis." *American Journal of Orthopsychiatry* 75 (2005) :3–18.

Torrey, E. Fuller. *Out of the Shadows: Confronting America's Mental Illness Crisis.* New York: John Wiley & Sons, 1997.

Whitaker, Robert. *Mad in America: Bad Science, Bad Medicine, and the Enduring Mistreatment of the Mentally Ill.* New York: Perseus Publishing, 2002.

My Mother and Me
(A Memoir)

John Laue

My father refused to tell me much about my mother, even when I was an adult, just that she wasn't the type of woman who should have had a child. At eight years old I came home from camp and she wasn't there. Dad told me that she'd had to go away. I remember shedding a tear or two, then going on as if nothing were wrong. After all, it was the 40's. In those days boys didn't cry.

Later, when he took me to visit her, it was an experience I felt rather ambivalent about. Although I was glad to see Mother, Greystone Park, The New Jersey State Hospital for the Insane, was a scary place. It consisted of several large buildings like warehouses with bars on the windows. Since anti-psychotic drugs hadn't been discovered yet these were filled with residents many of whom were bizarre in appearance, speech and/or actions.

We visited a few times over the next three years. Each time we got permission to take Mother out for an afternoon she seemed perfectly normal to me. I couldn't understand why she had to be there. Then Dad divorced her and decided to move the two of us out West. We came to California and Dad

1

married Cathy, my stepmother, who soon proved to be what I now call a "rageaholic." She even knocked him unconscious with a flung candy jar at one point. However, they stayed married. After my freshman year of high school in Salinas, California, the three of us went back to New Jersey to visit Dad's and Mother's home town, Belvidere. Cathy got into another of her rages and this time I hit her back, causing me to be left in my maternal grandmother's care until I finished high school.

All the time I'd been out West I hadn't seen my mother, but when I was left with Nanny (Mother's mother), she decided to take me to visit. However, after one or two times this ceased because, as Nanny told me, Mother got sent back to a worse ward each time she saw me. Soon I graduated from Belvidere High and Dad took me out west again where I lived with him and Cathy until I couldn't stand her. Most of the time while going to Hartnell Community College, where I edited the student newspaper and wrote articles for a local weekly paper, I lived with the family of a friend.

From there, at the University of California, Berkeley, I went on to major in psychology, a subject that had always fascinated me. At U.C. Berkeley, I worked on the literary magazine and won the Ina Coolbrith Poetry Award. Then I went to graduate school in Creative Writing at San Francisco State University, which at the time had the second best creative writing program in the country (after the University of Iowa's). I edited the school's literary magazine and wrote poems about being an orphan because that's how I felt. During this time I was also an Associate Editor of *San Francisco Review*, a national literary journal.

I didn't hear from my mother until a few years later, after I'd had a brief marriage and divorce and a death experience that was the beginning of my own psychosis. I was afraid of being committed because I thought that, like Mother, I'd never get out, so twice when the police came for me I hid from them. I was living alone in San Francisco and was in the therapy group of Dr. David Shupp, the head of San Francisco's Mental Health system who I called my "second father," when I got a rather pleasant letter from Mother, the first in many years. I can't remember the content but can still envision the stationery, which had colorful flowers on it. Then, in 1968, I was advised that she'd died while still in the institution. This didn't mean overly much to me because I'd been separated from her for so many years, but when I visited Dad and asked him again about Mother's illness he still would say very little about her. It was as if the pain was too much for him to bear.

So the mystery of my mother and her illness continued through my 20-year career as a high school teacher and counselor and into my retirement, during which I won a small national poetry award, got my first book published, and served as Chair of Santa Cruz County's Local Mental Health Board. I became an activist for mental health, developing a website, speaking to local high school health classes about mental illnesses and mental health, and even successfully lobbying in Sacramento to change the state's health curriculum framework to include more information about mental illnesses.

When I spoke to students I shared my experiences with my family including the little I knew about Mother. Often they'd ask me about her diagnosis. I would always say I thought she might have been schizophrenic or bipolar but didn't know for sure. Finally I resolved to find out what I could. Since I'd lived for 67 years, been through my own mental illness and survived two major cancer operations, I thought I ought to be able to handle whatever my father may have been protecting me from.

All the people I knew who'd known Mother were dead by that time, so I decided to go to the source and get her records from Greystone Park. To do this I had to obtain her death certificate. I sent for it and it arrived three weeks later. It listed Mother's cause of death as a myocardial infarction brought on by a blockage of the colon by a carcinoma. This much I'd been told by Dad. But also on that form was my mother's psychiatric diagnosis: "psychotic with psychopathic personality, sexual episode."

In all my experiences with her, even when visiting at the institution, she'd never by words or actions implied that she was seriously crazy. I'd spent most of my life studying psychology, had majored in it, and was still taking graduate level seminars. I'd seen several psychiatrists and been diagnosed at different times as schizophrenic, bipolar, narcissistic, and depressive, and had even had courses in clinical diagnostics myself. But I couldn't understand why my mother had been diagnosed as "psychotic."

And then there was the "psychopathic personality" portion. I'd always thought that "psychopath" was one of the worst labels a person could have. Was my mother that way? I searched my memory for evidence. Yes, there was an incident when she'd been bathing me in the kitchen sink and I'd gotten a shock from the radio that was on the lip of the sink. I'd read about psychotic mothers who killed their children. Had Mother wanted to hurt or kill me?

I did remember her saying over and over to me, "You are THE LIMIT!" One time I recalled shouting to Dad, "If she doesn't stop picking on me I'm going to jump out of the window!" I'd said this for effect rather than really wanting to do it. I'd just wished my mother would stop her harassment. Another incident I remembered was when at five years old I'd indulged in sex play with a girl of seven and told Mother about it. She became quite agitated and screamed at me, "That's the way you have babies!" I went around for months worried and upset, thinking, "I'm only five years old. How can I take care of a baby?" Yes, she was "beyond the pale" sometimes—but did this mean she was psychotic or psychopathic?

Another thought I had was that perhaps my mother, instead of being a terrible person, was merely a lesbian. I knew that in those less enlightened days homosexuality was considered a mental illness. And my mother and father's best friends were two prominent educators, my Godmother, whom I called Laloo, and her companion, Miss Anne, whom I called my "Grand-Mother." They were known as "Maiden Ladies," but after visiting them later I understood them to be a wonderful loving lesbian couple.

A final alternative I thought of for my mother's diagnosis was that perhaps she'd been promiscuous, like a female Bill Clinton. In those days men could have several affairs and come out of them pretty much unscathed by public opinion, but if a woman did this she'd have been considered a slut, perhaps even labeled a sexual psychopath. I suspected that if Mother had had affairs it might have been enough to make my father sign commitment papers for her.

I continued trying to dredge up early memories and anything else I could think of that might shed light on Mother's mental makeup, but couldn't come to any firm conclusions. Finally, after a month or so, I got a manila envelope from Greystone Park. In it were fifty-some copied pages of Mother's records. Although I suspect a few things had been omitted, such as medical records of shock treatments, which were hinted at in the material, most of the information they'd apparently used to diagnose and make decisions about her was there.

There were verbatim interviews with her and my father concerning her background and their life together, the opinions of psychiatrists, and medical records from her 23-year stay with notes on unusual incidents. I don't think I had the entire story, but I was able to piece together their reasoning for her diagnosis, the circumstances that had brought her to the institution in the first place, and form some opinions as to why she'd had to stay.

To understand her predicament, one has to know something about the era. The story commences in the early 1930's, around the time of the Great Depression. Although the plight of women in this society still is frustrating to many, for good reasons, in those days females had much less freedom and equality than they do now. Both my mother and father had been raised in the small provincial hamlet of Belvidere, New Jersey. My mother had been a sophomore at Montclair State Teachers' College when they got married, but if the college had known that she was married she would have been kept from graduating. So she and my father apparently lived apart until after she had her degree. And according to her later account, during this time she felt she was about to have a nervous breakdown but had an affair with another man, which she thought saved her.

After graduating she got a job as a school teacher, which only lasted one year because it became known that she was married. Women who were teachers, or "schoolmarms" as they were called, were expected to be single. In those early days men were considered to be the breadwinners and if a married woman were to be employed as a teacher, that would mean she was denying the job to a man who had or would have a family to support.

In 1936, I was born, and according to Dad, I was a planned child. Dad was the supervising principal of a small school district in Wanaque, New Jersey, and Mother had soon worked at several jobs including social worker, newspaper reporter, Macy's saleswoman (in New York City), and as a public accountant's office clerk. The birth had been hard for her and she'd told Dad she regretted it. She grew increasingly nervous and apparently had an eating disorder. At five foot three she weighed 218 pounds. Around 1943, she became very interested in psychoanalysis, read everything she could about it, and commenced what was probably a classical Freudian analysis in New York City.

The first psychiatrist apparently became so attached to her that he thought he shouldn't see her any more, so he recommended another analyst. While she was seeing this second fellow, she did lose weight. And she also accepted his interpretation that she was a masochist. In fact, she became obsessed with it, demanding that my father "dominate" her and beat her with a strap, which he refused to do. She said she needed this in order to have a healthy sex life and she'd made connections in the analyst's office with people who were like her. She offered Dad the alternative of them both living in the same house and leading separate lives but he refused.

In that era (actually not so long ago) Freudian psychoanalysis was practically the only type of psychology that seemed to offer hope to curious and worried individuals. It was the cutting edge of psychiatry. Nowadays we know that labeling people and focusing on determinants in their childhoods, as I believe psychoanalysis does, isn't a cure for most ills and can even cause or exacerbate mental illnesses in certain people. That may be what happened to Mother. Today she'd have a choice of several therapeutic systems, most of which would almost certainly be less damaging and more helpful than what she had.

Soon the psychoanalysis was costing more than my family could afford and my mother was going to it less often than the analyst wanted. But she was still nervous and upset, even more so than before. Finally she spent a summer in a private sanitarium, but that also was too expensive. She progressed to not wanting to be around men, since she was afraid she'd lose control and didn't believe she should have affairs when she was living with Dad. Then she joined several women's clubs and spent most of her time with them. Dad got quite angry at this because he thought she was neglecting our family, which she probably was.

Around this time she apparently became very easily irritated with me, to the point where Dad, according to his testimony, told her she'd have to leave the house if she didn't let up. Dad, in the meantime, was considering joining the army and going away, a fact which made Mother very upset. In spite of the fact that she regretted having given birth to me, she then said she wanted to have another child, but Dad thought that this was just an attempt to keep him home.

After spending almost all of her time with clubwomen,

mother became afraid of them for reasons that are unclear. She said that the only people she could be comfortable with were children, so she sat watching our little sandlot baseball games for hours. At this point, too, she was "taking vegetables from other people's gardens" because, as she put it, she was "lonely and needed affection." Finally, she apparently became unable to leave home at all and Dad convinced her to go to Greystone Park, where her intake interview revealed that she thought people were sadistically talking about her.

The above aberrations were seemingly what led to the diagnosis of "psychotic" (her paranoia about other people and inability to leave the house). The "psychopathic personality, sexual episode" seems to be based on the one affair she'd had after she'd been married. It also seems obvious to me that if she'd been assessed now, there would have been different conclusions and, of course, radically different treatment options. If she really were psychotic she'd have been put on anti-psychotic medications, as I am today, and sent home. If they'd had to hold her at the institution it wouldn't have been a very long stay. Dr. Shupp told me that in San Francisco they'd release almost everybody within four days since after that the patients were in danger of developing "an institutional psychosis."

In February 1946, she was assessed by a Doctor Skifman: "This patient was interviewed today on ward 37. She is neat, cooperative and apparently in good physical health. Her conduct has been good and she keeps herself busy with occupational therapy. Patient appeared to speak willingly and freely of her sex life. Says she is a masochist and possibly a sadist. Says her husband will not cooperate with her, thus making a happy home life impossible. Patient does not believe that she is mentally ill. Showed some signs of emotional instability when stating that she was satisfied with institutional life if her conception of home life were impossible."

In August 1947, after Mother had been in Greystone Park for two years, another psychiatric assessment was done. In part it was as follows: "Most of the patient's symptoms revolve around sexual troubles. However lengthy discussions failed to reveal definite evidence of fully developed masochistic tendencies. . . . There seems little doubt that this patient has reacted neurotically and that her relationship with her husband merely added to her conflicts. A review of the patient's past history shows little of psychopathic tendencies; in fact patient attempted extra-marital relations on only one occasion in a sort of therapeutic attempt to prove to herself that she was capable of normal experiences."

On the basis of this and other evidence, the authorities decided to grant her a year's parole in the custody of my grandmother, who had applied for that. On September 3rd a letter from Mother to Dr. Collins, a staff psychiatrist, is noted, asking for permission to take a course and start psychiatric training. There's no record of why she was returned to the hospital, but she was readmitted on November 4th. I suspect her difficulties at home had to do with conflicts with her stepfather, who was alcoholic and may have molested her.

Of the next few years there are few records, none of psychiatric assessments or treatments (the hospital's typical "treatment" for patients seemed to be no treatment at all), but some of minor health procedures. In April 1956 she was assessed by a Dr. Colonna. This time even I would agree she exhibited what seems to me to be a full-blown psychosis. "She said she believes in mental telepathy and people are talking to her by the radio and television. She admitted hearing voices when no one is around. . . . Patient said she has television in her eyes and sees many various things like 'phosphorus persons' glowing all over."

In September of 1956 she had another encounter with Dr. Colonna. "As soon as the undersigned (Dr. Colonna) found himself in the room, patient suddenly slammed the door in a violent manner and lifted her skirt. She asked the undersigned to hit her or do something to her. She talked in a rapid manner stating she was dreaming of being beaten and bodily punished.

When interviewed later, patient was much more calm. . . . In the opinion of the undersigned, patient should have shock treatment but there is no permit. This will be requested."

In those days, as was later pointed out in the book and play "One Flew Over the Cuckoo's Nest," shock treatment was used as a sort of disciplinary ploy or punishment for unruly behavior. When a patient's actions really annoyed the staff psychiatrists or others, he or she was likely to undergo that ordeal. It's rather suspicious to me that this notation is in her file and there is no medical record to follow it up—as if they forgot to take this out when they expunged the records.

On August 13, 1957, there's another saddening entry. "The instructor walked into the Affiliates' Kitchen in the Affiliates' Residence and saw _____ _____, Parole Janitor patient from the Main Building North embracing and kissing this patient. Incident was reported to Mrs. Longley, Miss Agnes McAndrews and Mrs. Winters. _____ _____'s parole has been lifted and he has been discontinued from working in the Affiliates' Kitchen." Apparently the last thing they wanted was for patients to have affairs.

Another thing that compelled my attention about this period of her life was that anti-psychotic drugs had been discovered and were in general use, but they didn't seem to be that helpful for Mother. In December of 1958 they said she was receiving "Thorazine, 50 mg, b.i.d." However she was still hallucinating and obsessed. "Admits masturbatory experiences which she enjoys mostly in connection with radio and television voices which tell her how to do it and how well she is doing, but does not believe to be over sexed or under sexed but just playing. In spite of constant stimulation it was impossible to direct patient's attention away from her sexual problem." I believe that she'd been in this hell-hole so long that she would have had to be superhuman to avoid having a psychosis.

More proof of this comes when she's interviewed on January 11, 1962. "When asked why she came to the hospital she stated that she went to a psychiatrist. 'I was so fat. I had an irritated vaginal section. I first went to my old doctor who had treated me for years and he sent me to New York City to see this psychiatrist. I did not know about mental telepathy when I came here. It was a great surprise to find that people heard voices. I didn't know anything about it until I had been here about five years. . . . I have such a difficult mental telepathy problem.'"

For the next six years there seem to be no records of her being interviewed, just notations of dental treatments, chest x-rays, and incident reports when she was slightly injured in two minor accidents. At this point I believe that she probably couldn't even conceive of living elsewhere. And for all this time the staff at the institution apparently confined themselves to giving only custodial care.

The end came for her in February 1968. "February 5. This patient is today being transferred to the Clinic Building from Main Building South, Ward 33, because of possible intestinal obstruction   February 21   CLINICAL IMPRESSION: Intestinal obstruction —Cause and site undetermined." "February 27, 1968. —She was placed in Oxygen, given Aramine and Cedilanid I.V. but failed to respond and expired February 27, 1968 being pronounced at 1:05 P.M. She was signed out Cause of Death: Acute Myocardial Infarction. Carcinoma of the Transverse Colon causing Intestinal Obstruction. The other significant condition: Psychosis With Psychopathic Personality, Sexual Episode."

I loved my mother. I still do, in spite of some of the things I've learned about her. When I look back at my life I know that, aware of it or not, I've been much influenced by her. I've been a writer for a weekly newspaper, as she was, a teacher, and have had a life-long fascination with psychology, as both she and Dad had. Dad was much influenced by her also. After their divorce he went on to take courses and be certified as a school psychologist. However he never had therapy, which I've had much of, so he stayed fixated on a certain type of woman.

My stepmother looked like my mother, was overweight, had constant rages, and even at one point was prescribed anti-psychotics by her family doctor. She also seemed to have absolutely no awareness or conscience about the chaos and distress she caused in our home, but blamed me for being "different." This fact seems ironic to me because, according to one interview with Dad at the hospital, Mother also clashed violently with her opposite-sex stepparent who came into her family at approximately the same age as mine did.

I also followed Mother's lead by becoming psychotic at about thirty years old, a condition that I believe was caused in part by my having inherited a predisposition to psychosis from my mother's side of the family. (There were two and possibly three close relatives on her father's side who were hospitalized for mental problems.) The precipitating factors were many, but according to Dr. Shupp, it was probably my first dose of LSD that sent me over the edge. When I contemplate this part of my life I still think that without LSD I likely would have found some other way to go crazy, in part as an attempt to understand Mother.

I haven't had the degree of sexual problems she had, perhaps because of (or in spite of) the medications I've been on, but I certainly can empathize with them. I wonder if she would have been better if Dad had been more accepting of her desires. (She apparently felt very depressed and perhaps guilty about having these urges—in one interview she said she'd wanted to move to New York because "Lepers live with other lepers.") The one positive thing that I got from my mother's illness, and still have, is a determination to make a difference in the world. For as long as I can remember I've seen her life as tragic and, in a certain sense, meaningless. I'm not sure why I took this as a challenge but I did. I taught high school Peer Counseling for fourteen years, bolstered by the sixteen years of experiences I had in Dr. Shupp's therapy groups in San Francisco. Much of the time Peer Counseling resembled a twenty to twenty-five person therapy group. I was able to affect the lives of many students in a positive way, getting some of them into therapy, others to the proper authorities because they were being abused or molested, and I believe literally saving the lives of a few.

I've also Chaired this County's Local Mental Health Board, an experience by which I was able to affect changes at the state and possibly the national level by using my knowledge of the state's educational system and the leverage I got by being on the Board. I'm presently on the Board of MHCAN, the Mental Health Clients' Action Network, as well as the Steering Committee of my Local of the National Writers Union. And I still frequently take seminars in different areas of medicine and psychology. My wife is a psychiatric nurse and has to have 30 units of coursework every two years to keep her license. We both attend these courses and usually take more than the minimum number of units because we enjoy them.

Now, at the threshold of old age, I feel unusually lucky in many ways. I've survived a major psychosis and two major operations (for lung and prostate cancer). At 67, I'm still relatively healthy and able to think and write. At one point a few years ago I changed my lifestyle, started eating non-fat food and exercising, lost more than 50 pounds and gave up my 47-year cigarette habit because of my lung cancer diagnosis (a step that seemed impossible for me earlier). I'm very lucky in another important way too. I married a beautiful woman thirty-three years ago who was never psychotic but whom I met in Dr. Shupp's therapy group. My relationship with her is one of the most satisfying aspects of my life.

In spite of my doubts about my mother, I believe she's had an overall beneficial effect on me. I'm now able to choose how to think about her and other past relationships. I can't explain it but I treasure her memory. It may seem ironic but some of her problems, i.e., her being afraid of me (as Dad was quoted as saying in one of his Greystone Park interviews) and her resulting behaviors, caused me to develop a certain freedom and confidence in my own ability to change things.

Like many mentally ill people, I've had to cultivate a sense of what would be healthy for me and what wouldn't. Not only did I choose to marry quite well, probably because of the knowledge and insight I got from Dr. Shupp's group, but I've often chosen situations, friends, and acquaintances that have encouraged and inspired me over the years. Many years ago I resolved never to be incarcerated like my mother, whose main identity for her last 23 years was as Case No. 44987. I don't think anyone should ever be reduced to that status. I'm still working to bring this about for others.

Some Further Observations

I'm now almost 70 years old and have had recent experiences that have caused me to think about this essay and consider what I wrote here. Two years ago my wife and I visited Greystone Park, my first visit in over 50 years. There were still many buildings on the 47 acres, but most were vacant and rather eery, with broken windows and other signs of disrepair. In front of the still-occupied main building, a massive grey stone fortress five stories high with four-story wings on each side, some wag had written on the official billboard, "Have a Nice Day." Its stark, oppressive façade and complete lack of human scale actually seemed to imply the opposite. I thought a more accurate inscription should say something like "Abandon all hope ye who enter here."

Although the complex apparently was built to house 7,000–8,000 patients, I was told that there are now only about 550 people there. We were stopped from taking photos of the Park by a member of its police force (it has its own police and fire departments), who told us that people were posting pictures on the Internet and making money from them—and that we had to get permission from the CEO.

During the past two years I've shared this essay with several people who are "consumers" (the legal term for mentally ill people) and "survivors" (those who've been ill). Their reactions have been positive; however, many seem to have had negative experiences with the public mental health system. I was able to avoid this for reasons I've earlier stated. And I was fortunate enough to be a private patient of Dr. Shupp's even before I became seriously ill—or (in psychiatric terminology) "decompensated."

Some of the people (consumers and survivors) mentioned above have told me that I've been too easy on the system that brought about the abuses my mother suffered. In fact I wrote what I knew and could piece together about her situation and for the most part let the reader draw his or her own conclusions. Still these will differ depending on what conceptual and experiential lenses one looks through. For instance some of my own thinking changed last year after I read Phyllis Chesler's excellent feminist book "Women and Madness." A quotation I saved from it (p. 85) is as follows: "Many women who are psychiatrically labeled, privately treated and publicly hospitalized are not mad. Like Plath, West, Fitzgerald and Packard [prominent women who've been labeled as crazy], they may be deeply unhappy, self-destructive, economically powerless, and sexually impotent—but as women they're supposed to be."

Having experienced a severe life-altering mental illness myself, I'm not one to deny that some people go crazy. I do think, however, that the above quotation probably described my mother quite accurately, at least at the time she was first hospitalized. That the treatment (or lack of treatment) she received was unmerited seems to be obvious. I also suspect that the circumstances of her death may not be as the institution would have us believe.

The best I (and any of us) can do is try to improve the situation as it exists today. It was a great injustice to incarcerate so many people in these hell-holes (Phillip Wylie called them "snakepits"—with some metaphorical justification) and then to turn them out into the streets without adequate support, as happened later. But now there's more hope because facilities like MHCAN exist where "consumers" and "survivors" can help each other.

Many of us are working to decrease the stigma surrounding psychiatric problems. One sign of our improving status is that in the June 2006 issue of *Atlantic Monthly* there's a feature on major psychiatric disorders among U.S. Presidents, something that probably wouldn't have been written about or published until recently. The magazine lists 18 past Chief Executives who apparently suffered serious illnesses, mostly mood disorders, i.e., bipolar and clinical depression. I believe this and other signs indicate that the situation for the mentally ill is improving. I just hope the world doesn't go any more crazy than it is before we attain our full measure of equality.

The Continuum of
Mental Health

Teresa J. Brown

In my experience as a psychologist, I have run across any number of people who think of "mental health" or being mentally healthy, as the opposite of mental illness or being "mentally ill." I discourage people from understanding mental health in this manner, because, in my own experience, I found that one can move from a point of mental wellness to a point of mental illness in virtually the blink of an eye.

During the course of one day, I took my daughter and myself on a psychotic journey, which I, although a psychologist, did not recognize as being a manic episode. I believed I had special wisdom from God. . . . I was to write a book—nay, we (my daughter and I) were to write a book—for it would be her job to complete it as I believed that I would "go with God" via an accident. Yet I had a "mission" to tell friends and loved ones that Christ was coming and to be ready. I abruptly left my daughter with "our book" at her great grandmother's (how I got there only God knows) and proceeded on my journey, "knowing" that I would be going with God. I fully expected that with the next car I passed, I would hear the grinding of metal and the breaking of glass—yet, in reality, I found myself in utter silence, in a snow filled ditch.

I proceeded to call friends with "God's message," while ignoring the good Samaritan at my window, until a friend found a way to get through my "insanity" by saying, "this is *your* message," and had me hand the phone to the man who had kindly stopped to help. Thus, law enforcement arrived at the scene, and I recall a handful of people milling around. I now wonder what they thought they were seeing—a woman out of her head from drugs or alcohol? Someone who was fleeing from the law in "Cops-like" fashion? No, it was simply me—a person in a mental health crisis—still a mother, a daughter, a friend, a psychologist . . .

After a week in the hospital during which I was brought back to reality by the power of medicine (and the wisdom of God), and another week at home, I returned to my job as "psychologist," more humbled, more in awe, more knowledgeable, and still able to help others as I was trained to do, as is my life's purpose.

I live today, still a mother, daughter, friend, psychologist, and also a client, consumer, recipient—a contributing member of society—who moves back and forth on the continuum of mental health or "mental wellness," which I understand to be far more "politically correct," and more accurate, than the polarities of being either "mentally ill" or "mentally well."

We can all help the fight against the stigma of mental illness by understanding that it's not "us against them." We are all in this world together, and we all can find ourselves on that continuum of mental wellness, shifting back and forth at various points in time. I beseech all of us to take time to understand one another and not to judge, but to give one another a hand or a "leg up" as we move along that continuum and on our personal journeys.

The Escape

Katherine F.H. Heart

I need to give you a bit of the story behind *The Escape*. For as long as I can remember, I have had this need to explain myself. Maybe because the beginning was complex, not your pretty, ideal family, though it may have looked so from the outside. Both of my parents were in the military until they got married, then Mary was expected to leave her career and have babies, while Ken supported the family. I was born to Mary and Ken in a now remote and forbidden place for Americans: Tripoli, Libya. At one-year old I contracted pneumonia and was flown out of the country for two months to receive treatment. When I was reunited with Mom and Dad, Mary had a baby brother for me, Kenny Jr., and then James came, in quick succession. I think the short time during which I was the only child may have been the only time Mom held me. I have no childhood or teenage or adult memories of her holding me or ever approaching me to give me a hug. If I wanted a hug, I had to go and scoop it up from her.

Dad was a different story. We moved back to the states and Mom had another baby, Richard Lee, and a baby boy named Robert, who died shortly after birth. We lived in a succession of trailer parks in remote country locations outside military bases. I was the oldest and the only daughter. I was expected

19

to "look after" the boys when they played outdoors. That was
fine while Mom was home, although not fair. When Dad
watched us alone, he put the boys down for a nap and played
sexual games with me.

Yes, I was secretly and deviously sexually abused. He got
away with it for nine years, until I was fourteen years old. My
"telling" was accidental. I became afraid Dad would make me
pregnant when my period started. So, one weekend when I
was heading out with friends on a camping trip, I left Dad a
slip of paper in his pants pocket, saying that if he didn't leave
me alone, I would run away. When I returned home from the
outing, Dad was stone cold distant and Mom was tripping all
over herself to be nice to me. The exact opposite of how
things normally felt around the house. Dad didn't utter a
word in my direction for two weeks and Mom seemed, at
every turn, to be bribing me with things . . . food, clothes,
money. I realized that Mom had probably found the note and
confronted Dad. He had always threatened me with beatings
if I ever told about the abuse. I kept waiting for that to happen. Meanwhile, Mom had another baby, named John.

After Mom's kindness wore off, and she had cared for the
new baby for about three months, she put me in charge of
him, too. I had my hands full, going to school plus worrying
about whether Dad was going to rape or beat me, then having
to care for an infant. Over the next two years, I became increasingly depressed, like wanting-to-kill-myself depressed. Instead of my parents noticing and getting me professional
help, they ignored me. I stole Mom's back pain pills from her
bathroom closet and snuck them into my mouth on the way
to school on the bus. No one noticed. The pills gave me a "little high" to get through the day.

One day I took some extra pills when the usual dose didn't
seem to work. I got sort of sick and mixed up, and felt a lot
worse about everything. I needed to confide in someone. I
chose Miss Green, a guidance counselor. I told her about the
pills and how bad I felt; when she asked why I felt so bad, I felt

embarrassed and just said, Dad "did stuff" to me. Miss Green called Dad to have him take me to the hospital. On the way, in the car, when he asked why, I couldn't answer. The tension made me want to throw up.

The hospital personnel took me into a private room and had me change into a gown. They took my clothing. They left me there by myself and I started to cry. I cried for three days straight from the relief of not having rape or a beating hanging as an unspoken threat in the air around me. Ten years of fear and finally, it seemed, I was in a safe place. A "psych ward." The older woman doctor asked why I was taking pills. "Because I felt so bad." And why did I feel so bad? "Because I couldn't take living with Dad." Why did I hate him? "Because he made me do stuff to him." Sexual? "Yes." She looked at me with no expression and walked out. I found out from a nurse that I was diagnosed as schizophrenic.

Apparently, in the early 1970's, the psychiatric profession believed that father-daughter incest was rare, and of course both Mom and Dad denied that it had happened. The only thing left to believe was that it was my delusions. One week into my stay at the psych ward, Mom took me out against doctor's orders, because she couldn't afford any more care at the private hospital. When she took me home, she put me in my room, hissing spitefully: "There is nothing wrong with you—you're never going back to that place." If it was possible to feel deeper hurt, anger and depression, I sank into that place over the next several months.

As a family, we were ordered into family therapy, where no one spoke a word out of fear that Dad would beat us afterward. I was seen by another outpatient psychiatrist, a middle-aged man, who diagnosed me with "adjustment reaction to adolescence." He, too, believed I had delusions about the sexual abuse by dad, this time caused by the onset of my female hormones. Finally, after a near suicide attempt, I went back to Miss Green. I told her that if she didn't help me get out of my home, I would run away. This time she called me a cab and sent me back to the same psych ward. Mom was mad. Dad didn't speak. But I was safe again. For thirty days. Near the end of the month, Mom visited. She took me downstairs for a soda and chips. As soon as the elevator door closed, she said, coldly and angrily: "You can't come home again. You have two choices—go to the state mental hospital or a group home until your aunt and uncle return from traveling and can take you in."

I was shocked speechless with the coldness of her "offer." How could a mother send her child to a state mental hospital? Not knowing what I was choosing, I told her I would go to the group home and then to my aunt and uncle, whom I only vaguely remembered. I was sent from the hospital to the new Group Home for Emotionally-Disturbed Adolescents, run by a prominent psychiatrist in the area. This type of adolescent treatment was considered "in vogue" at the time. Except that I did not receive anything but angry treatment from the housemother who decided that my quiet reserve and depression could be cured with ridicule and personal attacks, and tried to bait me to become angry at her. I was mostly relieved not to be going home. I only had to endure the three months in the halfway house, with kids sicker than me.

Finally, my aunt and uncle sent for me just before my senior year started. I moved to a different state and started over. They and their three daughters were kind and generous to me. They treated me as their own. It wasn't until I had graduated from high school and college, and was working on my master's degree, that I learned that Mom had told my aunt and uncle, in a conversation they had together before I arrived to live with them, I was schizophrenic. My aunt was studying for her master's degree in school psychology and didn't believe my diagnosis. She treated me as if I was well. I didn't tell her until we had the talk about my diagnosis that I had been sexually abused by Dad. She was very upset with herself—and Mom—at not getting me treatment sooner. But, she believed me, which was like a cooling balm on a still fresh wound.

I wish that my aunt's believing me had been enough for a cure. I moved to a big city in another state not far from my aunt and uncle's home. I worked at various professional positions in the non-profit field, including working on behalf of rape victims. For nearly 10 years, I saw one therapist after another—an older caring social worker, a Jungian-Feminist psychotherapist, a psychophysical therapist (body-mind worker), all in succession. All the while I wrote rageful poems and had haunting experiences with rageful people in my personal life. It was a whirlwind time. My moods cycled into deep troughs of lonely depression (where I withdrew and slept weekends away) and flew high in ideational flights of fancy (when I painted, made big plans at work and wrote in my journal for days, and when agitated or rageful, put myself into debt furnishing my apartment and buying designer clothing to make my life feel and look better).

In 1992, when I was 38 years old, I met and spent time with a social worker who spotted my patterns and suggested I see a female psychiatrist. I had avoided the psychiatric profession for years as an adult because of my experience of not being believed and being misdiagnosed as a teenager. I wasn't at all sure I wanted to subject myself to the same treatment as an adult. But when I was diagnosed as manic-depressive (bipolar) and the doctor fully explained the diagnosis and treatment, for the first time in my life my "ups and downs" made sense. I was also diagnosed with two other post-traumatic stress disorders, related to the unresolved abuse.

In 1992, I retired from one of my victim services positions to apply to art school. Even though I had three degrees, they were in the health and education fields, and I longed to learn to paint professionally. But instead of starting art school, I found myself on a plane going to see my Mom, who had gone into a diabetic coma and lost both of her legs at the hip. She wasn't expected to live and I had to face Dad, whom I hadn't seen or spoken to in years. Mom pulled through. When I returned home from visiting my family, the stress of seeing my parents brought the beginning of a long period of unearthing memories, of falling into deep catatonic depressions, of flying into self-harming rages, and of being out of control in ways I did not realize a human being could manage to live to write and tell about.

Between 1992 and 2006, I experienced 27 hospital stays as short as 3 days and as long as 3 months. I was given 57 electro-convulsive therapy (ECT) treatments and tried on 40 different medications, with the effect that I have permanent memory loss and medication-induced Parkinson's syndrome. I have worked with 7 different psychiatrists. My current female psychiatrist is the kindest I could find and she has patiently endured the wildness within me. Today, I mourn the loss of years and the thousands of dollars in failed treatments from both outside and within "the system." All was not lost. Along the way, a couple of doctors and therapists have stood by me as I exorcised the demons of the hundreds of damaging molesting episodes.

My mother and father died during the 1990's. I grieved for them, the relationships that never were, and for my own brokenness. I found space in my being to forgive the bad things they did and the good things they could not give. I forgave myself that I could not be there with them as only a daughter can, when they were ready to pass away. I forgave all of us for the wasted time it took to traverse the deep chasm of misunderstanding and disbelief.

Yes, I still have a mental illness, and the associated Parkinson's syndrome. I take a number of medications to keep my balance, so necessary these days in my life as a writer and small business owner. I go so far as to say that "I have disabilities." My head is up, as I can also count my strengths and abilities. I have survived my upbringing, hurting myself, an out-of-kilter brain and hormonal chemistry, failed relationships, and "the system" to come to a high quality of life and authentic sense of self.

My Story

Eric Davis

I was 38 years old and I had spent 20 years building a career in aviation. All this effort was destroyed by corporate downsizing in early December, 1995. I not only lost the best job I ever had but I lost my financial independence and lost the friendships that I had developed and maintained over a 10 year period in Phoenix, Arizona. My mind started playing tricks on me almost immediately after I was notified of the loss of my job that I held for 10 years. I had overwhelming feelings of hurt, fear, insecurity, loss, and despair that led to trouble.

I experienced a super high level of spiritual thought and activity. I had an emergency appointment with my family physician. My mom came to Arizona from Michigan and in two days she called 911 to take me to the hospital because of my behavior. There is apparently no history of mental illness in my family. Maybe there is but it was never discussed.

I have had a total of five hospitalizations in the past 12 years. The duration between each one has gotten longer over time. I hope that the worst is behind me now.

I loved my career choice and pursuing my goals to advance my talents. I have a Federal Aviation Administration–issued Airframe & Power Plant mechanic license, a Federal Aviation Administration–issued Private Pilot license, and a

Federal Communication Commission General Radio license. I took classes at Western Michigan University, completed Aircraft Maintenance Technology courses at Spartan School of Aeronautics. I hold an Associate Arts degree in Avionics from Ferris State University and recently took classes at Southwestern Community College. I have had some jobs off and on with little success. At one point, I tried to work in aviation with another airline. I only lasted about three years before the stress and anxiety negatively affected my job performance. I left that job voluntarily before any mishaps could occur.

One of my hospitalizations was in Minneapolis, Minnesota. I met a guy on the job who really pushed my buttons and put me in a terrible manic state. Things there were tough enough to deal with on my own. The manager on shift that day requested that I leave the department and go to another. I ended up with a week of inpatient hospitalization, after which I had two weeks of intensive outpatient therapy. After my release, I wound up in Detroit, Michigan, and this is where I had to face the fact that my career in aviation was over.

Before moving back to Michigan, I tried to coerce my parents into helping me bring legal action against the airline that fired me. We had an appointment with one lawyer and he talked them out of doing anything because of the time and expense involved in litigation. I feel I was treated unjustly by my employer when I became ill and I am still in debt today. When I think of all the lost years of wages, I would still sue the airline company if I could.

The other three hospitalizations were in Michigan. I went to Kalamazoo State Hospital first and later was hospitalized in Pine Rest in Grand Rapids. I participated in a bipolar disorder group in Kalamazoo for about 18 months and that helped me a lot.

I don't know what I will end up doing for the rest of my life. I am still interested in many of the things I felt passionately about before my mental illness started. I am looking into becoming a Peer Support Specialist and am interested in politics. I also donate my talents to help where they are needed and appreciated.

My Struggle with Depression

George Albert

I was raised in a small town outside of Philadelphia by strict Christian parents. I remember from a very young age living with a feeling of strong guilt whenever I performed some minor infraction against my parents' strict code of conduct. I never really misbehaved in any major way, but I remember always having the feeling that my parents' disapproval was likely to surface at any time without warning. I think I learned to repress my emotions from a very young age, until I was not aware of my feelings at all. My father was an extreme introvert who rarely showed emotion. He would come home from work every night and immediately go into the living room to work on his stamp or coin collections, hardly saying a word to anyone. Never expressing any feelings or emotion was how everyone in my family seemed to operate.

I went away to college at the University of Delaware after high school graduation and worked part time and studied diligently. I met a girl in the school chorus and asked her out and we soon became a couple. Deborah was raised by her parents to be a doctor. There was never any question of what her career choice would be. I completed my undergraduate degree and was accepted into the Wharton School of Business for graduate studies. Deborah was accepted into medical school at the University of Pennsylvania and we were married. Deborah's parents were against the marriage until they realized that I would not stand in the way of their daughter becoming a doctor.

After I obtained my MBA, I worked full time while Deborah continued her medical studies. When Deborah was accepted into a residency program out of state, I gave notice at work, we moved and I found another job. Shortly after this, Deb became pregnant and gave birth to our son. With Deb's schedule at the hospital, my work and caring for our son, we hardly ever saw each other. After completing her training in neonatology, Deb again found a position out of state and I was hesitant to quit my job since I had finally felt I was starting to establish my career in the health insurance field. I had grown close to a female co-worker and told Deb that I wanted a divorce. Our parents were very disappointed at the failure of our marriage. I will never forget the look of hatred on my father's face when I told him about the divorce. That ended up being the last time I saw my father; he died of a stroke shortly after.

After my divorce, I ended up getting a job in Michigan and asked Sherry, the co-worker with whom I had been having an affair, to come with me. Shortly after we moved and I settled into my new job, Sherry decided she missed her family and moved back home. I was devastated by her abrupt departure and felt deserted and alone.

Several years later, when I was about 31, my family doctor mentioned during a routine physical that I always appeared to have a flat affect and asked me if I was depressed. I had lived with a low-grade depression for so long that I didn't know it was possible for me to feel any differently. My doctor prescribed Prozac and in a few weeks I felt surprisingly better. I liked the feeling so much that I proceeded to increase the dosage on my own. When I ran out of pills ahead of schedule and requested a refill, my doctor was quite upset and extracted a promise from me never to increase my prescribed dose without his approval. He did write me a prescription for an increased dose and I did well on Prozac for several years.

Meanwhile, I started dating and eventually married a woman who was my barber. Terry was separated from her husband and had three children. She also had mental health problems much more serious than mine. She was a severe alcoholic and also suffered from anorexia. When Terry wasn't drinking, she literally starved herself, eating nothing at all for days at a time. Her body would go into ketosis so severely that the smell of her breath would nearly knock me over. Then Terry would start to drink again and she would relax a bit, start eating again, and gain some weight. But her drinking would very soon get out of control and I would come home to find her passed out in the middle of the living room floor. At times, I was unable to rouse her and would have to call an ambulance to take her to the ER for detox. On one such occasion, after Terrry was divorced and we were engaged to be married, an ER doctor took me in a private room and advised me not to marry Terry. This doctor told me that the chances of Terry ever recovering were slim to none and it would be the best thing for me if I got out now.

Unfortunately, I did not follow this doctor's advice. After Terry and I were married, I witnessed her repeated cycles of starvation and alcoholic binge drinking. When Terry would decide to stop drinking, I would recommend that she check herself into a detox facility to get some help with her withdrawal, but she always insisted on doing it on her own. She would become violently ill, with severe episodes of vomiting and dry heaves. This would last for about three days and would, of course, result in a quick weight loss, which would start her on the anorexic part of the cycle. When we went out to eat, Terry would take a trip to the restroom shortly after she had consumed what little food she did eat and would make herself vomit.

Towards the end of our marriage, Terry moved in with a fellow alcoholic who allowed her to stay in his residence in exchange for her sexual services. I finally realized that what the ER doctor had told me seven years before was true, and I filed for divorce. Although it was a relief not to have to live through the endless series of crises that existed while living with Terry, I was very lonely and was convinced that I would never marry again. Years later Terry called me when she was attempting to make amends through the AA program. She was finally sober, living in a small apartment, which was paid for with her disability payments and by a part-time job as a restaurant hostess. She apologized for what she had put me through during the course of our marriage and I told her I was glad she had called so that I at least knew she was okay.

After Prozac stopped working for me and my low-grade depression returned, my doctor added Wellbutrin to my medication regimen. Every couple of years my medications were adjusted in an attempt to keep my depression under control. Eventually, these adjustments in my medication regimen no longer resulted in any improvement in my symptoms. I found that I could no longer concentrate at work and was not performing my job up to expectations. After 27 years of working for a health insurance company, I was called in by my boss and told that I could either retire early with a reduced pension benefit or be fired. I was, of course, devastated, but also somewhat relieved since I had been struggling to perform my job duties for quite some time.

Shortly before I was forced to retire early from my job, I met a woman through an online dating service and fell in love. Stephanie was very understanding in regard to my depression since she suffered from a long-term low-grade depression herself. Shortly before I lost my job, she encouraged me to go to a psychiatrist and try some new medications. My current doctor is a neurologist as well as a psychiatrist. She has adjusted my medication regimen many times with little success. She suggested that I try vagus nerve stimulation (VNS), which is a device that is permanently inserted into the neck area, to simulate the vagus nerve. This method has had some success with people who are medication-resistant. Unfortunately, since I also have obstructive sleep apnea, VNS turned out not to be a viable alternative for me since it is risky for people with any sort of breathing problems.

My doctor and I continue to search for new treatments for medication resistant depression. Recently, a friend told me about a new drug, Amantadine, that has been successful with people who are resistant to antidepressants. This drug is used to treat patients with Parkinson's disease; however, doctors noted that some patients receiving the medication for Parkinson's who also suffered from medication-resistant depression noticed improvement in their depression as well as their symptoms of Parkinson's. My doctor has been on an extended vacation, but when she returns, I hope to have a trial with this new "wonder" drug. Before I learned about this new medication, I was considering whether or not to undergo electric shock therapy (ECT), which has also been quite successful in treating severely depressed people that are resistant to medications. I have been warned about the loss of short-term memory that often occurs with ECT, but it remains an option.

Currently, some days are better than others. I still go through several-month-long episodes experiencing a severely depressed mood with little interest in engaging in any activity at all, a so called "double depression," or major depressive disorder "on top of" the dysthymia or low-grade constant depression. It has been frustrating for me, my doctor, and the woman in my life but, although I am very discouraged, I still have hope that I will eventually find a treatment which successfully alleviates my symptoms.

Untitled

Mary Ellen Groat

I always knew that I was different. First, because I lived on the dead end of a back road, and second, because I was a farm-girl. I remember times when Mom's full attention was on taking care of us and the house, but later Mom worked with Daddy on the farm. (Daddy only had one arm.) I remember Christmases that were very generous, but later Christmases were skimpy.

I never knew why kids talked behind my back and made fun of me. But I could catch onto what the teachers told us and I relished their attention. I became what was called a "good student" and hoped to earn the grades I needed to go to college. I wanted to go to Michigan State University and major in music. I could play piano—I taught myself to play the first year of piano. Then I took two more years of piano. By my senior year of high school I could play what was required of me to major in piano at MSU. But what I really wanted to do was sing. So I signed up to be a vocal music major. I was voted "Outstanding Chorister" and I was named to "Who's Who Among American High School Students" when I graduated from high school.

My year of music in college did not pan out as I had hoped. But the man I loved had proposed to me and I married him. He was a good Christian man and I was a good Christian woman, so this was going to be a good Christian marriage—so everyone thought. We moved to Columbus, Ohio, and I loved it there. I began to sell Avon. I also began to notice something suspicious. My husband, who was in the military, was making purchases we could not afford. I told one of my Avon customers what I noticed and she told me that the government was court-martialing people under similar circumstances. (I thought the government put to death people they court martialed.)

One day, as I came in the laundry room after a day of selling Avon, I could hear other voices in the house and I could hear Charles's voice. "Oh," I thought to myself. "These must be the special guests Charles told me about. Let's see. The OSI [Office of Special Investigations—the military's version of the FBI] Yeah, that's it. Well. I'll just keep my nose out of this. I'll make dinner." Minutes later, I was called in and told that Charles was being investigated. The OSI questioned Charles about some things in the house. Then they went through the upstairs looking for evidence to use to charge Charles with Grand Larceny of the U.S. Treasury. They found it. Charles confessed to the crime.

Downstairs, I was reading the Psalms and telling the investigator observing me that Charles was a good man and that he was innocent. The investigator did not believe me. Later that night Charles told me that he was guilty. I hollered. "No!" "Mary." said Charles, "I did it. I'm guilty." I could not believe this was happening to us. I gave birth to our first baby one week later. Charles was found guilty and sentenced to one year at Leavenworth. I heaved a sigh of relief. The government was going for 55 years.

Life was not the same after Leavenworth. Charles could not keep a job and he had this idea about getting a divorce that I could not understand. He did not attend church any longer. This was hard on me because this was a time when I was getting closer in my relationship with the Lord Jesus. I had another daughter and a son. At a time when I needed Charles the most and didn't think he would leave us, he left.

Life settled down to an easy routine after Charles left. I was up at 6:30 a.m., ate breakfast, bathed the kids (a baby and two toddlers), cleaned house (the toddlers would mess it up as fast as I cleaned it), played with the kids, fixed and ate dinner, took a nap, then fixed and ate supper, played and watched TV. But that was not good enough. Protective Services started to call on me. My housekeeping was not good enough for PS. They often came before the house was clean, or if the house was clean, it was never clean enough. When a PS worker found out I was afraid of him, he would tersely reply that I should be afraid of what he could do to me. (That reminded me of what my dad used to say to maintain his authority.) I was told that I never should have had children and that I was a slob. I was screamed at, just like my parents screamed at me.

I began pre-nursing training and I was maintaining high grades. PS opened another case on me, accusing me of sexually abusing my children and asking me if I had a boyfriend (I didn't). Then I began to notice something suspicious. My oldest daughter's grades were slipping. She wanted to die and I didn't know what to say. My son frequently asked me what it was like to die. My training in pre-nursing taught me that children do not become depressed, yet my children were demonstrating symptoms of depression.

My oldest daughter was 8 or 10 when I took her to therapy. I showed the therapist her grades and the therapist could see that the grades were sliding. I tried to tell her the best I knew how that my daughter wanted to die. I also went in to see her. My husband was involved in a bigamous marriage while we were married. It was overwhelming me and I couldn't bear it alone. My therapist laughed at me. (My lawyer also laughed at me when I told him.) We talked about nursing school, about nursing, and the children. We never did talk about the bigamy.

One day, my youngest daughter told me that our neighbor's son was going to rape her. This boy also bragged to me that he liked some girl and that he was going to rape her and that there was nothing I could do to stop him. At that point I knew he was talking about my children. I saw our therapist and told her that my youngest daughter was being raped and I believed that my oldest daughter and my son were also being raped as well. Her response shocked me. "You knew these kids were being sexually abused and you did nothing to stop it," charged my therapist. "I did not know my children were being sexually abused." "You did know your children were being sexually abused and you'd better have a good reason for not reporting it to PS." At that point, I knew I was losing my kids instead of getting them the help they needed. PS was more interested in convicting me than finding out what happened. "You could have come to me for help, but you didn't," said the PS worker.

By a miracle and poor judgement on my ex-husband's part, I got my children back. But things were never the same. My children didn't fully trust me and I was afraid I would lose them again. I also learned that my friends discredited the things I said. They did not take anything I said at face value. I felt very vulnerable. The support system I had was now gone.

I began to hear voices. They told me that I was a waste of my instructor's time and that I would never make anything of my life. The voices had a definite accusatory, feminine persona and I had no resistance to the things they said. I withdrew from nursing school. I knew from the training I'd received up to that point that I needed treatment. I knew that mental illness was not my fault and was not due to a weakness in my character. But I also knew my children were under the jurisdiction of Probate Court and I couldn't tell a soul that I had a mental illness and that I needed treatment.

When I withdrew from nursing school, the voices stopped. But how could I support our family now? After a few months I decided to go into medical technology, so after I took a couple of years of chemistry and a year of calculus, I graduated. I graduated from St. Clair County Community College magma cum laude. I was also a member of Phi Theta Kappa (the honors fraternity of St. Clair County Community College). This was a high point in my life. I transferred to the University of Michigan–Flint.

I felt out of place at U of M–Flint. I did not fit in with the women in their chiffon and small groups of people engaged in intellectual discussion. For many weeks, I cried every day I drove the 60 miles to U of M–Flint. But gradually, I fit in. My boss, Mary Ann was very helpful and very supportive of me. When it came to problem solving, she was very level-headed. I regarded her as my mentor.

I was able to maintain nice grades—not the highest grades, just nice grades. In the early years of my study at U of M–Flint, I was confident I would get a Medical Technology internship. But as I closed in on graduation I learned that only students with high grades went on into Med Tech internships. I did not know what to do. At U of M–Flint, students with high grades went on to medical school or graduate school. When I received news that the State of Michigan could not place me in an internship I was crushed. But I decided that I would take some more classes and try again. I also had begun some research on antibiotic resistance in bacteria found in dairy cows and I would also complete that. I hoped to present the results of my research at a conference.

I graduated from U of M-Flint when I applied for the first internship. The highlight of my years at U of M–Flint was receiving the Nathan Oaklander U of M–Flint's Most Academically Courageous Student Award. It was U of M–Flint's acknowledgment that the playing field was not level, that some of us had more barriers to overcome than the average student, and that given different circumstances we would be winning honors with the best of students.

I returned to U of M–Flint to get another biology class and another chemistry class under my belt. I hoped that then the hospitals would look at me more favorably for an internship. Unfortunately, I was not placed in an internship by the state.

I decided to find a job at the end of the school year to get some job experience. I did manage to get an opportunity to present my research at the Michigan Academy of Arts, Letters, and Sciences, and the presentation went very well.

My success with the presentation had only faded just a little when I began to have flashbacks of my past. I had forgotten these things, but now I was remembering them in vivid detail; entrails outside of a dead cat, blood splattered on a tractor tire, and a cow being beaten continuously well beyond the time she went down. I always identified with the animals. They were my only friends.

I began to experience pain—not the kind of pain one has when he or she is physically hurt—but a heart pain, an emotional pain that is very intense and inescapable. There was only one way to escape this pain—death. But I wanted my children to know that it wasn't their fault I died. I knew they would believe it was their fault. So I wrote a note and asked my friend Judy to tell my children that it wasn't their fault that I died. She took my note for what it was. I was placed in treatment and my first contact with Sanilac County Community Mental Health was made.

Eventually, I recovered. I got a job. I also found out that gardening and singing were vital to my recovery. I was doing so well that my psychiatrist referred me back to my family doctor. Months later, something went wrong and my medical doctor could no longer provide my free psychiatric medications. I went back to CMH, and because I had medical insurance, they could not help me. (My insurance company would not cover my medications, but led CMH to believe that I could apply for and receive prescription coverage. Yet they had turned me down twice.) I began the slow descent into the abyss.

It was scary to enter the abyss. There was no hope. There was no hope that I would ever have an adequate income, no hope that I could make my home livable, no hope that I could ever pursue my dreams. The guilt of the sexual abuse of my children was crushing and was inescapable. I was hospitalized again and started back on the meds I took before. I began to learn some coping skills that helped me. But the meds were not as effective as they had been. Doctors tried new meds, but they were ineffective and they caused an increase in my blood pressure. My psychiatrist found a combination (I call it a cocktail) of meds that work. In months, I was feeling much better.

When I was growing up. I always thought that being different was bad and made one weird. Now I know that God made each of us different. Aren't you glad that not everyone is just like me? Aren't you glad that not everyone is just like you?

I always assumed that the challenges I would face in my life would be challenges that I gave myself. Challenges such as a new treatment for cancer or learning a new Beethoven piano sonata. Instead, it was my psychiatrist who was challenged and who would read the most current literature. You know what? That's OK. I didn't burden her. That was a part of her job and it's a part of her job that she accepts.

Last of all, I'd always believed that I'd always sense God's presence as He walked with me. My journey through mental illness was frightening and lonely. But just because I couldn't feel God's presence with me doesn't mean He wasn't there. I am never alone because the Lord Jesus Christ is always with me. I don't have to feel His presence for Him to be with me.

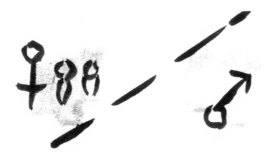

"God, Grant Me Serenity"

Sarah Coyne

Since the first day I can remember, I was a little off, mentally and emotionally that is. My father and mother divorced when I was two years old. I know they tried their best to stay together for the family, and I am also aware that my father put all his effort into living close to my older brother and me. Unfortunately, over time life took its course, and my father decided he could not possibly live in Arizona, where we lived. My mother is clinically depressed and my father has schizoaffective disorder, though I could not understand all of this at the time. Now I realize that our family could not ever have worked, and my father needed to find himself another home where he felt safe. My anger and resentment built up about my father's absence. My mother, suffering from depression, lacks healthy self-esteem and is overwhelmed with loneliness. She later remarried an abusive alcoholic. She finally came to her senses and divorced him as well.

Now, after having had two father figures leave me before the age of ten, both of them mentally sick, I had become an emotional wreck. This world terrified me; I developed into a timid and isolated little girl. I would spend my days alone in my bedroom, screaming and crying, praying to God to take my soul into heaven. As I grew older my anger grew as well.

Life had not only depressed me, but also caused my mind to be hostile and cynical. I hated my sad Mother, I hated my crazy Father, and I hated my mean ex-step Dad. I hated the fact that everything and everyone in my life had seemed to destroy me and abandon me. I started to project my psychological damage onto my innocent brother. Just for attention, I would attempt to physically hurt him, and then other times I would run around the house with a knife, hollering, "I'm going to kill myself!" After a while he refused to play the father model, and decided he would never come home, unless it were for food or shelter, and even then he seemed hesitant.

At this point I blamed myself for all the destruction in my life, and became infatuated with self-destruction. Obsessed with self-loathing, I started fasting and limiting the amount of food I consumed. I thought if I was beautiful and skinny then maybe I would be worthy enough for love and attention. But not letting myself eat was not enough for me; I needed to find an escape from life and myself. I could not relate to other human beings, so knives and razors had become my new best friends. Slitting my wrists and neck was my nirvana. I was in love with seeing my own blood and the euphoric high I got from losing the blood. I was completely amazed how powerful I was, with the ability to not eat and to slash my arms. Though it was not the attention I was craving for, heads were turning left and right at school.

Then puberty hit, and that is when it all went downhill. I was already emotionally unstable, and then adding PMS to the puzzle, my life seemed unmanageable. I was twelve years old when I first attempted suicide. I wrote a letter to my mother and brother, what I thought to be my last words, and swallowed a whole full bottle of Advil. Somehow my brother had come to check on me in my bedroom and found me lying there. All I remember from that night was spending hours and hours curled over the toilet puking up this acid my mother had given me. She claimed she knew I would try something like that and was prepared.

After the suicide attempt, my mother thought it would be a good idea for me to be psychologically evaluated by a psychiatrist. I had seen a therapist before, when my mother divorced for the second time, but this whole psychiatry approach was very new to me. I was diagnosed as clinically depressed, just as my Mother had. It was then that the doctor prescribed me my first batch of "happy pills," Zoloft. It was the newest drug on the market, and was known for the least side effects. I thought it was a miracle, a single pill that would vanish all the horror in my mind!

Three months passed and the medicine was completely in my system, and should have been working. During this period I lost all my friends, they told me "I was different now, and they liked me better off the meds." I could've cared less, though; it was the first time I ever felt love for myself. I thought I loved myself. I'm not sure if it was the "happy pills" or if it was the fact that I developed breasts and guys were throwing attention at me every which way, but life seemed complete. I began hanging around high school guys, who introduced me to alcohol, marijuana, and sex. I fell in love with this life, I not only had any guy I wanted but received free booze and weed to up the high of the Zoloft. I was sneaking out every night to party, and ditching school every day. The rumors had escalated at school and my family began to worry more than they ever had before. The excitement of my new partying scene crumbled, and I couldn't bear the sight of myself anymore. My crying spells and irritability had intensified. I was not only bursting out at home, but at school too. When I wasn't ditching school I was either in detention or suspended, for fighting, ditching, or wearing inappropriate attire. The school empathized with my situation and decided it would be in my best interest to put me on a 504 plan. This alternative plan is specifically designed for mentally troubled adolescents, giving them personal attention and attempting to keep them out of court, for mischief and absenteeism. The psychiatrist had also came to the conclusion that the one pill I was taking wasn't sufficient, she claimed it had caused a manic episode. My dose was elevated, and another drug was added, a mood stabilizer called Trileptal.

Finally, high school came around, and I felt anxious, just as any other teenager would. Though in my case, for different reasons; I had already built a reputation for myself. I was the notorious Sarah Coyne, the slacker, man hitting, arm carving, pothead, lush, slut. To my surprise, I wasn't rejected by my peers, on the contrary, despite my negative identity my class-mates were lured by my "fuck off and party" persona and at-tractive exterior. Utterly confused as to why anyone could be envious of me, I was still petrified of mirrors and suicide pos-sessed my mind, body, and soul. My partying and absenteeism continued, and the Doc was convinced there was a perfect medication to clean up my mess. So we went from one anti-depressant to the other. Raising the doses, switching mood stabilizers, and experimenting with ADHD pills.

I remember it precisely, it was my freshmen year and it was my third day in on Ritalin, an ADHD drug, I had at-tempted suicide for the second time. I had come home from a day of sexual harassment, a suspension for smoking on cam-pus, and realizing I was failing half of my classes due to my lack of attendance. I saw no hope at the end of the gloomy, torturous tunnel. It was the definite end of my existence. Even though I didn't succeed the first time with pills, I still thought it was the best way for me to go down. I was thrilled by the thought of slowly watching my life fade away. I also consid-ered my family's reaction, and would enjoy them seeing me in all my glory in an open casket.

I failed; my brother found me once again. This time the ambulance was called and I was rushed to the emergency room. With bright lights surrounding me, and a room filled with pretty nurses and doctors, I was being connected to wires and tubes all throughout my body. Since I was still con-scious, they took the charcoal approach. I had come to the conclusion that a poisonous acid that my mother had given me the first time was the worse it could get, but that is not so. I was literally forced against my will to swallow this black, thick, tar-looking liquid. The social worker came to visit with me, with the means, I suspected, to psychobabble all my problems away. All she asked though was what I was thinking, no how are you, why have you done this, it's all going to be okay bullshit. How I responded with such honesty with my brother, mother, and aunt present, is beyond my belief. I grunted, "I can't believe I'm still alive, and my brother should STAY THE FUCK OUT OF MY ROOM!" After that comment, there was no looking back, I was shipped to a psych ward, or in sugar-coated lingo, a behavioral correctional facility.

I spent only four days in there. Therapists and psychologists were prancing all about. It was ironically baffling though, there were two types of counselors in there. Type one, the egotistical asses who thought they were God and would tie strings to my shoulders at any given moment. And Type two, who were truly compassionate. I refused to really give myself up to the help, and ended up leaving with a new diagnosis of bipolar disorder, and a new collection of drugs. The psychiatrist had prescribed Lamictal, a mood stabilizer, and an anti-psychotic, Seroquel.

Even then, with professional help and new meds, I proceeded on with my destructive behavior. My father had so much concern, he moved all the way from Michigan to Arizona to bring some hope into my life for a few months. I was aggravated at the thought of him trying to make amends, but at the same time nervous and ecstatic, I finally had the chance to have a real father. This transition was almost the cure, but unfortunately I found myself incapable of loving and being loved. My ways were set in stone and I could not possibly give up my troubles.

Once he left, as all men in my life seem to love to do, my heart was shattered and this world appeared to be worthless in all aspects. All the drugs I was being prescribed had not been

effective and my feelings of sorrow and rage were still lingering. Though I knew mixing my medicine with alcohol and
weed could potentially damage the results of my mood and
thought processes, I could not simply bear life without them.
I could not let these quacks control my life. If drugs were the
answer to happiness, as they all had promised, then drugs can
have me. My sophomore year was a new beginning—my cocaine and crystal meth fetish.

If being diagnosed as clinically depressed, then bipolar at
the age of fifteen wasn't brutal enough, my latest counselor
told me I suffered from a minute case of obsessive compulsive
disorder. I drew the line at that, after the third diagnosis I was
completely fed up with psychiatry and psychology as a whole.
There would be no more therapy in my book. Although I
would love to say that was true to the full extent, it was not
so. I could not let go of the glamorous happy pills I took recre-
ationally whenever I had the "fuck it all" mentality, which
was quite often. No part of psychiatry and psychology made
sense to me. I felt as if all these doctors were treating me like a
test rat, experimenting on me with all these new toxic drugs.
One pill causes anxiety, so they add another one for the anxiety, but that medicine causes lethargy, so then they add another pill, but that drug causes insomnia, so we'll just keep
adding more drugs until you forget your own existence. It was
all a joke, one doctor says I'm a depressive and then the next
says I have OCD. In Europe and Canada some of these pills
were recognized to be so dangerous they have been taken off
the market. That fact was all I needed to justify my beliefs.

My insecurities, type A personality, need for control, or
whatever the reason is had bloomed, and my eating habits
were defective. I put myself on the Sarah diet, which consisted
of only five hundred calories a day. I was rapidly losing weight
and in less than six weeks I had lost over twenty pounds. I was
down to only one hundred and five pounds. I knew I was un-
derweight, but the horrid girl scolding me in the mirror was
too fat and ugly to be fed. I felt so guilty even letting myself

eat those five hundred calories a day I started to force myself to throw up. After every meal I would rush to the bathroom as if there were a bomb in the room, pull out my handy dandy toothbrush (it took me a while to find the right instrument for this), tickle the back of my throat, suck in my stomach, make myself cough, and "blaaaarrrr" puke. I would go through this process about three times a purge; just to make sure all of the catastrophic nutrients were missing from my ungrateful body. The whole school was in a rant about it, and my teachers would not get off my case. The nurse gave me a card for a nutritionist and encouraged me to exercise instead. None of it meant a thing to me; yes, I was unhealthy and the whole world knew, but fuck man all the guys wanted me and all the girls wanted to be me. I had no choice but to keep up this appearance, the crowds loved me, and I loved all the attention they blessed me with. I was well known before, but now I was one of the most popular girls in school.

With all the stress of my new look, I began drinking more and harder. On the weekends I would starve myself, so I could drink all that I wanted with out gaining weight. Being deliriously wasted every Friday and Saturday, I had developed a routine of dancing, crying, slapping guys, hurling, and then passing out. It got so bad, it was to the point that my friends had to lock me in rooms to hide me from all the guys, and carry my sad sorry self home. Every now and then, when there was availability, I would snort cocaine. My friends were not at all fans of coke, and were embarrassed to be seen with me. This routine ended quickly, for my friends realized I was no friend at all, but rather a bottle of gin. I could not possibly be alone, and sought comfort and reassurance elsewhere.

I started using meth and cocaine daily, and I was in love. These drugs were so much more than I could have ever dreamed. Better than any anti-depressant, and so much more than marijuana could ever offer. It made me think I was the Goddess of it all, that I was the most beautiful girl to breathe air on this earth. I was alive for the first time, till I discovered withdrawal. It wasn't a simple comedown like all my friends, I couldn't just sleep it off. I was physically paralyzed from not eating or sleeping for weeks, and all I was capable of doing was bawling my eyes out and punching the girl that glared back at me in the mirror. After coming down several times, suicide was my only answer. I attempted again, but this time with a little twist.

I had been constantly waking up every hour of the night, and one of those times I swallowed all the drugs the doctors had sold me. I lied in bed waiting to drift off to another world. Time passed and my mother came in to inform me of my continued existence and the school's. At that point I thought God was informing me that my time on this earth was not complete and more terror was to be evoked. So I figured the pills would just get me loaded, and all the people at school would appear a little less nauseating. Within the third hour I started dozing off, and couldn't keep my head up and eyes open. They sent me to the nurse. The nurse and counselors at school, knowing my story, weren't shocked that I had overdosed again. Once again the ambulance was demanded, and everyone at school was reassured that all the gossip about me was justified.

This time the social worker requested an intensive outpatient program, which I actually enjoyed. The therapist was young, insecure, and gracefully empathetic. Her heart was the only heart I could confide in. With a miracle at hand she had gotten me to expose my wounds, admitting to the rape and molestations that corrupted my soul. Though I truly appreciated her care and worry, psychology had deceived me before and devotion to anything healthy repulsed me. Confronting this disoriented life of mine was surreal and I needed more, an abstract painting. Just a little something to hide the bruises and gloss the mirrors. And that something of course would be my favorite escape, crystal methamphetamine.

My junior year of high school I went so deep into the rabbit hole that I was dating the biggest dealer the white suburbs had to offer me. We would smoke hourly and went to great extents to get that blissful crystal. How I kept a slight glimpse of morals is astonishing; I never technically committed armed robbery or car theft, but I sure partook in the process. Meth had possessed me and had bestowed me with a great friend of Satan. Soon, my boyfriend at the time, was sent to jail for armed robbery. My drug abuse was very transparent, the extravagant weight loss, the generous holes I was scraping all over my body, and the ghastly mood swings.

I was coming down, from what I recall, a month-long binge of meth. There was not even a single second I was sober during this month, and with scarcely any sleep and food. This comedown was foggy and unfamiliar, because for over a year I had always had access to drugs. I encountered a panic attack and made a trip to the good old urgent care. One glance at me, and the docs knew I was tweaking. With just a few hours clean, I was enlightened that my drug life was not an indefinite nightmare and I was living in reality again. I was freaking out, screaming at the top of my lungs with madness. In courtesy to the other patients, the nurses shoved me away in a private room. To stop my head from spinning and my lungs from exploding, a tranquilizer was enforced. Oh, how it all seemed perfect at that moment. My mother could no longer handle me, and shipped me off to my Father's in Michigan.

The first week I was there was insanity. I was slitting my wrists again and painting the walls with blood. I was on strike, never left my room; I was determined to be sent back to Arizona. My father had denied giving up on me, and offered more love than my cynical mind had ever allowed me to dream. The transition was incomprehensible, and suicide was the only thought that I dwelled upon. My father, being a huge fan of the science of psychiatry, recommended a local psychiatrist. We started with another anti-depressant, Cymbalta, again the newest drug out, created with the intentions of confined and tolerable side effects. Though I had previously turned down psychiatry, too, my self-medicating had failed me, and I had no willpower left in me to stop crying myself to sleep. If my father, who I felt was the only other human who understood me, firmly had faith in these chemicals, than so would I.

Even though I was sober, depression bewitched me, and the Cymbalta was no help at all. I had entered the rat race all over again, upping the dose, adding mood stabilizers and anti-psychotics. The suicidal thoughts had finally drifted away, but the psychological issues had not. From all the medication, I had become entirely fatigued, and slept for days on end. Waking up for school was practically impossible, if it were not for my father shouting and nagging every second of the morning there would have been no hope of my ever leaving that forsaken bed of mine. Lethargy was not the only fatal side effect; my lack of concentration was another major underlying factor. When placed in the structured classroom format, I just could not simply sit still and focus in on one single topic. I'm not sure if it was anxiety or mania that the drugs were producing, but either way my mind was mayhem and I was crawling out of my skin. The doctors would have typically prescribed me an ADHD pill, but knowing my drugs, I was aware of the suicide risks and rejected even the sight of a stimulant. My side effects of lethargy, anxiety, mania, and fogged thoughts, did not stand-alone. Irritability had strolled along, and every person who looked my way would have to pay for wasting my air.

Despite all the craziness from the drugs, my life was pretty healthy. With the love and care from my father, my mind had molded from masochistic to a purity activist. I became involved in a Japanese Buddhist yoga studio, where I practiced religiously three times a week, and again every Sunday for a guided meditation session. I joined all the clubs at school that peaked my interest; which consisted of the Young Democrats, the Gay Straight Alliance, and the Diversity club. I also found my heart calling for the arts, and took an A.P. literature course and got back into theatre. I was getting straight A's for the second time in my life, and a B on any paper or test drove me to tears. My father had saved my soul.

My path was everywhere I wanted to be, but me being an attention whore, I made friends in a heartbeat, and all my old partying antics crept back into my life. I had rationalized my thoughts by telling myself that abusing alcohol and weed were harmless in comparison to meth and coke. This time I controlled it, and saved my using for strictly weekend celebrating. Then occasionally, when I was down or stressed, I would drink my aunt's wine alone on weeknights. Midyear in my senior year I quit the yoga, quit the clubs, and I should have failed my favorite class, A.P Literature (but my teacher loved me and my poetry so much he let me slide.) How I was never kicked out of school, and how I graduated is absolutely a phenomenon.

Before I moved to Michigan I was dating this musician, and thought it would be perfect in every way if I moved back to Arizona for him. He was a starving artist just like my father. I hadn't been with a male in a year, and figured he would be the love of my life. I pictured how beautiful it would be with him and his rock band, and me with my poetry. Plus, he was twenty-one and could buy me my booze whenever essential. So Arizona was what I was to call home. Being the hopeless romantic that I am, I believed that love would rid me of all my bruises. I was out of my father's sight, my mother was naïve, and I was eighteen, so I decided I could take my life in my own hands. I quit taking all the psychiatric meds.

I was supposed to be living with my mother, but my boyfriend's house was basically my own. It was great, I thought, twenty-four hours of male attention and art, I couldn't ask for more. Coming off the legal mood altering drugs was just as hard as coming off meth and coke. I cried constantly and suicidal thoughts were my closest foe. I was filled with hesitation, and it took a couple of tries to actually get myself to quit. With a daily affirmation prayer that I had created from my days in yoga, I wrote uplifting words all over my mirrors with the intention of turning my life around. The weeks passed and the messages in my reflection did too. Though I was capable of shaking off the pills, my drinking habits remained, and my dieting habits launched as well. Although I do admit to having an eating disorder before, this time I felt that I had gotten my weight and eating under control with the Atkins diet.

After a long period of procrastination, I finally registered at Mesa Community College with a double major of Psychology and the Fine Arts. Off the meds, I was able to dedicate myself completely to my education. All my teachers adored my eagerness for knowledge, and I received straight A's. But there was trouble in paradise. I had come to another healthy enlightenment, and the relationship I had been in for over a year was not one of them. Ultimately, my eyes soon opened, and I recognized how sadistic my boyfriend really was, and I needed to escape my masochistic self for eternity. Though I cannot go into full on detail about this relationship, all I will say is I was following my mother's footsteps, but with twists and turns of my own. Brutal it was, I broke it off with him, or so I thought.

A few weeks went by with tears of remorse, but being my old codependent self was not what I desired. I needed to cleanse myself from all weaknesses. Living on impulse, I pierced my nose, tattooed my foot, and cut my hair. I was at one hundred and five pounds again, and felt invincible and amorous. Summer began, I was single, and I thought I would party every night. Loneliness slithered back in, and the first guy who showed me any attention at the time was my ex coke dealer. He declared he was clean, so I contemplated for a while, and gave into him. After a few weeks of binge drinking with him, my fear became reality. I was entirely wasted, he had some coke, and I relapsed. I promised myself it was only one slip, I had stayed clean for two years and I wasn't going down that road again. The next night came around, and that night we finished a whole eight-ball.

The day after, feelings of shame gnawed at my door. I called my ex boyfriend, who had been urgently trying to get hold of me for a month, for some comfort and reassurance. He took me back without a second thought, and enabled my drinking with longing. Eventually the truth was exposed, and I found out he had been sleeping with two other girls. Any other sane, healthy person would have left him the moment the secret was unraveled, but I just craved this self-mutilation. One of the nights I had passed out deliriously drunk, I awoke to him kicking me, shouting, "you need to leave!" In a nutshell he told me, I had crossed the line with my drinking, and my pathetic behavior was detestable.

Once those words left his mouth, I went home and threw a hissy fit. Not caring that my mother and brother were around, I went straight to the bottle. In an inebriated rage with tears, screaming at my family, my mother swiped the liquor from me, and I headed to the bathroom. There, I put a knife up to my wrist in preparation for my death. Without indecision, Mother broke down the door. My heart was pounding, I couldn't breathe and I was weeping "NO NONONONO I CAN'T DO THIS, I CAN'T LIVE!" I was going insane; I needed help and knew it. That night I spent in the emergency room, waiting for a room in a mental hospital. When I arrived, therapists, psychologists, psychiatrists, nurses, and social workers were all in a frenzy. When not flattering me about my maturity and wisdom, they were preaching to me about how I was a manic-depressive and needed to take my meds. I rejected any idea of these dependent chemicals, but ironically I did little more than worship fermented grapes. Since I denied medication there was no reason for me to be under the care of the hospital. I was referred to an intensive outpatient program for chemical dependency, and was sent home after four days.

I am currently in this IOPCD, it is three hours a day, four days a week for seven weeks. On top of that I am attending three AA and CA meetings a week. With a therapist I see once a week, enforced by my other therapist. I too, found a sponsor, and am working on my first step, which consists of me admitting that my life had become unmanageable and I am powerless over drugs and alcohol. Although I wish I could say I am cured and this therapy is what I needed all along, I am still confused about the twenty-first century psychology theories. Am I a manic-depressive, am I an addict, do I have these diseases, or do I just make poor choices? If I am so sick, as they claim, why am I getting a full-ride academic scholarship? Am I just weak, an escapist who can't handle this world? Is my situation more the nurture than the nature? My father was gone, my ex stepfather was a violent alcoholic, I had been deprived of the right to my own body by several predators. My mother was incapable of any mothering whatsoever. Wouldn't any other human feel insecure and diet compulsively? Do I not have the right to my angst? The Freudians would view my behavior as normal according to my past, but now everything has gone down to a science and I am "sick." Whatever the reason may be, I am abstaining from any mood-altering drugs at this time, and have sixteen days under my belt. Though I do not recommend everyone should quit their meds, I just believe I am one of the few who was treated early and understands her troubles. Psychiatry is not for me, but for the time being, therapy is saving my life. I have picked up writing and acting again, this time I am hoping the arts will redeem my soul. I wake up every morning now with meditation and prayer, and the mirrors are becoming less and less torn each day.

My Story

Margery Wakefield

I was nine years old when I first knew something was wrong. I was at a large family picnic in Dell Rapids, South Dakota. The other kids were all playing and happy, but I did not feel like playing. Suddenly I had the sense of being different. I knew I was not like the other kids. Something was wrong. I called it "the shadow."

All was not well at home. My parents fought a lot. I hated the sound of their voices, from the time my dad came home from work, until late into the night. The fights were about different things, but mostly about money.

To escape the fighting, I learned to dissociate. I learned to "go out the window." If I would stand near a window, I could project myself out the window to a place where I was no longer aware of what was going on in the room. I could no longer hear the fighting. It worked in the car as well. I always had to sit near a window. That way, if the fighting started, I could go out the window.

I was a piano prodigy, but I hated to perform. The music was mine, my secret world, my escape, and I didn't want to share it. I remember sitting in the back seat of the car and being driven to various competitions and musical gatherings at which I was to perform. I had terrible feelings, horrible feelings. I didn't know it at the time, but I was decompensating. I was experiencing the first stages of psychosis.

At about this time, I started to see faces in the windows of our house. I called them my Halloween faces. They were monstrous and disfigured. They scared me. I would hide under the telephone table in the hall until they would go away.

I was an unhappy child. In particular, I hated dolls. If anyone gave me a doll as a present, I would take it upstairs, get a scissors, and hack the doll to pieces, all the time fantasizing about growing up and having babies and killing them. Is it any surprise that when I did grow up I did just that? By the time I was thirty, I had had six abortions. No maternal feelings for me.

The shadow followed me throughout grade school, throughout junior high school, and into high school. I knew that something was terribly wrong. I went to two of my teachers. "Please help me," I pleaded with them. "I don't have a personality." That was the only way I knew to describe what was wrong.

I was seventeen when I had my first major break with reality, my first nervous breakdown. I graduated from high school and traveled to England to study piano with a teacher there. I started to have terrible anxiety attacks, more like terror attacks. I started to hallucinate all the time. I would go to art museums and stand and stare at pictures for hours, seeing beauty that no one else saw in the pictures. It was like being on an LSD trip.

I would wake up in the middle of the night screaming with fear. My roommate took me to the local hospital, but they could find nothing wrong with me. Eventually, I lost contact with reality altogether. I remember standing in the living room of our rented flat in London, and seeing nothing but wavy yellow energy. All reality had disappeared.

My friends realized that something was wrong. They took me to my piano teacher. Together they decided to take me to the airport and send me back to the States. All I remember of the trip was sitting next to a little boy who had a teddy bear.

I made my way to Philadelphia where I had a male friend

named Lorenzo. He put me up in his apartment. In the morning I went into the living room and looked out the window. There was London! It was actually the middle of December, and there was London in the fall with the red buses, and people walking and the Thames and turning leaves. I knew that wasn't right. I went to the front door and opened it, and there was Philadelphia and snow and cold. I went back into the living room, and there was London again. The mind is truly remarkable.

The next night, I was in bed and I woke in the middle of the night to hear a beautiful symphony playing on the radio. It sounded like Schumann, but I didn't recognize the symphony. I heard a chorus of voices coming from the ceiling, singing and talking to me, saying different things, all at the same time. I turned over in bed to find someone with dark hair sleeping beside me, yet when I tried to see the person more clearly, they faded away.

The next morning I woke up and discovered that the radio was not plugged in. I had composed my own Schumann symphony in the middle of the night.

I told Lorenzo what was going on and he took me to the Philadelphia City Hospital. I was examined there, and of course could not answer any of their questions (what was the date, day, who was President, etc.), and was promptly admitted to the psychiatric unit. That's when the pain started in earnest. Until then the pain (anxiety) had been sporadic and difficult to manage, but now it was constant and unendurable. I was in excruciating pain from the moment I woke up until I went to sleep. I want everyone to know that mental illness can be cruelly painful.

Somehow I had smuggled a pair of fingernail scissors onto the unit. One day, unable to bear the pain any longer, I went into the bathroom and began to cut my wrists. A nurse discovered me in time to save my life, and she confiscated the scissors and bandaged my wounds.

At some point I was walking past the nurses' station and I saw my chart in the window. On the chart was my name, and on the corner it said, "schizophrenic." My reaction to this was unusual. I wasn't afraid. On the contrary, it was a relief to me to know what was wrong. Finally, the shadow had a name. And if it had a name, then maybe something could be done about it.

I stayed in the hospital for six months. I witnessed horrors. Two women on my unit had lobotomies. Every day, patients were taken for shock treatment, which in those days was given without anesthesia. My father had mercifully refused to sign the papers authorizing shock treatment for me, so I was spared. But the experience of seeing people dragged away screaming, held down on gurneys by orderlies, and taken away every morning scared me.

Scarier still was the illness. What if it never went away? That was the thought that frightened me the most. I saw patients that had been hospitalized for years, and I wondered if that was to be my fate. My father later told me that on one occasion, the psychiatrist in charge of my care told him that I would never live outside an institution. Although the doctor was partly right—I was to spend ten years in institutions—my father lived to see me happy and productive in life.

In all, I have been hospitalized fifty-five times, more or less. I have lost count. I have had that many nervous breakdowns. But in later years my luck changed. Once out of the hospital, I earned two college degrees, including a Master's in Social Work. I have worked productively for many years. I have written four books, been to Europe four times on my own, and have generally had a happy life.

Part of this is due to increasingly improving medications. Today, I take three medications: Abilify for the voices, Lexapro for depression, and Klonopin for anxiety. The voices are still there, but I have learned to ignore them. The shadow has always lurked in the background. I will never be completely "normal," whatever that is. But today I work, go out with friends, write, read, and travel. I am, for the most part, enjoying a happy life.

And that is the best revenge.

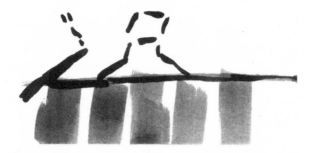

Jumping Off the Fence

Gary Brotman

Part 1 of 4

There are many titles that could head this story but this is the one I chose because it is one that I can mentally picture with respect to the life I have lived. The subject matter is not comfortable, yet there are many people in this world that are suffering what I have suffered and still feel vulnerable with nowhere to turn. The subject is mental illness and it not only affects those afflicted with it, but also the family members who try desperately to understand. This story is dedicated to those still suffering, with a simple message: DON'T GIVE UP!!

It is my intention in this story to tell you about the road I have traveled and the decisions I have chosen to make. Many of the decisions I made only exacerbated the illness I have finally overcome. By reading my story and identifying with behaviors that are common with mental illness, and the medications that doctors insist we take to feel normal, yet manifest unpleasant side effects that make our lives less than adequate, the title to this story will come to have a meaning for you as well. In jumping off the fence, there are four steps. This story will address each step by including a part of my life that corresponds to those steps and the choices that led to each subsequent step. It is my hope that you, too, will examine the choices you have made thus far, to find out where you are with your own personal fence, so that you can build the courage to take the next step to finding the true, happy person inside. Before I go on, I want to mention that each person's case is unique and that you shouldn't stop any prescribed medications without first discussing it with your doctors, because withdrawals from any drug could be dangerous if not monitored carefully.

The first step is called the Observation Step: Looking at the fence. It is the beginning and the first sign that something isn't quite right. Like most kids, the earliest recollections of my childhood were normal and happy. My childhood photos show me as a smiling and well-adjusted kid. I remember being shy, quiet, and sensitive. When I was about five years old, I had a security blanket. What kid doesn't? I used to suck my thumb and carry it around with me all the time. As the normal next step in growing, my mother said that I had to throw my blanket away. Being rather attached to it, I felt like I had lost a best friend. I was hurt and sad.

In 1967, my parents got divorced. I realize this happens in a lot of homes. When this happened, no one told me about it. All of a sudden, I was uprooted from a way of life I was comfortable with, taken from friends I had fun with. My whole life turned upside down, and for the first time I felt the stirrings of rage. Like all kids, I bounced back and focused on this new life. My parents had joint custody of my siblings and me so I still got to see my dad. The new school was nice and I began to be more sociable again. I discovered that I had a gift for athletics and I began to play sports. I was good at them and the exercise was a way to deal with the anger inside so that I didn't notice it so much.

My mother, now a single parent, was forced to work. I became resentful that she was no longer there for me. She would come home tired and was often moody and unpredictable.

She began to yell and scream at me a lot and was always angry. I didn't understand but I felt like I wasn't good enough for her. Eventually, she began to date other men and this always made me uncomfortable and insecure. I felt they could never be good enough for her.

My siblings and I still got to spend time with Dad. He always took us to eat out and then we would do other activities like bowling, miniature golf, and frequently, we would go to the movies. On one such occasion, we found a puppy and Mom let us keep her. She named the dog Bonnditt and I loved this little dog. At that time and later in life, this sweet little dog gave me a great deal of comfort.

As the years wore on, I became immersed in school activities and sports. I loved the competition that sports provided and I was very talented at it. In the fifth grade, I was elected Vice President of the entire elementary school. It was probably the first time I was proud of myself. I had put in a lot of work to be elected and it was a great accomplishment. The next year, I was elected President and was also chosen for the Little League All-Star team, where I started at second base. Everything was going great.

In 1973, I began Junior High. It was a bigger school and I was uncomfortable there. I was 13 and began isolating, spending more time alone. I was lonely and unhappy. My mother took me to see a psychiatrist for the first time, but because I refused to acknowledge my feelings, he refused to see me again. I began to feel anger for no reason and would take out my anger on my younger siblings. I didn't want to hurt them, but I couldn't stop and became angrier with myself. It seemed this emotion was taking me over. I also developed distrust toward people. My father took a new job farther away, and though he continued to see us, the visits became more infrequent. I began to feel abandoned by my dad. It hurt more than I thought it would. I became more isolated and depressed.

Even though most kids in a similar situation feel these strong emotions, it is a grieving process and once the situation stabilizes, life goes on. With me, this was not the case. Some experts believe mental illness is a genetic disease and that it is often inherited and manifests in each generation. As I look back, I can see this tendency with my mother in her fits of anger. My anger was similar and I acted out just as she did. I didn't understand why I had these intense feelings within me. I just knew, at the tender age of 13, that I didn't want to live anymore. I had my first thoughts of suicide. I looked ahead and saw the fence; the very object that manifested itself in my mind in the form of mental illness. I would keep moving forward to the next step—the beginning step—climbing the fence.

Part 2 of 4

In the first part, I introduced the first step to Jumping Off the Fence, the observation step—looking at the fence. This is when I first started to notice that things weren't quite right. I had begun to isolate myself and withdraw. Everyday life became a struggle and suicide became a part of my thinking process. While this happens to many adolescents, they usually grow out of it and go on to live normal, happy, productive lives. This wasn't the case with me. As a result of this, I saw the fence ahead of me, an imaginary obstacle, if you will, but very real to me. As with any obstacle, I wanted it out of the way. But first I had to get there.

This article introduces step 2; the beginning step—Climbing the Fence. It was never my intention to begin taking drugs or smoking. In Elementary school, we were shown films on the subject and our teacher mentioned that some of us would probably experiment with various drugs. I had vowed that it wouldn't be me. There was a certain babysitter that stayed with us on occasion while Mom would go out. It was during one of these nights that she went out to her car and I followed. She lit up a joint and began smoking it. Out of curiosity, I asked if I could try and she passed it to me. I couldn't inhale, but there was a buzz just from her smoking it. It was the beginning of an addiction that hadn't manifested yet. Some experts believe, that for people who suffer from mental illness, addiction often goes hand in hand as we try anything to ease the suffering.

In 1976, I began High School. I was becoming more and more isolated and had no friends or close relationships with anyone. I was painfully lonely and felt like giving up. I had no desire to live and just wanted to kill myself, somehow, some way. My life changed again when a new kid moved into the neighborhood just up the street from me. Billy and I were the same age and in the same grade. We became friends and would smoke marijuana together. One day in particular, Billy and I took a drive. We were listening to music and smoking pot. For the first time I really got high and completely stoned. I couldn't stop laughing. It felt so good to be high. When I was stoned, I felt less inhibited and all of my senses were heightened. Everything seemed better when I was stoned and I didn't seem as depressed, either. I became more sociable and formed a circle of friends. Unfortunately, my using didn't stop with pot. I began to drink alcohol, smoke regular cigarettes, and experiment with other drugs such as quaaludes and cocaine. My friends could relate to me on this level and I could relate to them.

In my senior year of High School, my mother sold our house and we moved to a larger, four-bedroom condominium. I wasn't happy about the move, but I was allowed to continue attending my current High School and finish out the year so I could graduate with my class. It shouldn't have mattered, because I hated school. When graduation was just around the corner, I was five credits short of graduating. My parents were adamant that I get my diploma, so I went to summer school and earned my five credits. I was tired of school and burnt out but my parents were proud of me. I couldn't concentrate in school, was bored, and my attention span was practically non-existent. I would smoke marijuana in the morning and go to school stoned.

From that point, things escalated. I tried Junior College but dropped out after seven weeks. I was still living at home so all of my expenses were paid for but I still needed money just to pay for my growing marijuana and cigarette habit. My first job was at a heating and air-conditioning business as a foot canvasser. After two months, I quit. By now, I was smoking a tremendous amount of marijuana and didn't care where I did it; sometimes in my own room. My life began to revolve around it. It would numb the pain inside. It made the depression go away for a while.

My father remarried and she was a nice lady. I became resentful of her, feeling that she was taking Dad away from me. Then Dad got a job for me where he worked. I packed my things and moved in with him. I thought, perhaps this environment would be good for me. I worked the evening shift and met two other guys who also worked there. We were all the same age and we all smoked marijuana. We would get stoned on our breaks. My new routine consisted of sleeping in and getting ready for work. Soon, I began to feel like a stranger in my father's house. We couldn't communicate. Since the job was temporary, I moved back to my mother's.

I took different jobs that never lasted long because I got bored, or did things wrong. My mother suggested I take an Erhard Seminars Training course. It had made a difference for her. It taught a new way of thinking, teaching empowerment and how effective action could make a lasting impact on important concerns in our lives. I connected to the people there and began to feel like I belonged. I took a better job as a telephone salesman that was straight commission and really began to make some money. I was growing up. I moved away from home, began wearing glasses. Things were looking up. By 1981, I considered myself a financial success. I had earned the pride of my friends and parents.

Like most things in my life, this, too, didn't last. I moved around. First, back to Mom's temporarily; then with a roommate in a small apartment. I decided to become an actor. I took classes, had pictures taken of me for my portfolio. I began wearing contacts. I really enjoyed acting. I had another social group and we would go to a local restaurant and talk about our dreams and aspirations over food and drinks. One morning, I woke up with a pounding headache. There were blisters and rashes running down the right side of my face and eye. The pain was excruciating. I went to a doctor and was diagnosed with shingles. Antibiotics and creams took care of the problem but I was left with a scar on my forehead. I was self conscious about the scar and quit going to acting classes. My second biggest dream, being a professional actor, came to a screeching halt. As a result, I picked up bad habits again. I felt the world was against me. I had climbed the fence.

Part 3 of 4

In part one, we took a look at the first of my four-step process; the observation step—looking at the fence. This was a recollection of early childhood memories up to the point when I turned thirteen and first noticed that things weren't quite what they should be with regard to how I felt and responded to others. The second part, the beginning step—climbing the fence, was the beginning of bad habits that became an established pattern. I experienced a series of highs and lows with regard to events in my life but no matter what I did or how successful I was at something, it was fragile like a house of cards. When the ill wind of fate blew in, my house of cards crumbled and I ended up right back at square one. In this part I'll introduce you to the third step of the process; the decision step—Sitting on the Fence.

It is now 1983. I am 23 years old and my health isn't very good. My diet and nutrition was poor and I wasn't sleeping very well. I was very thin and continued to lose weight. I really wanted to get better so I decided to quit smoking, began drinking healthy drinks, and began to exercise. In spite of these changes, I still had no energy and could barely function at work. On March 29th, I woke with horrible stomach pain. When I went to the doctor, I was telling him about my pain and began to cry uncontrollably. The doctor felt it was best to admit me to the hospital. While there, the pains got worse and I would scream for the nurse, who would run in and give me a shot of some strong pain medication. The sensation from the medication was wonderful, warm, and comfortable. It was also temporary. The doctor ordered tests that revealed that my bladder was descended and I needed immediate surgery. After the surgery, I was wheeled back to my room where I felt comfortable, nurtured, and taken care of. I didn't want to leave. While there, I wrote a will. Since I couldn't stay, I wanted to die.

The doctor suggested that I talk to a psychiatrist, so I walked over to another room and met with the psychiatrist on duty. Again, I began crying uncontrollably. After talking to him, I went back to my room. I was diagnosed as having a nervous breakdown. Eight days in the hospital was all I was allowed and when I left, I was dazed and confused. I could no longer go back to my job and filed for state disability insurance as well as workers' compensation against my company for stress.

I began to see a psychiatrist I will call Doctor Jones. He diagnosed me as having major depression and dysthymia and put me on medication. He also suggested I go to group therapy once a week. I had not smoked marijuana in quite a while and made the decision at this time that it would be best if I stop all together. Dr. Wilson was in charge of the group therapy sessions that I attended. I liked group therapy. Everyone there all had similar problems in life. I continued to see Dr. Jones even though nothing relevant happened there. He would listen while I talked and continued to recommend the group therapy and that I continue my medications. The medication had bad side effects. My appetite increased and I gained 20 pounds. My mouth was always very dry and I was constipated. I really hated the side effects.

My brother lived with me in a one-bedroom apartment. It

was a comfort that he was with me. After several months of not working, I finally found the courage to start looking for employment again. I found a job as a teller trainee at a savings and loan. I had to dress up for this job, but that had never been necessary for any other job I had worked and I found it very uncomfortable and irritating. The new job was far enough away that I could no longer make it to group therapy. I also stopped taking my medication and no longer saw Dr. Jones. The side effects of the medications had become unbearable.

Shortly after beginning the job, I received a settlement from my stress claim and used it to buy a nicer car and to move into a larger apartment. My brother moved with me and added a cat to the mix. I was allergic to the cat, but he wouldn't get rid of it. While working at the bank, I helped an older lady with a safety deposit box that was very heavy and I strained my back. My neck became stiff and I had to take time from work, filing a worker's compensation claim for my back. I began to see a chiropractor and felt better almost instantly. The staff was very friendly and I took advantage of the other services such as massage and yoga. Everything was paid by my employer's insurance company. Even with all the treatment, I constantly suffered with backaches and stiff neck and other muscles. I returned to work and transferred to a closer branch. My brother moved in with his girlfriend and that hurt. The lethargy and depression returned and I went to see Dr. Wilson. He diagnosed me with major depression and I found myself on medications again. I was constantly in pain now and had to leave my job. The medication I was taking made me irritable and shaky. I wasn't sleeping and felt like I was going to jump out of my skin. Mom rushed me to the hospital after I called her and the doctor put me on medication that counteracted the symptoms I was having. I stopped taking medications and vowed never to take any more.

In 1989, I discovered a 12-step program called Co-Dependents Anonymous (CoDA). Based on the Alcoholics Anonymous program, it was in its infancy. The people there shared their stories and how the program had benefited their lives. I began to relate to and identify with them. They became my social circle and were the human contact that I desperately needed. I opened up with my own story, eventually became the main speaker, and found I was popular again. Making a difference in the lives of others made me feel good. In 1990, my brother got married and I was the best man. Things were looking up for me again.

Most people, when they experience the presence of God, have usually been searching for him. He actually found me. I began to cry then I got angry. Why did this have to happen to me? Shortly after, I realized my life was spiraling out of control and then I prayed very hard for the right answers. At CoDA, one of my friends pleaded with me to seek help. Even though it was the last thing I wanted to hear, I recognized it was also the truth. I went to a different psychiatrist, was diagnosed with the same as before and put on more medication. I had hit rock bottom, having no money. I applied for Social Security Disability benefits and food stamps. I was now in the system and was assigned a social worker. I continued to go from one psychiatrist to another and was put on different drugs to treat the same diagnosis.

In 1993, I was accepted into a program that was doing research on a new anti-depressant at UCLA. I was a good candidate and I did feel better on the medication. When the research ended, I was asked to continue to see the psychiatrist, Dr. Caldwell. During the study, they did a PET scan of my brain. On one of my monthly visits with Dr. Caldwell, I noticed there were pictures of brains on his wall. He explained to me that one of them was mine from the research study and that based on the results of that study, there was a noticeable change in the chemical makeup in my brain. Dr. Caldwell told me at this time that I may have to stay on the medications for the rest of my life. Due to my diagnosis and history of relapse, there was an 80% to 90% chance that I would relapse again should I go off of them. I was feeling so much better and the idea of sinking into that black hole of depression scared me. I was convinced that the medications were working for me. So, I decided to continue with them as Dr. Caldwell recommended.

I tried working again only with the same results. After a short relationship with a young woman I had intentions of marrying fell through, my anger resurfaced in a big way. I couldn't take working anymore and cashed in my 401K, using the money for Lasik eye surgery and a tattoo. I sought and found female companionship that was meaningless and for only one reason. I started a business venture with my brother that failed. I was living with Mom at the time. A therapist I was seeing at the time urged me to move out on my own. I moved in with my cousin. And so things continued in this vicious cycle of working, quitting, moving, doctors, and medications. It was as if I was on a nightmarish carousel. Instead, I found myself sitting on the fence. It was decision time.

Part 4 of 4

My journey with mental illness started in part one, with my four-step process, from early childhood to the first realization that something was wrong. Next, I had to deal with the fallout from the divorce of my parents, the beginning of my descent into the world of drugs and addictive behaviors. The third part dealt with the endless cycles of trying to fit into society by working as a responsible adult, only to find that I needed the help of psychiatrists and fell into the routines of counseling, group therapy, and medications. I couldn't handle any of it for long and it became a vicious circle that spiraled downward until I found myself sitting on my figurative fence. It is time for a decision. Either I stay on this cycle of negativity that is going nowhere, or I decide to believe in myself and God. Actually, I am rather straddling the fence, weighing the options of where I have been against the unknown. In this part, I make a decision. This is the Action step—Jumping Off the Fence.

The beginning of the end of this story finds me in need of a job again since the state disability is drying up. I took a job at a large health insurance company as a claims examiner. I worked long hours. I was living with my cousin in a tiny bedroom where I would spend all my off time. I had become a loner. I also found myself falling back into depression and was referred to another psychiatrist. Dr. Garza diagnosed me with major depression and advised that I continue with the medication. I was under a lot of stress at work and he also recommended that my hours be reduced to no more than 40 per week. I also began to see a social worker by the name of Lynn Thomas. Lynn was a therapist, and during my time with her, it was determined that I should move out of my cousin's place and get one of my own. The apartment I found was nice and it was also very close to work.

I still had close ties with my brother and we went to Las Vegas one weekend and shared a hotel room. He observed that I snored extremely loudly and made weird noises as I slept. A few weeks later, I woke in the middle of the night gagging and gasping for air. I began having a harder time waking in the morning and was exhausted after work. The fatigue got worse with each passing day. Because of this, I entered a sleep study at the recommendation of my internist, Dr. Brown. The results of this showed I was suffering from severe sleep apnea. The doctor at the sleep center prescribed a CPAP machine, which would help me breathe at night. I tried it but found it intolerable and so I quit using it.

At work, I was placed into a new position as a Systems Support Coordinator. I needed the change because I was bored where I was. After a short time I was transferred to a brand-new unit with a raise in salary that had me making more money than I had ever made before. On the other hand, the sleep apnea was growing worse. I was so tired all the time and I just wanted to sleep. My family dentist referred me to an ENT and plastic surgeon, Dr. Cohen. At the time, Dr. Cohen was the only surgeon performing a relatively new and innovative surgery to treat and cure sleep apnea. I made arrangements at work to take some time off and on January 19th of 2004 I underwent the 4½-hour-long surgery. Several procedures were performed and I spent four days in the hospital recovering. It was very painful. I returned to work on February 9th. I suffered through two more follow-up surgeries in the next year and the results of the next sleep study showed a significant improvement. I was very nearly cured. However, work began to weigh on me, causing stress, and I found I could no longer work again.

I continued to see Dr. Garza, who put me on disability for two months. The diagnosis remained the same, and he recommended that I stay on the current dose of medication and see him in one month. This was 2005. I began to taper off the medications under the supervision of Dr. Garza and suffered terrible withdrawal. Once again, I vowed never to take psychiatric medications again.

During this time, I applied for Social Security benefits. I also hired a lawyer to negotiate a severance package on my behalf from my employer. I knew I could no longer work. Depression is like a bad penny. It just keeps turning up. I went to see yet another psychologist for weekly therapy and was referred to another psychiatrist who diagnosed me with bipolar disorder. He put me on a very different medication that gave me bad side effects and I stopped taking the medication.

In July of 2006, I received the severance compensation from my employer, but by the time everyone had their part of it, I was left with little. Fortunately, my health insurance would continue for a while. I continued to see the psychologist on a weekly basis but quit, feeling that it was doing no good.

In March 2007, I was awarded Social Security benefits with a review of my condition in another year. In May, I went to see a medical doctor who recommended marijuana for my depression. I was given a special license that would enable me to legally smoke it. Next door to the doctor was the co-op that actually dispensed the drug. I walked in and was greeted by an armed guard who asked to see my license and ID. I was then escorted to a locked security door that was opened for me. Inside was a showcase that displayed different varieties of marijuana. The clerk explained the different varieties and I purchased the pot and left.

I seemed to have come full circle. I smoked the marijuana several times and did feel pretty good. The depression lifted. I was experiencing some severe social anxiety and began to develop a sore throat. I was also afraid to drive while under the influence and in less than two weeks, I quit smoking it and discarded the unused portions.

In June, I decided to try again, this time going to a store recommended by the doctor who issued the license. I was greeted by a guard, filled out paperwork, and was then escorted inside, where I talked with employees who seemed more knowledgeable and courteous. I made my purchase, was given a cannabis brownie for being a new patron, issued an itemized receipt, and went home. I resumed smoking the pot.

On June 14th, I volunteered to participate in the filming for a documentary on the use of medicinal marijuana as a treatment for my clinical depression. We met at a co-op store that sold it and commenced with the filming of the entire procedure from purchase to my explaining the condition that I had and what I was attempting to achieve. I went home with a small baggie of samples, and a peanut butter edible all packaged neatly in a white bag complete with a prescription written on it. After smoking the pot, I had the same sore throat and finally concluded that I could no longer continue to smoke the marijuana. I decided that there would be no more marijuana, period.

Upon my decision with regard to psychiatric medications and medicinal marijuana, I decided on a holistic approach to managing my mental illness. I changed my diet, began taking nutritional supplements, started an exercise program that included yoga and meditation, more sleep, and lots of water. I also began using positive affirmations, prayer, and chiropractic treatment and massage. I jumped off the fence into the unknown and have found that this approach is working well for me. I take life one day at a time and find that I am grateful for the life I have. I have discovered that I love myself in spite of my imperfections. I looked inside and found self acceptance, which led to happiness. This is my true self.

Everybody has their own journey with their own decisions to make. I just wanted to share mine and give you the message that I discovered by jumping off the fence. Never quit, never give up, and never lose hope.

Life in Mental Health

Cheryl A. Stephison

My daughter is watching cartoons. It's Kim Possible and she's immersed in the dialogue. I'm hearing voices again. "It's you," says the television, "You're the one." I can't eat, I can't sleep, and I'm talking too loud. I have bipolar disorder and I'm in the manic phase. My ears are ringing, my thoughts are racing, and I think I'm a Muslim saint. This is the reality of my mental illness. I'm seriously ill but convinced otherwise. I think the medication is killing me. I'm dangerously close to being admitted for another 10 days. How did I get here? I'm middle class, college educated, and my IQ is off the charts. I was a mental health employee for 11 years. How could I now be mentally ill?

My family was dysfunctional. I was sexually abused as a child, and my mother always viewed me as a rival. No wonder I thought I was the only normal one. It took years of therapy for me to take responsibility for my illness instead of blaming everyone else. Acceptance, my doctor says, is the first step toward recovery. In a week or two, I'll be well enough to work on my person-centered plan through my objectives. I've been diagnosed for 12 years, and I have a lot of objectives.

I believe recovery means functioning in the community with a minimum of support from Community Mental Health.

It's not so easy. When I make friends they are put off by my silences. My behavior is just eccentric enough to make people around me uneasy. I have church to attend. It's mostly older people who have surrounded me with care without knowing about my illness. I'm afraid to tell them. My most profound and most rewarding relationship is with God. He is always merciful, always forgiving. I spend a lot of time by myself, in meditation or prayer. I believe prayer is a healer and that it can lift me out of mental illness. I've been to workshops and conferences and I believe I have built a solid foundation for recovery. I haven't had a relapse in seven or eight years. I've been discharged from counseling and my behavior is stabilized. I feel very fortunate.

My day to day life is simple. I don't work so I just stay home and keep house. I have very severe arthritis so a person comes in to help with the heavier work. I nap and work on the computer. I can't do handwritten drafts any more. I spend an hour or so daily on research on the Internet. I look up medical research on my illnesses and various other topics I'm interested in. I go for a small walk and I spend two or three hours on my writing. It's just enough activity in a day for me to stay stable and unstressed. Lately I've been working with Michigan Protection and Advocacy to press my landlord for accommodations such as handrails and extra insulation. I start each day with the expectation that this will be the day I have completed my recovery and found a cure.

It's a constant struggle to stay healthy, both mentally and physically. As I've said, I have to accept that I'm mentally ill. It's a big challenge. In bipolar disorder you can get just well enough to say you don't need doctors or the medication. There's constant internal pressure to chuck the whole treatment program and head out on your own. No one wants to have a lifelong health problem, especially one with the stigma of mental illness. It's far easier to pretend nothing is wrong and that your latest crisis was caused by some circumstance beyond your control. Denial, as they say in AA, is more than a river in Egypt.

I've found I have to be vigilant with my sleep schedule, my exercise and my eating habits. Moderation is the key to everything. I often read about herbal treatments for my illness, but after several experiments sent me to the hospital I stay away from everything that would interact with my regular medications. Instead I eat a balanced diet, exercise as much as I can, and regularly sleep 10 or 11 hours a night. I have kept a journal for 30 years. It has been a place to pour out my frustrations, my fears and my hopes. I've become so much calmer as I've grown older, and my journaling is now an outlet that gives me great pleasure.

I was in counseling from 1983 to 2006. Those years were spent with a variety of psychologists and social workers. I thought it was all going nowhere until one day I realized I had no more problems to discuss and my greatest objective was to get free of Community Mental Health and to get well. I go for med checks every eight weeks or so, but I am happy to be free of regular sessions. I have integrated my mental health care with my physician's care, and I think I am closing in on the elusive cure. Instead of meeting with a therapist I meet regularly with my minister for spiritual guidance. I've decided my great work is writing, and I'm satisfied with the solitary time and regular deadlines.

Mental illness has had a profound impact on my life. Not only did I work ten years in a state institution for the mentally ill but I have also been privileged to witness unprecedented changes in the treatment of the mentally ill. When I was a young child my mother used to tell me "you are a mental case" and assured me I was destined to end up spending my life at Pontiac State Hospital. These unfortunate words have stayed with me throughout my life and prefigured my eventual diagnosis. When I later began working at Pontiac State, I met many patients that were not so different from me. In those days people with even the mildest symptoms might find themselves condemned to a long-term commitment. When the medication revolution became widespread these same patients no longer needed hospitalization. The result was not

immediate, but about a decade after the advent of medications, patients began to leave the hospitals in great numbers,
moving into adult foster care and individual settings.

Over the years I worked at Pontiac State, the patient population dropped from 3500 to about 800. Thereafter, Community Mental Health was born. The Michigan Department of
Mental Health faced a second revolution, focusing on serving
the patient through the development of the Community Mental Health system. Patients received more individual attention
from therapists, but were left to their own devices regarding
medication compliance. Over the years that Community Mental Health has been in existence, patients came to be called
consumers and developed a list of consumer rights, including
refusal of care and appeals of proposed treatments. Consumers
developed peer groups and came to have a substantial voice in
the Department of Community Health. As budgetary constraints became a major factor in mental health care, patients
began to be discharged from Community Mental Health altogether. Where previously the system had been reluctant to let
go of the control of patients, it was now forced to discharge
many patients who were merely lingering in care for the sake
of medication compliance and funding.

Community Mental Health as we know it is about to come
to an end. Its bloated, expensive form is being dismantled by a
state government forced to reconsider services available to its
population. Advances in modern science are making changes
as well. Research in gene formation raises the possibility that
gene therapy may be the wave of the future in mental health
care. There is some possibility that medication use will end
and gene manipulation will become the preferred method of
treatment. In the realm of therapy, I believe there is increasing
emphasis on treatment of the family dynamic. Consumers are
sometimes recognized as the identified patient, while the rest
of the family is considered dysfunctional. Individuals and
families are encouraged to consider how family interaction
affects the consumer's condition. Mental health support ser-

vices therefore focus on making the consumer comfortable both individually and in a larger family system. Support is also provided by groups founded loosely on conditions such as depression or schizophrenia. Planned sharing of experiences among consumers allows them to understand that they are not isolated individuals and helps them learn coping mechanisms from other consumers.

I am much different than I was when I was first diagnosed with bipolar disorder. I am firmly convinced of the benefit of medication. I also believe that talk therapy, in whatever form, is one of the most important parts of treatment. Mental health treatment is changing rapidly and is certain to take a much different form in the 21st century. I believe people with mental illness are well served by increasing public knowledge about the illness. Moving consumers outside the realm of stigma and into the mainstream of human experience is a compassionate treatment that allows room for their eventual recovery. That's the best outcome for a mental illness, and one I fervently hope for.

Why Do I Feel So Crummy?

Bernos "Bernie" J. Bliss

I've been feeling weighed down lately. Feels like I am moving through marshmallow cream. I am just stuck—can't go back or forward—just stuck. I don't like it one bit. I think that my anti-depressant may not be working. I know that medications sometimes stop working. I just feel so worthless. I find myself crying at times and I can't explain what it is that I am crying about. There are things written on my white board above the computer that I really should be doing. But I just slump over the keyboard and play another game of solitaire. It is so hopeless. I am not even excited about Christmas and it is only a week or so away.

I guess I will give my doctor a call and see what he says.

Our whole family has been affected with mental illness in one of its various forms. It is a story unlike that of other families. I'm the Mother, Ben is the father. The children are Shari, 40, Gretchen, 38, and Brent, 32. What a joy these children have been . . . even though there have been a few bumps in the road.

Brent's problems surfaced in early grade school. He would not get up and go to school. Nothing I could do seemed to make a difference. When I came home, in the afternoon, he seemed to be fine. His father was angry. I was hurting so much inside. You see, I was convinced that something was out of balance for him.

We had him tested for dyslexia, but that was not the problem. Still he didn't do homework and often didn't go to school. Teachers tried to be helpful. At someone's suggestion, we took him for a complete physical. High cholesterol. No other problems. He and I met with a nutritionist and we tried to change his eating habits.

His father and I disagreed. I still thought that there was something chemically out of balance.

My son lightly ticks off the questions that he is asked about his mental illness. "Have you been feeling hopeless?" "Do you sleep a lot or not very much?" "Are you having trouble remembering things, concentrating, making decisions?" I laugh and shrug it off, but several days later after thinking about those questions, I ask him again what they were.

One of his male teachers came to our house to see if he could get my son to come to school. Brent hid in the basement. When I came home, he told me that he had run out of the house, had jumped on his bike and the teacher had driven after him. He said he had fallen, even told me where it happened. How did I know if this was true? I didn't. Now I know that it may have been true in his mind, but not really real.

We saw therapists separately and together. He would be his best and brightest at these appointments. And I had to pay the bills. The assumption always was that he was choosing to behave as he did.

I still thought that there was something chemically out of balance. But where do I turn?

After his father and I divorced, Brent was living with me. His dad would take him every other weekend if it was convenient. The stress increased, as I was the one to deal with his behavior on a day-to-day basis. He joined the soccer program and I attended all of his games. Then he just quit. We now know that he had a panic attack and locked himself in the bathroom, curled up in a ball until the starting time of the game had passed and it was safe for him to come out. Nothing would make him return. He joined the Boy Scouts and did well, participating in their activities and programs. Then he quit going. Nothing could get him to go back to the scout meetings.

Money continued to be a problem. His father would periodically stop paying the $250 per month child support because Brent was not going to school. I would return to the lawyer who would write a letter to get things going again. Then I not only had no child support, I had to pay the lawyer!

My doctor calls me back and tells me that it is probably time for me to see a psychiatrist. He makes a couple of recommendations and I am left to follow through. I am leaning toward one doctor, but he is not on our insurance list. I don't recognize the names that are on the insurance program list, so I must decide if I will go with a name I know and pay more, or if I should go another route.

Somehow we survived junior high school. In 9th grade, Brent was active in the choir program at Lakewood High School. He was the youngest boy chosen to sing in the show choir. He bought a tuxedo, bow tie, and cummerbund. Again, I attended as many performances as I could. He was a little shy around the older singers. Then he quit that too. Didn't go to school and was dropped as a student because of excessive absence. I tried to be as supportive as I could. I knew that school just didn't work for him, but I didn't know why. I cried a lot, worried a lot, and tried to explain what was going on to friends who just didn't seem to understand.

Then, there were the jobs he tried. He was successful selling frozen yogurt for over a year. I drove him to work before he could drive and picked him up after work. He could be impressive at an interview, be hired, go to work for a day or maybe a few more, and just walk away or just quit going. From April of 1991 to December of 2001, he held twenty-two different jobs. Some lasted a day or so, the longest a year and five months.

Two weeks! My appointment with the psychiatrist is not for another two weeks! I am ready for treatment NOW. Christmas is coming and I have little desire to participate in activities that I love. Somehow I muddle through. Dozing off at the computer at work in the middle of the morning . . . struggling to do what I need to do, depending on John and Brent to do things that I am not able to do. I make a list of the symptoms that I am experiencing.

I remarried in 1990. My new husband had not been married before and he found that his learning curve with my three children was a steep one. He did not understand my son's behavior. He repeatedly suggested that Brent just straighten himself out. I had little idea of how to answer him. My stress grew even more.

Then my oldest daughter shared with us that she was in treatment for post-traumatic stress disorder because of nightmares of abuse by her father. I began to read books about abuse so that I could understand her situation. I had a lot of problems keeping myself together with two of my children suffering hurt and low self-esteem. Taking care of myself was not even on the radar screen during that time.

I still didn't have a name for my son's problem. I had no idea what was going on with him. My older daughter, who was on medication for her PTSD, urged him to get on some kind of medication. But he refused. I did not know where to go for help or whether he would go with me. I still believed he suffered with a chemical imbalance.

Finally it is the day of my appointment. I arrive early to do the paperwork that the office wants for my file. The room is dimly lit—is that supposed to be to mellow us out as we wait? I find it oppressive. I like the light much better. "Hi, I'm your psychiatrist." We enter a small room with a loveseat and several other chairs. I choose the loveseat and the interview begins. I give him my list of symptoms. He asks what I mean when I say I can't multi-task. I reply, "Like doing laundry, working on the computer, and cooking dinner, all at the same time."

My son passed the test for his GED, with honors. He is a very intelligent young man, but something was wrong, and I couldn't find out what it was. Jobs came and went. Friends came and went. He came to us to tell us he was engaged. It didn't work out. Then came the shooting at Columbine High School where my second daughter was a teacher. She was able to get her class out to safety, but there were many difficult days following that event.

I became totally consumed with the particular difficulties of each of my children. I was adjusting to a new marriage and I don't think I had any idea that I was struggling to keep myself together.

Money was constantly a problem. At one point I paid for my son to go to a community college. We paid for classes and books; he didn't go; he didn't withdraw. Several years later, he secured a student loan to attend another school. He told me he could get as far as the parking lot and couldn't get out of the car to go into class. Another panic attack. Again, he didn't withdraw. The student loan people wanted their money. The school had been paid, but it had not been used by my son. We refinanced our house to pay off the student loan. We continued to get letters from collection agencies for bills that were not paid.

Cars were another problem. Most years we used all of the towing from our AAA memberships for my son's car. Cars were abandoned, repossessed, and payments were not made in a timely manner. Pets created another problem. They chewed on furniture, barked a lot, and were not welcome in our home because of my husband's allergies. But one of them lived with us for a time, spending his time indoors in his cage or my son's room. My husband was tolerant during these difficult days, and I was caught in the middle between my son and my husband. It was so hard to hold myself together.

"Is there a history of mental illness in your family?" he asks. "Could be, I don't know for sure," I answered.

Well, we have here a case of bipolar type II. "That's what my son has," I reply. "I thought I probably gave it to him, since there is some thought of a genetic connection with mental illnesses."

Brent met Alex at one of his jobs. They wanted to get married. She has bipolar illness in addition to several other problems. We didn't know much about mental illness, but we did know that her behavior was sometimes hard to understand when she visited with us. She would get very upset when someone was engaged in conversation with my son. She was able to help my son because she knew the mental health options. He started on antidepressants just before their wedding, but they did not have time to kick in. He did a great job caring for her that day; she does not remember the wedding because of the stress and her medications.

But she tended toward the manic side of her illness and my son tended toward the depressive side. She always wanted to go *out,* and he always wanted to stay *in.* They eventually divorced.

Following the divorce, my son was transferred to a nearby city to manage a shoe store that was having some difficulties. The company thought that he could straighten things out. I helped him get moved to an apartment and things seemed to go well. He was lonely with no friends, managing a struggling store and only two dogs for company.

The doctor recommends that I stay on my anti-depressant and adds a mood stabilizer. I am to start with a small dose for a week, then increase it and return in three weeks. I know it will take time to adjust to the right dosage for me, but I am relieved to be on the way to getting better.

The depression hit my son and it hit hard. He didn't go to work. He didn't answer the phone. He didn't take his dogs out for a walk. He took too many pills. I don't even know if he ate. His regional manager was concerned that the store was not opened one morning and he drove 60 miles to find out why. He knew about the mental illness and when he got no response at the apartment, he contacted the manager and the police and entered the apartment. The paramedics, who were also present, took him to the emergency room where he was held in observation. He was given a medication to help with the panic and anxiety and sent home. It was very hard to be so far away and not able to be helpful.

Many stresses surfaced during this time. My husband and I moved farther north with his job. I continued to drive an hour and a half to my office and back. Then I was terminated from my position after twelve and a half years of employment. It was ugly and was not settled until nine months later. My stress increased and increased and increased. In September, we were out walking one morning when I began to cry and just felt an urgent need to go home. It was later in the morning that we learned of the bombings of the World Trade Center. More sadness.

We invited my son to move in with us. We moved his belongings to a storage unit near us and had his beloved 260Z towed to our home. That fall, I went to the hospital with chest pains. I remained overnight and after answering the questions asked by the doctor, he suggested that I was suffering from depression. I guess I wasn't surprised! I began taking an antidepressant and continue to this day.

We began to seek help from the local Behavioral Health facility. My son sees a medical doctor and a therapist/case manager regularly. He has changed his medications a number of times as we struggle to find the right combination. Another medication for sleep disorders gets him back on track in that regard. He can now go to the pharmacy and pick up his own medications without anxiety and panic.

We learned of a class called Family to Family by NAMI, (National Alliance on Mental Illness) for family members. We attended the twelve weeks of class and have a notebook full of material. This was a wonderful experience for us to begin to understand mental illness, meet other families who have similar situations, and learn how to relate to persons with mental illness.

I began to attend a support group meeting held once a month. The programs were informative and the conversation with other families was helpful. This involvement led to my election as president of NAMI in my county in 2003. My son has also served on that board of directors.

The adjustment to being a consumer (one who uses mental illness services) was a difficult one for me. I pictured myself helping others as I listen to them tell their stories. Now I am one who is asking for help, the one with mental illness not just depression. I try to tell my church family on a Sunday morning, but break down. I feel strongly that we need to let others know so that we will bust the stigma that is attached to mental illness.

My son makes another try at community college, but he struggles with attendance, grades and finances. Another bump in the road.

I was right . . . his problems were all due to a chemical imbalance. Bipolar, anxiety, depression, schizophrenia, ADHD, OCD—all are becoming key words in our vocabulary. We probably have tough days ahead, but we are much better equipped to survive them with our education about mental illness.

I am feeling so much better this week. It feels like I am coming out of a thick cloudbank into a thinner haze. I have another appointment with my doctor. I am going to take my mother's book and show him that my grandfather on my Dad's side died of a nervous breakdown and other illnesses. Nervous breakdown in those days is what we now call bipolar, he explains.

We continue talking about our diagnoses—that is one way to begin to reduce the stigma surrounding mental illness. We are sick, just like someone with cancer or diabetes.

Small accomplishments give me hope that my medication is working. I will continue to increase my dosage until we achieve the right balance for me . . . this week.

It feels like I am a new person—most of the time. I still find myself very tired or heavy with sad thoughts. But I will get better; I know that for sure. With support and prayers from my family, my church family, my NAMI family and other friends, I know there will be brighter days ahead.

Impoverishment

Dream Merchant

A dark cloud hovers over my head. The cloud is poverty. Its black rain of depression, thunderous fear, and frightening lightning of no money in sight means there is no reason to be hopeful. Still, I work to make my life better.

It all started when I was eighteen, just graduated from high school and in a fit of what they don't quite call insanity, I drove into a forest at seventy-five miles per hour on purpose.

No car, no money, and everybody thinking I'm crazy and avoiding me, for fear I was dangerous. The dark cloud started to form. (A bit of information, I've never been out of poverty and I am now thirty.) I realized I was in the hell of impoverishment just after moving out to the city with a drug-addicted stripper. I thought, "I'll just work, support myself, and enjoy life." The reality was I couldn't hold a job and after getting four or five different ones and losing them rapidly, I found I was out of money, had no way to pay rent, and there was no place I could go. My mom saved me as she had several times.

It didn't seem that it was the work itself that was the problem but rather the immensely gigantic number of matters on my mind. I then began to seriously develop writing, my favorite hobby. It was heaven to me while the workforce was hell. Life, besides writing, was sort of a limbo seeming to have no purpose or reason. Writing was something people just did. Something they felt like doing. I still didn't have any money.

The impoverishment has been the sickest part of my life all along. Some psychologists say that if you have an extremely traumatic experience you can develop mental blocks. My block was work and I was powerless to battle the forces that kept dragging me away from the many jobs I hated.

The connection between poverty and illness was time. For me, not lasting at jobs was a reflex, like jumping away from a fire that burns. I did last in poverty, though, and by looking at the dark cloud it was clear that a storm was brewing. My life was thunder and lightning with a vague memory of being broke. I tried to determine what was due to mental illness and what the other hidden factors were. Job after job, seldom lasting for more than a week. (How can one resist the instinct to jump out of the fire?) I found that poverty was a lifestyle I had to accept and might never escape. Many, many times I worried that I would be unable to escape homelessness.

I have long been on government disability. I want to make money but I do not wish to burn alive to do it. At most available jobs I can make enough to get off disability but not enough to raise me out of poverty.

It began to rain black drops of sickness again. The drops were a reflection of the many who called or considered me a loser. I thought I had a brilliant mind but that the only way to get money was to work a job that would kill my creativity. In poverty, I spent months with only thirty dollars a week to get food, cigarettes, and to go out twice for coffee. At the coffee shop, I would irritate the waitress because I did not have enough money for food. I had a desperate need to go out. All of my friends had ditched me because I had no money.

Poverty, there were millions of voices screaming in my ear, "Loser." Surviving on disability the voices screamed, "User".

I was in a group home for a year. I had ten dollars a week to spend on my social life. With no money, visitors were few and far between. I felt I was going more and more insane every second. During all this time frame I was never far from suicide. Many wanted me dead and I was broke.

There were influences. I said something nonthreatening to one guy I ran into. He replied, "I don't like you. Don't talk to me." Many people have many hateful thoughts and vendettas they seldom reveal. I am paranoid that there is a worldwide conspiracy against me by those who do not know me and my situation and who surmise that I am stupid and a loser. There are people who later confessed that they really did want me to commit suicide. My ex wanted me to kill myself. Her voice matched perfectly with the sound of the other voices I heard. Hatred is usually a secret, at least until the hatred is gone.

The dark cloud of impoverishment burst, dropping rainy darkness on my mind. Depression, regardless of how deep, is seldom as bad as having others hate you. Poverty is a way of life. For me it still is and I don't see any way out. I haven't owned or driven a car for four years. I've never been able to afford television or the internet. I do not know what it is to be middle class or even out of abject poverty. Work promises to drive me insane. Work has never told me that it could get me out of insanity. For many years I've looked for work. I have found that muscle is far more valuable than mind.

I'm one semester away from earning an associate degree in Liberal Arts. I just received a letter stating that they are stopping my disability. My case manager and psychiatrist have told me not to worry, they'll take care of it. I've been burned many times before. It seems no one cares about me.

The clouds of poverty are beginning to pour. My dreams of becoming a successful author, a musician, and an entrepreneur, and getting off disability permanently and never missing it are all delusions. While it is true I may get off disability, the likely real consequence is that I'd be homeless or drive my family crazy and then be homeless. It seems that many point to work as a savior. It's not that I don't want to work, rather that I have a severe case of insanity that is swiftly triggered by work. I'm trying though. I'm trying. My dream of becoming a successful author and musician are the only possible paths I see to make it as an entrepreneur. My dreams are seemingly a joke to most, a pipe dream. They think it's completely unrealistic. What is realistic is that I'll be mentally ill my entire life and I will be on medication ever more unless I can no longer afford the pharmaceuticals. Then I'll become street trash.

The reason this seems so horribly sad is because of my past, my childhood, my upbringing, and that sort of stuff. In grammar school and in high school I had been an A and B student all the way through. I graduated from high school with a 3.1 grade point average. They always told me I was a good kid. They said I was smart and bright and I remember my father saying "Your future is so bright, I gotta wear shades." It seemed I had so much going for me. Now, I have been in poverty for a decade and still I can find no suitable way to make money. I can try to force myself to work fast food, or push grocery carts, but I honestly haven't been able to resist the powerful effect it has on my mind.

My future looks dim and grim. Although college is going good, work and a career are eluding me. I feel that I am at a dead end and my reality is terrifying. I feel powerless. I can get a 3.8 in a fulltime college semester but I can't last a week at fast food. What does this mean? What should I do about it?

In summary, I think it means that they want me to be a good little zombie. Intelligence is only used in society when you are thinking for the system. You are only thinking what the society wants you to think, never thinking for yourself. Some think there is no wickedness in the world, but look at how our society determines success and failure. Impoverishment is my reality even though I have a mind that does honor society–level work. Still, society is pushing me back to fast food employment. It feels abusive, cruel, and hateful, but it's my reality. Push carts. College is useless. Your mind is useless.

Did my insanity cause impoverishment or was it the other way around? I'm used to being treated like trash. The dark clouds are raining, it's thundering and lightning but still there is little more I can do. It seems it will not just blow through. Poverty doesn't end. I can't escape the cloud. It follows me everywhere I go. I am waiting for lightning to strike me but it seems others enjoy seeing me poor.

Tears, Tests, and Triumphs

Diana Miller

People say that the experience of suffering, pain, and disappointments make either a bitter or better person. I choose to believe I came out a stronger, more confident, more caring, and much better person from living with a mental illness. Working on my recovery has strengthened and enforced this belief. A favorite quote of mine is by George Washington Carver. It states, "How far you go in life depends on your being tender with the young, compassionate with the aged, sympathetic with the striving and tolerant of both the weak and strong, because someday you have been one or all of these." It's my opinion that both good and bad life experiences are opportunities to mold, shape, and allow you to grow.

My first memories were feelings of abandonment as my father passed in and out of my early life. My family lived a very isolated life of poverty, neglect, and abuse. We resided in a small rural town. We had electricity but no indoor plumbing. We used an outhouse and as we did, we were careful to avoid stinging nettles. All of our water came from a pump and we carried the water to our house. The water that we carried was used for cooking, dishes, bathing, cleaning, laundry, and to fill potty cans for use during the night. In our lives in the

1960's, food, clothing, and necessities; taken for granted by most, were hard to come by in our lives.

After my mother passed, both of the children in my immediate family were placed in foster homes. I was almost three at the time. Six years after my mother's death my sister and I were adopted and my father's parental rights were terminated. My family never became complete again because my sister and I were adopted by different parents. We did, however, have an open adoption that allowed my sister and I to visit each other occasionally.

I believe our minds work like recorders throughout our lives as they take in all that is occurring. I think that when our lives become too painful our body's defense mechanism kicks in and our remembrance of painful memories are buried by our minds. These buried memories can be of inappropriate behavior, cases of trauma, head injuries, electric shock, dementia, Alzheimer's, or psychosis.

In 1986, I opted to study the field of occupational therapy assistance with an emphasis on mental illness and developmental disabilities. How ironic that I, myself, ended up with mental illness! However, I did earn an Associates of Science degree in Occupational Therapy Assisting. During this time, I learned that both my mother and my father had suffered from depression. Oh joy! I always have wondered how much of my family's problems were genetic or environmental. I've wondered if there was a predisposition that was activated by trauma. Regardless, my life in 1986, while studying at the junior college, was the best I had ever known. I met the love of my life, classes were exciting, I had many friends, and I was living in my first apartment.

By the second year of college, I was aware of things that had become glaringly obvious. Yet I hoped these things would not become my reality. I had goals, hope, dreams, and lofty and noble ideas that would make the world a better place. I had ideas for research. I thought about possible surveys that would support my theories. Ironically, eight years later one of my theories was researched at Johns Hopkins University and a paper on the research was published. (This is not to imply that I submitted my ideas to Johns Hopkins.) But my friend told me there was no such thing as original ideas. Her response did give me food for thought. It was during my second year in Junior College that I became symptomatic. Changes in my behavior included a dramatic decrease in self esteem, erratic sleeping patterns, loss of interest in people and events that I had once held dear, irritability, anxiety, frustration, and feelings of being overwhelmed, as well as a great sense of loss.

After graduation I ended precious relationships without explanations. I thought it was unfair for these friends to bear the brunt of my illness. My solution was to run from my problems and my running put a distance between myself and others that I thought was necessary in order for me to lick my wounds. I wanted to avoid being pitied. I tried to ignore changes in my relationships due to my disability. Somehow, I managed to hold simple home health aid positions that helped maintain a degree of sanity for a period of time.

As my life unfolded, my behavior interrupted my ability to work. So, I stayed with friends while I developed feelings of paranoia along with fear, anxiety, and frustration. I seldom left the house because I had developed a fear of crossing streets. I became a prisoner held in by the invisible bars of my illness. I recall staring into space, measuring the value of my life (a life I wanted to end). I developed constant ideas of suicide that I acted out. I was scared that my insurance would not cover the cost of my funeral.

I began experiencing visual and auditory hallucinations. Some were grisly and they were abundant. There were no psychadelic colors or the hoped-for euphoria. A friend later likened my experiences to a bad trip. It sure wasn't my idea of a vacation. It felt like the interior of hell. These occurrences continued for many years before they subsided

As my first hallucinations set in, I was flown to Michigan for the first time. My parents had relocated to Michigan. My parents tried to deal with me for a period of time but they lacked resources in terms of knowledge, moral support, financial resources, and the ability to navigate through the mental health system.

I was hospitalized for roughly nine weeks. I remember feeling like a zombie or like a tranquilized elephant. Later, they applied the term catatonic to my experience. The doctor was going to apply electric shock therapy if I didn't respond to medication. It was confusing for me. I didn't understand what was happening to me. Nor did I receive any explanation. I was highly medicated and barely able to function. I awoke in a very scary, dark, lonely, cold room. I was without blankets and I was tied down by leather restraints. I was in the isolation room.

Time passed in the hospital as in an unconscious daze or fog. One of my friends in the hospital said that mental illness is a living nightmare with your eyes wide open. That was so true for me for several years to come. By the time that six or seven weeks passed in the hospital, boredom began to set in. I took up smoking instead of the opportunity to feel sunshine and fresh air on my skin. It was during this time that a fetish concerning patterns set in. I thought that if I only could solve the patterns I would be released. Then I discovered the hospital snack room. The snack room brought comfort and compensation in a trivial way. I enjoyed the free cookies, ice cream, fruits, drinks, and crackers. As time passed I began to feel better and my memory started to return. I drove my family bonkers with asking them when I could come home. (Later, I thought that my frequent calls to my family indicated feelings of insecurity and abandonment.) Anyway, my hospital stay became more bearable as family and friends came to visit. My fondest memory of my hospital stay was when my little niece came and turned summersaults for me. I remember how those summersaults touched the very core of my heart. They were such a normal experience to share in a world that made no sense and was chaotic. In the hospital I learned the ropes of surviving a psychiatric stay. The ropes were schedules, routines, demands, and activities. I became acclimated. I adopted a hospital mind set from being in a regimented environment.

After my release, I was placed in a good foster care home. My guardians were great providers for two years. They were caring and supportive. We still keep in touch. Even though I had emotional troubles while I stayed with my foster parents, I took away some good memories. I had some new friends. When I left the security of my foster home to be semi-independent I was frightened and I felt vulnerable.

I tried independent living but I had horrible experiences with my roommate. As if the wrong roommate was not difficult enough, while in independent living I experienced a cycle of high mania for the first time. In the past I had been unable to function because of depression. While in mania, I thought I was invincible. I had no sense of judgment and I foolishly spent money on unnecessary things. When mania set in I was the energizer bunny, jumping from one relationship to another. I developed a sense of numbness, no self worth, and a feeling of just being a piece of meat on the market. Later I found that promiscuity is common in mental illness. I am glad that I found this information regarding promiscuity and mental illness because until I acquired this information I felt like the world's biggest tramp. I could still count the number of my relationships on two hands. Since this time I've had conversations with both male and female friends who've had hundreds of relationships and who are lost in the never ending trap of seeking comfort through promiscuity. Later in my life, guilt about my sex life became a burden I carried for many years, because I had hurt myself as well as some very good people. After ending this life of promiscuity I went through all of the tests for sexually transmitted diseases and for HIV. I chose to become sterile because I did not want my history of mental illness to be repeated in children. Some people thought being sterilized was a selfish choice but I thought it for the best. I get angry when people judge me for the choice I've made but they will never know my grieving. They will never know the personal expense of the sacrifice I made, to do what I thought was best for others and myself. I no longer feel as though I owe the world explanations for every page and chapter of the book of my life that is written deep in my heart.

Life offers no guarantees. I don't know if my horrible experiences from mental illness will happen to me again. To accept me for who I am would take a person who is very special, and knowledgeable and educated about mental illness. It would take someone who thinks I, at age forty, am a risk worth taking. I am experiencing great loneliness. My blessings come from my cat, Smokey, and my family and friends. I try to keep myself busy and I try not to be self-absorbed because I think being overly concerned with self can create a very narrow world.

To date, I recollect being hospitalized six times, with the third time being the worst. My third hospitalization caused emotional, mental, and physical problems. It almost cost me my life. In this third hospitalization I was in a state mental institution for six months. I didn't speak for three months and I didn't eat for a long time. I didn't even know my own identity. If someone had asked me to give him or her personal identification such as my bank account number or social security number, I would have had to use sign language to give them the requested information. The difficulties I was experiencing were from a bad reaction to Haldol (an antipsychotic drug). It caused my body to go into a frozen state and caused my heart and kidneys to fail. I was in a coma for ten days in a private hospital. As I recovered and left the hospital to return to the state mental institution, I witnessed people in the state hospital burning, cutting, scratching, and slashing themselves. While I found these self-inflicted mutilations repulsive, they also caused me to feel compassion. No one knows the depths of despair one reaches from mental illness. Hurting oneself because of being overwhelmed by life can be a cry for help.

Enough is enough. Everyone carries wounds of the heart. After going through so many years of my life with mental illness, my life has begun to change and opportunities have come my way. Somebody once told me that illness is only part of life and not the total sum of life. I needed to live life and to have a quality of life other than subsisting. As I thought about what this person had told me, it was as if a seed of hope had been planted in the dry soil of my heart and soul. I thoughtfully questioned whether illness was only part of my life. I took steps to find out. I had to admit the reality of my illness. I had to allow myself to grieve for all that I had been through. I let go of things I had lost, people who were no longer part of my life, and relationships that had been destroyed. I wanted the shattered pieces of my life to come back together to form the beauty and purpose for which it had been creatively and lovingly designed.

Education became the focal point of my life. It was the central key that led to a better life. I took advantage of training, conferences and books, videos, movies, and other peers who were consumers of mental health care. I listened to the experts in the field of mental health. I attended clubhouses and drop-in centers and I did volunteer work. I tried to develop supervisory skills. I wrote successful grants. I participated in accredited training in mental health provided for police officers. I joined support groups. For three years I co-led a therapy group. I raised over $12,000 for various projects. I did public speaking and served on different boards and committees. I traveled out of state by winning an essay contest. I also left the state on an all-expense-paid trip to a conference. I've learned to speak up for myself and to advocate for others.

So, what I've learned through it all is that the gains far outweigh the losses and the pain. Dare to live your life. Have a dream. Set goals. Be persistent. Shoot for the moon. If you miss you'll always hit a star.

Life Interrupted

Teri Syms

I left my husband in February of 1978. He was involved with a woman ten years his senior. Nine years earlier it was my best friend, while I was pregnant with our son. After my son was born I was depressed. My husband sent me to a shrink to get my head examined. The doctor put me on an antidepressant and a minor tranquilizer. I was smoking like a fiend and I was in the depths of postpartum depression.

So, some time later, when I left with my ten-year-old daughter and my eight-year-old son to see my childhood friend in Texas and to start a new life, I didn't count on flipping out! In Texas we celebrated a last supper of veal parmesan. While sitting outside after dinner, I thought my friend's son was killing my son with rocks. I sat there thinking, "This is how Mary must have felt when Jesus was being killed." I went to bed that night, but I couldn't sleep as I thought about my husband. I dreamed he had a car crash and I woke up screaming his name. An armadillo went running past the window. I decided to get up and take a shower in my nightgown. I dragged my son and daughter out of bed because a plane had landed in the front lawn and everyone who loved us was on it. I thought God had stopped time. I felt the earth move under my feet. On the way to the hospital I tried to jump out of the car. While we were waiting, all I could hear was loud march-ing. It was deafening and it wouldn't stop. I saw my son and cried out, "My son, you're alive." Someone dropped some-thing that made a loud clatter. My friend jumped a foot off her chair. I sat in a catatonic state.

When they took me down the hospital hall I saw a black man weeping. I went running toward him, yelling, "My sav-ior." They grabbed me and my head hit the wall. They gave me stitches and a shot of antipsychotic medication. One big black girl walked around taking her clothes off. A Hispanic guy kept fighting with other male patients. They put him in a padded cell. Once I hid under the bed. I thought the room was on fire. When my husband came to visit I was in pieces. He didn't want to be there. He would have rather been golfing in New Jersey. Most of all, he didn't want to be around a crazy lady. We toured a Victorian home. He was nice to me. In the hospital I had the beginning of my life's story with me to show my friends. They may have read it and determined I was only partially insane. My friend visited me in that hospital in Galveston, Texas, every day. I was there thirteen days. Then I went home. My shrink diagnosed manic depression and put me on Lithium that May.

Twenty years later the doctor took me off Lithium because it was damaging my kidneys. They call it bipolar disorder now. I'm now on a different medicine. As long as I take my meds everyday I will remain stable.

In 1979, my husband left me. He married his woman friend in 1982. My second husband and I got together through a matchbook cover that read: *Sociability*. He was nice enough. We fell in love and we got engaged. He moved into my house. Then he lived in the basement, celibate, because my children were in the house. We married in July 1983. My daughter went into rehab in 1984 and my son went in 1985. My husband moved out for a year.

When my second husband and I met, he lived above a vet-erinary hospital, with only an American Express card. After we married he had twenty-eight more cards. He bought me flowers, candy, trips, and tickets to shows. I bought him a car. This was all on credit. He worked in a jail as a guard and had guns. He was a recovering alcoholic tenor who sang a very good *Danny Boy*. He had a quick wit and a cat named O.J.

I sold my '57 Chevy to have a nice wedding. I refinanced my house to pay some bills in 1984. I sold my house in April 1986, to pay $50,000 worth of bills. He got his half of the bills down to $15,000. He paid me $100 per month for a total of $6,500. He's gone now and so is the $8,500 he owes me. He left me many years ago and I never knew why. Whenever I hear a train whistle I think of him. He loved trains.

I met the next love of my life at a manic depressive meeting in a Bergen County hospital in February 1994. The same month my father died in that hospital. This lover was different from the rest. He was like me, bipolar, vulnerable, and childlike. We hit it off and started dating right away. He lived in one room he rented from a man he knew. I was living in my mother's house. I had a car. He didn't. We had a good time together. We went to movies, ate ice cream, and went to meetings. We held hands and he told corny jokes that were so sweet. By August he was hospitalized for a bipolar episode. I went to visit him but he didn't know I was there. In October 1994, I had a tumor removed from the optic nerve of my right eye. He was there for me. Our love for one another was real. Finally I had a man I could trust. In February 1999, he went into the hospital again. This time the doctors added schizophrenia to his diagnosis of bipolar disorder. I hated to see him behind locked doors.

It seemed that when he was ill, I was well, and when I was ill, he was well. We couldn't seem to get it together. I would get angry and annoyed when he ended up in a psych ward but he was always so supportive of me. I wished we never had this illness so we could live our lives without medications and monitoring. Maybe in another time and place we could live free and happy.

In November 1999, I moved to Pennsylvania and I maintained a long distance love affair with the same man. We took turns going back and forth from New Jersey to Pennsylvania and back again. While we were on the brakes in our relationship, he strayed once with a homeless mentally ill woman he took in for the night. He strayed another time with a woman from his temple who was attracted to him. So much for trust. Did I want to marry him? In April 2004, we started talking to my pastor to see how we would go about it. He wanted a rabbi and I wanted a priest. Could we have both? We signed the applicable papers. He needed some information from his ex-wife and I needed to send my second husband a paper to be filled out.

On Memorial Day of 2004 my intended called me and told me "I don't want to marry you but can we still be friends?" I replied "NO WAY." By the next Wednesday he was in the hospital. He'd been involved in three different projects at the same time and our breakup was the straw that broke the camel's back.

I visited him almost every weekend for about seven weeks. I stayed at my sister's in Clifton, New Jersey, when I came for visits. I held myself together by comforting my body with food and prayer and I comforted my soul with the Holy Eucharist. If I had gotten sick, I might have ended up in the psych ward too. I prayed for the doctors to make him stable but they couldn't snap him out of it this time. He was in a catatonic state most of the time and he was hallucinating about everything. He barely knew me. One time he read Psalm 41 to me and my son.

When his meds finally started to kick in, would he start to remember things he may not want to remember? Would he recall that we were thinking of marriage? I thought, "After he's well it will be difficult for me to accept an amended relationship. What will happen to us? Is there an us?" He had been through a little bit of hell and I had been through it with him. Only I was on the other side of a locked door. I was faced with the brutal reality of living life without him. I continued my thoughts. "He may be coming home soon. What will I do then? (No more weekends back and forth from New Jersey to Pennsylvania.) We have a ten and a half year history. What do I do with that? How do I stop loving him?" We said our last goodbyes and I took the bus home to Pennsylvania. I prayed that God would bring me to where He wants me to be. He has answered my prayers.

I remember better days. Back in 1994 he was my eyes when I couldn't see. He was my feet when I couldn't walk after I broke my ankle in 2002. The radio plays, "You're only someone I used to love."

My Life with Mental Illness

John Laue

I am a mentally ill person diagnosed on different occasions as schizophrenic, manic depressive, borderline, and as a narcissistic personality. I've chosen to call myself a schizophrenic because the label seems to fit my symptoms best. When I diagnosed myself as schizophrenic (yes, my psychiatrist let me do that), he said it's not the diagnosis; it's how you take it. You have a choice. You can either be depressed about your diagnosis, think it's the absolute truthful voice of doom. Or you can say, okay so I'm probably schizophrenic (or bipolar, schizoaffective, etc.) But I'm much more than that. And the much more is more important than the illness.

I'm well aware of the stigma attached, but not ashamed of being mentally ill. It's just one of the labels I've had through the years (I'm 70 years old). I've been called just about everything by this time. The important thing is I try to remember that I am a human being first, much more than any of my smaller labels, of which there are an infinite number. And as a human being, I am entitled to respect myself and not let labels get me down.

The portrayals of mental illness on TV or in movies I have seen often appear to be inaccurate and misleading. The media never shows the majority of us who are working full or part time, leading uneventful lives, and maybe suffering some, but getting along. What is published in the newspapers except crimes and tragedies? It's not news if you're mentally ill and doing okay.

The fact is that psychiatric diagnoses are rather imprecise and quite fallible. They do provide some guidelines for what kinds of medications can help people, but even these are not precise because we're individuals. Many times medications need to be changed over and over again.

A college student recently wrote to me that he varies his medication depending on what type of assignments he has. If he has a task requiring intense concentration he reduces it somewhat. Then for the lighter tasks he resumes the higher level. I've tried this strategy myself at times, but if I reduced it too much and encountered stresses I'd find myself getting paranoid and over-reactive to minor annoyances.

I owe what sanity I have today and probably my life to Stelazine, a first generation antipsychotic. At one point, I attempted to switch to Zyprexa under the supervision of my medication doctor, but this didn't work. I do take some of it now along with the Stelazine because it helps me sleep better at night. The problem I had near the end of my teaching career was that when I increased the dosage of Stelazine enough to get me through the day easily, I had to fight to stay awake after lunch. Now that I'm retired I can usually take a nap if I feel sleepy during the day.

I've been lucky. I have had no major side effects such as tardive dyskinesia (frequent compulsive movements of the mouth and tongue). However, I did gain weight and lose some of my sexual responsiveness when I first went on the drug. I also gained more weight when I retired, but now, because of a low-fat diet and fast walking almost every day, I've lost nearly forty-five pounds and am thinner than before.

I've known several people who went off their meds and got into serious trouble. When I decrease my dosage too much I start reading the wrong messages into what people are saying. I can recognize this before it gets too severe and go on a higher dosage until things calm down. I consult with the medication doctor if I make major drug changes in my meds. To stay on an even keel and be productive is my goal. If I don't accomplish this not only do I suffer, but also my relationships with my wife and friends deteriorate. So I believe it's only good and fair to all that I stay properly medicated.

There was a time when the label schizophrenic meant to doctors that you had no future. Now all enlightened physicians know this isn't the case. Schizophrenics can recover, can be stabilized on medications, can have decent and productive lives. I and many people I know are proving this every day. I had about two years of very severe symptoms during which I couldn't work. Later with the support of a very fine psychiatrist, Dr. David Shupp, I became a high school teacher and counselor and had a 20 year career. Now I'm retired, a nationally published poet and prose writer, a member of the Steering Committee of my Writers Union Local, and Co-Chair of my county's Mental Health Board.

In spite of the fact that I had some rather difficult symptoms, I was able to succeed at my job as a high school teacher without most people knowing I was mentally ill. Why? Because I had a good "face." What I mean by "face" is the ability to not look or act crazy even when you are experiencing symptoms. I'd be on a low dose of medication because the goal of medicating is for you to be on the lowest dose possible, then every once in a while I'd begin to think crazy, get paranoid. I'd increase my dosage, but the higher dose didn't kick in and give me relief from my symptoms for about 2 weeks. During that time, I was still somewhat crazy.

Even when I am feeling fairly paranoid and nuts, I can act as if I'm "normal." That's what I did. And, luckily, I was able to pull it off without many people knowing. The only ones that really were aware were those who had gone through craziness themselves. And there are more of those than most people think. But they're not about to tell on us.

Appearing "sane" when the occasion warrants is one of the best abilities to have when you're mentally ill. I know it's impossible for some people, since they're out of control at certain times. But most of the time we can put on a good "face," seem to the uninitiated to be "normal." This can do many things for us; let us keep our jobs, keep us from being committed or detained by the police, keep up relationships that otherwise wouldn't continue because we would scare the other person, etc.

One of my friends has had a bad time because she often "loses it," looks and acts crazy. She's lost jobs because of this, and been detained by the police. I hid from the police twice when I was going through my worst period. I was afraid that if they picked me up I'd never get out of a mental institution, which is what happened to my mother. Of course, I didn't realize that now they just keep you on the psych ward until you're stabilized, as short a time as possible. And my mother was incarcerated before they discovered the new medications which are often quite effective in getting you into shape to get back into the world.

For much of my life I blamed my father and stepmother for my problems. I had the idea that they "should" have been different. There's always a "should" in blaming, i.e. what the person (or thing) "should" have been, or done, or not done. "Shoulds" dominate the lives of blamers yet "shoulds" are irrational and all too often contrary to fact.

Sure, my father and especially my stepmother were pretty horrible at times. Their attitudes and actions probably played a part in my illness. And as long as I could blame them, I could be content with how I was instead of growing and taking responsibility for my life. After all, if I became a success couldn't they say they'd done a good job?

I want to reiterate I'm not saying forgive and forget as a formula for getting well. Sometimes it can be good not to lie to yourself. I never kidded myself about my stepmother's dislike of me. She'd probably have been happier if I were dead. But I was lucky on one count; she was honest enough not to pretend she loved or cared, at least not enough to fool me. If she had I'd have been a lot more mixed up.

A popular misconception which results from the publicity given to one particular school of psychology (psychoanalysis) would have us believe that labeling our problems and locating or trying to locate their causes in our childhood will somehow cure us. The fact is, according to Dr. Shupp and my own and others' experiences, it doesn't do any good at all, and may even hold us back. I've met people who insist that because of what was done to them as children, they're ruined for life. Even if these experiences really did contribute to their present behavior, what good does it do to "know" them when their only function is to serve as excuses to not get their lives together? As a person of the "psychiatric persuasion" I can also assure you that for us, psychoanalysis has been proven not only to be useless, but to aggravate our symptoms. Who wants to waste time obsessing about things that happened in his or her childhood when there's life to be lived in the present?

Yes, we have wounds, perhaps very deep ones that originated early in our development. But isn't it better to get help and work on healing them rather than letting them fester and bother us for the rest of our lives? And if they can't be completely healed, they can at least be reduced to manageable size by the proper present-centered therapies. They may even become sources of creativity and strength for us. The secret here is getting the help that allows us to grow out of our absorption with the past and concentrate our energies on dealing with our lives right now.

I was very lucky to have found Dr. Shupp as a mentor and guide for 16 years. It was by sheer good fortune that I went to him in the first place. I was worried about some symptoms my ex-wife had, and a neighbor suggested we go to his group. My ex-wife soon dropped out and our marriage dissolved, but I kept going through all the acute phase of my illness and for many more years. If it weren't for this doctor and his group, I might not be here at all. I was suicidal for about two years of that time.

Dr. Shupp once said to me, "You're too strong to be a schiz-ophrenic; you must be borderline." That was when the con-cept of borderline personality first came out and it was very unclear. Since then I've realized that I don't fit the criteria for that diagnosis. But the concept of strength has always both-ered me. What did he mean? Was it mental strength, emo-tional strength, personality strength?

According to my unabridged dictionary, the word "strength" implies durability and resistance to stress. I'd hardly qualify as a strong person since I broke down into psy-chosis when confronted with the serious life problems of that time. But since then, I've had many years to recover and face myself (to get my strength back, as the old saying goes). I now feel stronger than ever. Of course, the medications I take are in part responsible for this. Without them I'd probably be dead or at least homeless. But there's also the strength that comes from going through things. I made it through the worst of madness, through a "death" and a stint in "hell," and still am alive and functioning. That's a source of strength.

Whether mentally ill or not, it's an exceptional person who finds his or her mission in life, who knows where he or she fits in the overall scheme of things. Missions come from develop-ing one's talents, from being alive to possibilities. Many times we don't consciously plan for or choose them, but they call us and we respond. Not that a sonorous voice comes out of the sky and commands us to do this or that, but as we follow our interests, talents and skills, we find that opportunities open up, and we gain greater and greater conviction as we go.

I wanted to make an impact on the world partly because my mother, who was institutionalized for most of her life, had little chance to do so. But our reasons are unimportant. What-ever our motives, I believe that satisfaction lies, not in the ac-quisition of things or the pursuit of power, wealth or fame, but in service to our fellow human beings. We can be successes in this realm whether or not we fit the common definitions of suc-cess. And we may get more out of life than the people who do.

A Dream Keeper's Victory

Ginger Novelle

My parents' eyes seemed to dog my every waking moment and my nightmares as well. My mother's eyes, cold as steel when she smothered me with my pillow. My father's eyes, icy hot with rage, during his drunken knife attacks. To defy them meant death. I learned that lesson before I even started school.

What had I done? Cried? No, that was forbidden. Put too many peas on my fork again? Or too few? If only I were a perfect daughter. I would try to be. I must not get their attention. Stop breathing. Stop existing.

My guardian angel had always stepped in whenever their eyes turned cold. They couldn't see her and I sometimes remembered nothing more for as long as a year. Was that why my parents called me "Mental Case" ever since I could remember? Did they know my real name anymore? It didn't matter. I was named after my mother. I had no name of my own.

I whispered to my guardian angel because there was nobody else to talk to. Her name was Mogell, pronounced Moe-ZHELL. But my preschool tongue couldn't twist itself around her name so I called her Suzanne. Suzanne taught me to read the words in red in the Bible and to pray to God. But that had to be done silently and in secret because God and all things religious were forbidden in this household—unless my father made them the butt of a dirty joke.

The red-faced shame of it. Getting kicked out of church because my father had spiked the punch with whiskey, smoked cigars during services, told dirty jokes in Sunday School class, and flirted with the minister's wife. My father's house was not a safe place for an angel to tread, but tread she did.

"Why did God make me a mental case, Suzanne?"

"God made you a Dream Keeper, Child," she would always respond.

I didn't know what that meant, but I was definitely a dreamer. Even at six, I dreamed of getting a job and moving out of my parents' house.

My mother laughed, "Nobody in their right mind would ever hire a mental case."

So I stopped sharing my dreams. I became a selective mute. But I didn't stop dreaming.

My parents got a lot of mileage out of my silence. Every year they argued with my teachers that I was not to speak or participate in music, recess or physical education, anything that reeked of self-expression. The teachers couldn't take the pressure. By November, I would end up unofficially home-schooled. My mother became my 24/7 companion.

She did my homework for me, except for the math, which she hated. Whenever she got an A, she praised me for it; then she praised herself for my A's. When I tried to straighten out the confusion, she'd bawl, "You have no right to criticize me!" I let her keep my A's.

I identified more with my father because he didn't try to claim my identity. Not lining up the labels on the canned goods perfectly got me beaten. Smiling got my nose bitten. Begging him to let me use the stool after he'd sat there three hours masturbating and reading pornography risked a broken bone. But I could count on his reaction. He was my stability in the midst of my mother's insanity.

I reserved my love for Suzanne, God, and our cats and dogs.

"Don't tease the animals," my parents admonished me daily, even though they teased both the pets and me mercilessly.

Pretending the cats and dogs were my audience, I'd mouth the words of a speech because someday I was going to be a writer and a public speaker. I also wanted to be a busi-ness*man,* despite being a girl, because women discussed bot-tles and diapers while men discussed money and power.

My parents unknowingly contributed to this last dream. During the summer of my tenth year, my father took me to a barber who cut off my luxuriously long black hair and gave me a butch haircut. Then Dad bought me a cowboy outfit, complete with hat and boots with spurs. Not to mention the undershorts with a fly. When a little girl displayed her crush on me, my mother went into raptures over her handsome "son." I didn't want to be a boy, despite my confused dreams, but I would try to be a good boy anyway. After all, my survival depended on these people.

However, my perfection crumbled when they yammered at me to pee standing up.

My mother still bathed and dressed me when I was six-teen. I didn't dare to anger my physically brutal father—who gloried in sharing his pornographic films with me—by defy-ing my mother. So one day, I held my breath and very quietly asked her why she was still bathing me. She looked startled and said, "Because your father doesn't get clean." Then she bawled for an hour. After that, my "dirty" father bathed me.

I had to get out of there. I quit school and started job hunting. But every time I called an employer I had applied with to see if I got the job, he'd hang up on me. My mother stared at me grinning whenever I made the calls. Then one day she burst out laughing. "I called them all and none of them hires homicidal maniacs!"

Without money, I despaired of ever escaping. But hope rose up within me when social workers showed up unexpect-edly to ask questions.

"She quit school to work," my mother repeatedly assured them.

Then one day, my parents drove me out to a small country house that lacked running water, on a dead end road in another county where the social workers couldn't go.

"You're going to run our dog kennel," my parents told me.

Busy taking care of forty-two animals for four years, I barely noticed that I never saw another human being except my parents on weekends. I occasionally acknowledged to myself that I never got to go to a slumber party, dance, or date either, but then I wouldn't have gotten to do those things anyway if I'd stayed home.

Instead, I had five days a week without my parents' supervision, forty-two sources of unconditional love and productive work to do, even if I never did see a paycheck. I could even line up the labels on the canned goods any way I wanted to.

After the fourth year, I read an article in the paper about a new high school equivalency diploma for dropouts. On one of my rare trips to town, I sneaked in all five tests in one day at the local college without any preparation. With 35 rated as a passing score, my lowest was 95, with a perfect score on the math test. The administrator invited me to enroll in the college and handed me a family financial aid form to fill out.

But when I took the form home to my family, they laughed. Pointing out the intelligence tests that had scored me as borderline mentally retarded when I was ten, they weren't going to pay for me to flunk out on their money. To back up their point, my parents had a lawyer draw up papers stating that they weren't legally or financially responsible for me.

Undaunted, the college administrator pointed out this made me an individual with no income and that I could get all four years paid for. I majored in math with the intention of getting a PhD in statistics and psychology to become a psychometrist. I intended to rewrite intelligence tests without cultural biases. But even more exciting, I could live in a dorm!

My roommate was from South America, which threw me

into the foreign crowd for a social life. I may not have graduated except for that divine intervention. Communication problems were taken for granted. Failing to understand the culture, especially during the riotous sixties, was a given. Silent women were appreciated.

I started dating a man from the Middle East. I don't remember our sex life, but assumed most women didn't remember theirs either. I experienced sex as a "blip" which I assumed everybody did. A blip resembled a movie with several frames missing. Suddenly, positions and conversations jumped and I might even end up in a different place.

We planned to marry after I got my BS degree and he his PhD. He wanted me to go the diapers and bottles route, while I wanted to aim straight for a job, money, and power. But familiar with silencing my dreams, I said nothing. After all, my mother did what she wanted without consulting my father.

My first doubts crept in when he flunked his PhD orals, started drinking more heavily, and offered my body to his friends. But he didn't drink as much as my father did and his friends didn't take him up on the offer, so no harm done.

Plus, the good days still happened. On one of those days, he picked me up by the waist, twirled me in a circle and beamed, "Do you know why I love you so much?"

I shook my head no, eager to hear his response.

"Because you're like a hunk of clay. I can mold you into anything I want you to be."

I never went back.

Burnt out on studying by the time I finished college, I let go of graduate school. But my passive silence and lack of work history wouldn't get me past any job interviews, even when I hid the information from my parents. Without an income or financial aid, I had nowhere else to live.

A bill for hospitalization for depression fell on my parents' shoulders. They thought up a perfect solution to prevent future billings. I should have four illegitimate children and go on welfare to get the health insurance.

"Why four?" I dared to ask.

My mother glared at me. "Because that's how many kids I always wanted."

"I don't know anything about raising kids."

"I'll raise them," she yelled. "You just have them."

The next boyfriend was intended to get me away from home, not to father my children. Unfortunately, he made my parents look like innocent children themselves. He was openly outraged when the parents of a mentally retarded girl threatened him with charges if he didn't stop having sex with her and openly bragged about sneaking around behind their backs. At the same time, he threatened my life—and the lives of some infants in my extended family—if *I* didn't have sex with him. I told my parents, who berated me for not trying harder to please him. Though terrified for the infants and the mentally retarded girl, I reasoned that I didn't remember the sex anyway and I probably wouldn't remember dying.

I returned to school to escape both him and my parents. But I was addicted to calling them both every day to find out if anyone had died. I didn't share my trauma with my roommate. She wouldn't have understood it had I tried. None of the other students talked to me either.

Then one day in the big university where everyone was just a number, I got called into the administrator's office. Three men talked to me while my roommate sat silently in the corner. They pointed out I could never have a career as a psychometrist because I didn't know how to talk or put people at ease. I might as well quit school.

Bewildered why they'd even care, I quit. I hadn't been studying; I wasn't going to pass my courses anyway. I had just been escaping the inevitable trap at home while job searching out of town.

Back home, I returned to slave labor for my boyfriend until suddenly one day he announced I wasn't perfect enough: I had made too many mistakes and he needed to get rid of me. As I got in his car, I welcomed the peaceful thought that I would be dead soon and not have to deal with either him or my parents. But shock overwhelmed me when he ordered me out of the car and drove away. I stood in front of my parents' house, my heart loaded with dread.

Another depression sideswiped me, but since I had no insurance, I had to go to the state mental institution. Some people had been there thirty or forty years. Rumors abounded that the alcoholics and drug addicts, as well as some of the staff, raped the mental patients. I worked hard at getting out of there.

The only good result of that trip showed up in the mail when my disability checks started arriving. With both income and medical insurance, my parents stopped bugging me to have illegitimate children and I could afford to rent an apartment.

Except my parents handled landlords the same way they did employers. Nobody wanted to house a homicidal maniac and as hard as I pretended not to exist, they always noticed when I was gone.

All I had were the dogs to console me. When I was twenty-seven, my favorite pet of all died and I sought help. The counselor insisted on seeing me only in group therapy where he gently teased me into sharing in front of others. Soon, I had friends from the group and started talking conversationally in whispers. Soon, the counselor introduced me to his wife, let me hold his baby and frequently invited me into his home.

While he was attempting to set up another living arrangement for me, I met a man I really loved and he proposed. I flew high and giddy right up to the point where he brought out my father's type of pornographic magazines so he could teach me something.

Blip!

Suddenly, we stood facing each other at the bus station. White and trembling, he told me he felt too sick to drive.

The next day, his mother called me to report he had been admitted to the state mental institution for depression. I wrote him eight-page letters every day telling him that we were going to make it, that I would stick by him no matter what. I heard nothing back.

Finally, three months later, I got a card without a letter from him. I was so excited! I was on my way out the door so I momentarily tossed it aside. But the moment I returned, I wrote another long epistle.

About the time he would have received it, his sister-in-law called me. He had hung himself. *Then* I read the verse on the card: "If you love someone, set them free . . ."

My parents responded to my tragedy with sick suicide jokes. My counselor left town overnight to practice in another state without so much as a good-bye. My best friend was raped and murdered soon after. Despite the rape, my family turned me into the police. I was assigned a new counselor who informed me at our first meeting that suicide was not as traumatic as giving birth to a stillborn. So we spent all our sessions talking about her baby who had died thirty years before. My psychiatrist ordered shock treatments. When I begged him not to discharge me to my parents' care, he pointed out that child abuse did not really exist, let alone adult abuse.

I was thirty-one years old now and the doctor committed me to the County Home for life because I didn't heal fast enough. With rumors that the County Home suffered the same problems as the state institution, I spoke up and asked to go to a halfway house instead.

The halfway house catered mostly to alcoholics, drug addicts, and criminals with the same threat to the residents with mental illness as the county and state institutions. But the word "halfway" meant not permanent and my age and obesity kept me safe from predators. I flipped from silence to nonstop talking and let the staff know where I had come from. Overnight, I was rediagnosed manic-depressive. But best of all, it was out of town and they taught independent living there. Thrilled with the potential ticket away from my parents, I stuck to it.

After fourteen months, I entered the phase of the program

where I could go out job and apartment hunting. One day, when I returned from a job interview, they informed me I was on house arrest because of the interview. Confused, I pointed out it was one of their rules and showed them in my own records were I had jumped through all the hoops and gotten permission. They immediately banned me from seeing my own records and informed me they had changed the rules while I was gone. Too many people were graduating from the halfway house and becoming dependent on the county. They were afraid they'd lose their funding. So from now on, every graduate had to move home with his/her parents.

"No way. Have you been listening to me this past year?"

I called a lawyer who said since I had come in voluntarily instead of being committed, they couldn't tell me where to live. But when I quoted her, the staff banned me from incoming and outgoing phone calls and mail. I was to remain on house arrest until I agreed with them.

Normally, whenever I had free time, I was gone. After two weeks of confinement, I couldn't take it anymore. I agreed they had a point and I understood. After my graduation ceremony, my current boyfriend loaded up my stuff and drove me to another town where I knew no one. Conceding they had a point was not the same thing as agreeing to go home.

Shortly after my arrival, I fell on the ice and hurt my foot, requiring surgery. Afterward, I repeatedly complained to the doctor that I couldn't breathe. He reminded me I was a mental patient and, no doubt, was hyperventilating. Breathe into a paper bag and quit bothering him he told me.

Four weeks later, I walked into the hospital to visit someone, when a nurse pulled a chair out into the middle of the hall. She told me to sit in it and not to move until she called a doctor. He immediately shipped me off to intensive care with eight blood clots on my lungs.

By the time I was released more than a month later, I realized that, being named after my mother, I could have died with my mother's name on my tombstone. So, the first thing I did after my discharge was to legally change my first and middle names.

The blood clots caused a ripple in the relationship with my boyfriend, who had continued seeing me on weekends after I left town. He was a smoker; my lungs were suddenly too fragile to handle that. But we managed to keep the relationship intact for nine years, primarily because he was impotent. Sex would never become a ripple and that was more important than breathing.

Then he lost his job and began drinking. I feared abuse, but desperately held things together for another two years, until one day, he forced me to my knees, ordering me to pray to him instead of God.

The boyfriend had to go. But suggesting that only turned him into sticky glue.

I decided to tell him I was having an affair with another man to chase him away. He would either kill me or leave. Either way, I would be rid of him. But he knew me too well to believe a lie—I had to really have the affair.

The landlord had been feeling me up in the laundry room, just as he did all the female tenants, so that was the easiest route to take. It got rid of the boyfriend, but the one-nighter became a perpetual problem. This problem didn't care about me and he had the keys.

At the same time, my psychiatrist stopped accepting government insurance, which left me without a prescription, and on several waiting lists for a doctor. I stopped eating and sleeping, and lived on beer for a month. Finally, I broke.

In my twisted psychotic state, I decided to tell the police that I had bombs planted all over the city. Then, when they came to arrest me, I would tell them about the landlord and they would arrest him instead. I sent notes to the police via the landlord himself, but no one came to investigate. Then I went to the landlord's office to see if the police were interrogating him, but he was alone. He ordered me to take my clothes off.

I heard voices near the ceiling scream, "Oh my god! He's going to rape a two-year-old!"

I took off running. All I accomplished was to lock myself out of the building without my keys. The lone buzzer rang into the landlord's office.

I ran to a nearby hotel and called the police. They hung up on me. Desperate for room and board on a cold night, I decided to get myself arrested until I could think through what to do.

So, I verbally harassed the nearest officer until she got angry enough to take me in. They booked me on a criminal trespass charge, but spent the entire night trying to release me. I charged at the door every time they approached it. I had nowhere else to go.

I either had a blip or slept, because suddenly, it was morning. I had a hearing and was committed to a mental hospital for observation. I had a 'why didn't I think of that?' reaction.

I hadn't bathed in a month. My first moment in the hospital, two nurses offered to help me take a shower. I screamed, "No, Mama! No!" Another blip.

I came to in a cell in the "Quiet Room" with my head stuck out the unlocked door. I got up and approached a patient and a staff member who were playing cards, expressing an interest. They folded their hands and walked away. Everybody I came near walked away.

Only the doctor seemed unafraid. I told him about the landlord. He said to take my medicine and the landlord would go away. I told him about my parents. He said to take my medicine and they would go away. I told him I needed to see a counselor. He told me to take my medicine and the need would go away. I told him I needed a new place to live. He told me to take my medicine and that need would go away too.

I had almost forgotten that, before my hospitalization, I had been scheduled to attend day treatment. After the police dropped my charges, the doctor let me go to treatment during the day, returning to the hospital at night. My plans were to continue treatment after I was discharged, hunt for a new apartment in the evening, and return home only after the landlord was asleep.

But when I woke up on my day of discharge, my clothes were missing. I had come in with just the clothes on my back, which had been laundered for me every night. I slept in a hospital gown. A staff member actually let me approach him. He informed me that my clothes had been hopelessly lost in the laundry and there was no way to get them back. He suggested I resign myself to being committed to the chronic unit.

I went ballistic. I forced my way into a classroom and climbed on top of the conference table, pacing and yelling. The leader cleared the room and asked me what was wrong. I told him as loudly as I could. Then, when my back was turned, sixty seconds later, my clothes were neatly folded and piled up on the end of the table.

I got dressed right there. The staff rushed me out to a cab for day treatment. On my return, I was greeted in the hallway with an announcement that my psychiatrist had ordered me to see a counselor.

Miracles abound. The counselor believed me about the landlord. She suggested that I confront him with consequences if it continued.

Again, I was met in the hallway, discharged there, and ushered out to a waiting cab. I avoided going home until the landlord was asleep. Then, I waited until another tenant let me in through the security door. I slipped a note under the landlord's door that if he even talked to me, I would be discussing his consequences with my counselor. He never bothered me again.

Besides literally sobering up, I decided that the whole thing was my parents' fault. They had set me up for this. But every time I mentioned ending my relationship with them, the psychiatrist would say, "Oh, we're still paranoid, are we?" and increase the dosage of my medication. I could hardly swallow, walk, or talk. I learned to shut up. However, even knowing I would get medicated for it, I legally changed my last name.

It took me two years to find a psychiatrist who would listen. The new doctor put me back on the medication for manic depression. He spent three months helping me role play the confrontation with my parents, which I was determined to do face-to-face. I also took courses in beginning and advanced dirty street fighting for women in case my father got violent.

I met them in a public place in my old home town. When I told my parents I wanted to sever ties with them, they both smiled their let's-placate-the-mental-case smile and my mother informed me what I really wanted was to give my father a heart attack. I countered that I wasn't accepting any guilt trips. There was another round of asserting that I was severing ties, followed by a guilt trip and a firm refusal to accept it. Finally, my mother pulled out her checkbook and asked how much money I wanted.

Totally unrehearsed, I slammed the checkbook shut and hissed, "I don't want your f**n' money. I want you the f**k out of my life."

She and my father, who hadn't uttered a single word, got up and left.

It took six hours to make the one-hour trip back to my own home town. All the extra counseling sessions scheduled to pick up the pieces were canceled on me. I thought what I had done was so powerful that I alone caused the flood of '93 that contaminated our water supply less than one hour after my return. Despite my temporary homelessness during the flood and a fire that destroyed everything I owned six months later, I was the happiest survivor in the city.

All that energy that had been directed at my parents for forty-four years had to be diverted somewhere else. I joined a psychosocial clubhouse for people with mental illnesses. For the first time, I shared my dream of being a writer and a public speaker.

They said, "Go for it! We believe in you!"

When a professor called the clubhouse, asking for a mental health consumer to give paid talks to his classes, they sent me.

All went well for two and a half years. Then, a distant relative showed up to tell me my father was dying and I'd better make up if I was going to. After much inner turmoil, I impulsively mailed my parents an unsigned note that said, "I forgive you."

I put down boundaries that we were to communicate only by phone and letter. As far as I was concerned, part of forgiving them meant not setting myself up to accept the same behaviors from them over and over again. Their first response was to try to commit me for having feelings about the fire and my homelessness.

I almost severed ties again, even though I realized I had too strong a support system to be committed and their stand was unreasonable. But then I had a flash of insight that their childhoods, which they had been obsessed with, had actually been worse than mine. In fact, I had copied many of their behaviors, and I couldn't rid myself of them despite thirty-eight years of therapy.

I decided that, just because I hadn't received the unconditional love I always craved, I didn't have to deprive them of the only unconditional love they had never known.

I ignored all their attempts at control. I repeated all the stories about their childhoods they had ranted about to show I was listening to them. Commenting on how I would have felt if I had been them, I lauded their courage and thanked them for passing their stamina on to me.

Six months later, I was on stage in front of an audience of 400 medical students, spotlights, and cameras. But the real highlight of the moment was the letter from my parents in my back pocket.

"Have you given that keynote yet? We know you can do it. You've come so far and we love you so much."

I still didn't go home because of distant relatives' reports that my father was still violent. But then he was placed in a nursing home in restraints. I visited him. I held him in my arms before he died and told him I loved him. He cried.

My mother began sharing her own emotions with me after his cremation. When I told her I planned to write a book, an autobiography called "A Dream Keeper's Victory," she sent me a word processor to write it on.

I visited my mother in person while the woman I was riding with visited her own mother. Stuck there during a storm, I had to endure my mother going into gross detail about how my father's body was cremated, especially the way they had to grind down his skull into the fine powder in the urn. I asked her several times to stop it, but she only laughed and escalated it.

When I returned home, I called a crematorium and asked about the details. They very gently said that the entire body was consumed by the flames until the bones became ash. When I repeated this to my mother, she laughed once more. "I knew that. I was only trying to get to you and it worked, didn't it?"

Perhaps she had frightened herself with her own vulnerability or I had frightened her with the book. But I couldn't forgive her this time.

In my anger, I responded to the flirtations of the janitor in my apartment building, unthinkingly once more getting involved with the man with the keys. Regretting my own behavior, I became threatening with him.

Suzanne/Mogell reappeared at this point. She had predicted my autobiography a decade earlier, saying it would change the way people with mental illnesses were treated. But now she informed me that if I persisted in threatening people, the book would be taken away from me. I broke off the affair.

The first draft of my book had been pure ranting and raving. The second draft became an objective report of everything that happened from beginning to end, leaving out all proper names. Then I began to move into the third draft in which I changed first person to third, revealing only in the last two paragraphs that I was Mental Case/Dream Keeper.

I started dating a man who finally heard me say no to sex. Feeling empowered, I got a job as a peer counselor. My psychiatrist took me off my medication because I seemed to be doing so well. But, still trying to connect with my mother, I heard one too many stories of sexual harassment at work and quit my job before I got started.

In my now-twisted thinking, I knew I was psychotic and needed my medication back, but believed that I had to trick my doctor into giving it to me. I had signed up for a conference he was hosting. By the time I got there, six of us were present—I was trying to crawl out of the body Satan occupied while Mogell and John the Baptist fought to prevent violence. A small child was clawing at the walls beneath a table trying to escape. And an objective note-taker hovered near the ceiling, taking notes on what behavior needed to change between psychoses.

I sent many notes to my psychiatrist to meet me in his office afterwards, signing them as Satan. He kept ignoring me. I stationed myself by the exit and stopped him.

"Does your daughter like sushi?" I asked him, using her name.

"I don't believe so."

"That will be a little difficult when she goes to Japan, won't it?"

His knees buckled. I wouldn't have recognized his daughter if she had walked up to me. But I knew he wouldn't know that the professor I spoke for had mentioned in passing that his son was going on a school trip to Japan with the doctor's daughter.

In his office afterwards, my psychiatrist informed me that I couldn't threaten him or he'd call the security guards. The police were afraid of me so I wasn't afraid of the security guards. But he was a man with boundaries and I had hit one. As I turned to leave, he reminded me I had an appointment in two weeks. I was so excited he wasn't going to abandon me.

But once again, I assumed no landlord would house a psychotic and verbally harassed the police for room and board until they arrested me. This time, it took a lawyer to get me out of jail. After another hospitalization under my own doctor and antipsychotic medication, things went well for another year, until I developed fluid on my lungs and had to switch to another brand of medication. The replacement kept me out of jail. That was about all.

Between the third and fourth draft of my manuscript, I decided to go directly to God to verify he really wanted me to write this book. I took two full bottles of medication, intending to return—and I did—four days later in intensive care. My psychiatrist declared that if I was going to pull a stunt like that, I didn't need to be on medication.

My first day home, I woke up horribly physically sick. I asked the man standing next to me if I should go to the hospital. He replied, "I don't see the point. You're dead. You just don't know it yet."

Because I could see right through this man, like a ghost, I called my psychiatrist instead. He said if there was an emergency, I should call an ambulance. So I did. But by the time they arrived, the symptoms had passed and I felt alienated from the world. I announced in a bizarre accent that I was an alien. I had come to bring love and peace but the world demanded sex and war so I had given them what they wanted.

The hospital psychiatrist angrily told me I should win an Academy Award for acting because everybody had believed me. I was startled. I wasn't an alien?

Discharged, I knew better than to share my assumed homelessness with the police this time. But it made sense that, if everybody believed me, the CIA had been called. I saw them in every face, behind every cloud. Finding solace by planting my feet in an outdoor church fountain centered by a larger-than-life statue of Christ, I suddenly saw the truth. I really *was* John the Baptist! My outlandish behavior was meant to draw people's attention to the second coming.

Okay, God. I've done my part. Now take me home and let Christ do His.

The next thing I knew, an angel was tugging at me, insistent that I was floating face down in the fountain. I thought it was weird for an angel to question hypothermia, to offer to return with sandwiches and blankets, and to call an ambulance. But while I waited, the police showed up and told me to move on, which I meekly did.

I meandered to the homeless shelter and stood in line for the doors to open. But the people in line were telling dirty jokes. Obviously, they could read my mind and knew it was one of my father's tactics to disturb me. Once inside, I could hear the staff plotting to send in the National Guard to get me out. So I walked out, intending to demand an MRI to detect what kind of brain damage I had suffered with the overdose. Instead, I ended up in the psychiatric unit again—the one where the staff lost my laundry. But I got a different doctor, one who was scared of me and made no demands.

Satan kept popping out all over the place whenever John the Baptist disappeared. But over time, the new medication began to take effect and word reached me that my long-term psychiatrist was still willing to work with me.

I continued to have momentary symptoms for a few months. One day, I was broadcasting my thoughts to the CIA who had electrodes implanted in my brain. While they were monitoring this powerless mental patient, somebody was going to take advantage of their turned backs and attack from behind.

In the middle of that thought came 9/11.

I put that coincidence together with the flood I had caused and panicked. Maybe I had tapped into some kind of evil power in all my flirtations with Satan. I had better quit it.

I countered every delusional, paranoid or negative thought with *Block. Block. Block.* Then I deliberately substituted positive thoughts. I worked hard at establishing the missing components of my life: sleep, exercise and nutritious food.

I was performing better than ever and my doctor knew better than to take me off my medication. He said I had taught *him* to be med-compliant.

Then one day, I returned to my mother's house for a family reunion. I listened to my family in silence as the anger mounted. *I have to be either a victim or a perpetrator in this family—there's no other role for me here.*

I continued to sit in silence during the car ride back home. As she dropped me off, the friend who was driving quietly commented, "I think you have the capacity to be homicidal."

Zap!

The strange confrontation in college! My fiance's suicide! The counselor who left town without a good-bye! The police officers' fear of me! The patients and staff at the hospital walking away from me!

I was a psychopath!

I had never heard of a psychopath healing, but if it were possible, I was going to be the first! Strangely, both my doctor and counselor trusted me to make the decision how to heal.

Every time I got angry, I took an extra antipsychotic and read for 24 or 48 or 72 hours, whatever it took to get past my own thoughts. Then, I redirected myself back to my routine.

And my dreams—I was going to get a job! I took a computer course, then traveled out of state alone to take two weeks of training to learn benefits planning for people with disabilities.

"Don't tell your mother!" everybody counseled.

Then one day, a drug addict who had a crush on me pressured me to give him a hug in a social gathering. I said, "No!" a dozen times but he wasn't listening. In the middle of a sentence turning the druggy down, a man I had been friends with for years walked up and gave me a bear hug. I hugged him back.

Suddenly, the drug addict was wedged between us, screaming, "You give him a hug! But you won't give me one?"

Calmly, firmly and loudly, I said, "That is not an option."

The druggy turned and walked out. I could protect myself against sexual harassment! I could protect myself against my mother too!

I called her and told her I was working. When she threw me a curve ball, I tossed it back. I told her I was going to work and not listen to her anymore. She was entering a nursing home the next week and I was moving to a two-bedroom apartment so I could have an office to work in. I didn't give her my new phone number or address. Our karma had been resolved and I was content not to stir up more of it. Her reaction to my autobiography would be hers alone without me.

My relationship with my mother had run parallel to my relationship with men. I had assumed my triumph meant saying "No more!" and being heard. Instead, it meant not being heard and standing my ground anyway. But as a Dream Keeper, my true victory had been overcoming my own behavior—no one could take that away from me.

For the first time in fifty-four years, I cried.

"What I See"

Jennifer Houchins

As I see it, depression is engulfing. I never thought I would be depressed. I thought of it as an illness that happened to other people. I had seen it in my friends but not in myself. I thought I was strong enough to withstand anything and that I had all of my mental faculties under control. Mental illness, as I am told, is not necessarily within one's self. Rather, it is a chemical imbalance. It is not my fault and I will get better. I mean, I'm depressed, yes, but I can function and make it through; at the same time, it has been somewhat debilitating. Does that mean I am crazy or just lonely or that I don't have a life?

I want so much to be normal again so I can live my life. When there are negative thoughts running through my head I am tortured, and these thoughts sometimes run through my mind every waking moment. This is how bad it has been for me the last six months. My life has been a total mess.

In the last year and a half I have been seeing a male therapist. It was suggested by a female therapist that I get the male perspective. I had often conversed with my female therapist about men, and she noticed a pattern in me regarding bringing up the pain I have experienced in my past relationships. I discussed with her how I had been disappointed time after time. I recall a particular question she asked me. "What is it you are expecting from men and why have you always ended up disappointed?" I could not fully answer the question. I could not conjure up a response. I just did not know.

Don't get me wrong, I like men and I'm glad they exist. However, I have not found a relationship that could be considered real or great or even satisfying. I think what made me realize that things had gotten pretty bad was when I entered a particular insight in my journal. I can't believe I'm even allowing myself to write this. Part of my depression stems from the fact that opening up and revealing myself to a man, or for that matter anyone, means defeat, and I'm afraid it will be used against me. This is difficult for me to write this. Here goes. Here is my journal entry dated November 2004.

I start out feeling confident at the beginning of a relationship then slowly I become incompetent, insecure (and) not knowing which way is up. These men seem to think women are beneath them and they (men) tend to hate them. Men want total control over women to feel better about themselves. They degrade women and have no problem putting women in their place. . . They start out prince charming because they have to hide the fact that they are really not nice people. They will use many words to confuse women and will expect sex quite early in the relationship. They will pretend they understand and care about you when actually they are incapable of loving you. The more you try to please them the more control they have. It is like a dance, a sick, sick dance you play back and forth. They will treat you bad to bring you down and then act so nice so that you will be grateful for it. Even if it's only for awhile, once they have you there is a switch and you are left wondering what really happened. You wonder, "what did I do wrong?" . . . I've been threatened with violence, told he wanted to cut my throat, been told "I don't really want to commit but I want sex with you." . . . that I should stop being fourteen and put out, been yelled at in parking lots, churches, shopping malls, been thrown forcefully onto a dryer, been pushed and told I am fat, (that) I am stupid and that I don't know what I'm talking about, been cheated on and when a man has you wrapped around his finger he proceeds to take control of your life including finances, sex, everyday stuff, what to think, what to wear, . . . to have you under his thumb. You will no longer be who you are or allowed to have an opinion and if by chance you happen to do something better than he does you will have to pay for it because it is not allowed. If you are sick you are seen as weak. If the house is dirty they will make you feel inadequate about it. And if you attempt to really please yourself sexually with him he will make sure that you never enjoy it more than he does, ever. It is an endless cycle and you become numb to it . . . after awhile you do not even realize you are being abused.

I cannot believe the hatred I sometimes feel for men. I feel confused and frustrated and I have a lot of pain. These past few months have been some of the hardest I've had to endure. Emotionally I'm a basket case. I am in a fog. I have crying spells almost every day, sometimes for no reason at all and sometimes from loss of hope. Did I deserve to be treated like a piece of meat? Did I deserve to be subjected to endless pain by these men? Of course not, although there definitely are certain patterns that follow, all from a painful childhood.

To feel my emotions again and to be in society would be something I haven't done in a long time. Depression to me is a struggle for peace, a need to feel that I belong in the world at age forty-one. I still feel somehow that I am not a piece of the puzzle. Everyone sees the outside of me and they have a mental picture of the way I am, but I have built a wall around me. I am trying to break down these walls through psychotherapy.

I can function on the outside pretty well but underneath the façade is a person wanting the world to know she hurts. I want to reveal myself without being a victim. Why do I somehow sabotage getting well? When will I ever get it? Well, as I see it, never. I am afraid to even acknowledge that I have severe depression. To admit it would be defeat. I am telling others I am doing fine while I am crying on the inside. I feel like I should just get over this and be grown up about it. Men are people too. Somehow I have allowed men to exploit me. A man has never truly committed to me. Even my marriage was a sham. I never really said, "Look, this is for the long haul. You need to commit." I was very open minded but did not think that I deserved to be treated well. I allowed so much to transpire because I was afraid of doing the wrong thing and in the process I lost myself. I inevitably have succumbed to the realization that happiness will never be mine. (At least not in the sense that others see as happiness. I might get by . . . but deep down inside I want more.)

I have an awful lot of negative thoughts. I am tired but tired of what? Is it living or the fact that I cannot see the end for what it is? When does what I want begin to matter? With my ex-boyfriend my needs were second to his. My needs did not matter. Years went by and my situation never changed. It's not so much that my thinking is unrealistic but I can no longer allow myself any hope because every time I do it's dashed. When something good does happen I am glad but my joy is fleeting. Why could he not tell me up front that he did not want a relationship with me? Would I still have gone out with him? At least I would have known. Men want to keep their options open. Somehow there is always that magical woman who will be a perfect size four. She'll be the perfect girlfriend. The perfect everything. I am not the perfect girlfriend or the perfect mom or the perfect friend. I am me—take it or leave it.

I went into these relationships with hope and of anticipation of a new beginning. There's nothing wrong with that but somehow it always ends up in hurt. Maybe this time I will do the exact opposite. Maybe I shouldn't look upon a relationship as a guarantee. Maybe this time I will put both feet on the ground and instead of wishing upon a star, I will wish upon reality—that somehow I will enjoy the moment and whatever happens will happen. It sounds reasonable but I don't know. I put too much emphasis on happiness and not enough emphasis on reality. My ex-boyfriend told me once, "Why does it have to be so complicated?" Did he mean us? Or did he mean, "Why can't I just have sex with you?" I just wanted him to see me as a person and not a sex object, but as usual, I was asking too much. So, I sold myself short. I settled for less. I was tossed crumbs and I fetched.

So where do I go from here? I am dealing with this pain head on. Writing is therapeutic for me and I write because I want to. I am not on any prescription drugs at the moment, although a few times my therapist has brought up the use of antidepressants to help me out of this ordeal. At present I still want to refrain from the use of pharmaceuticals. I do not want to hide the pain, only to find the cause of my pain. I want to get better and I want to discover new parts of me. As I see it, happy endings happen to other people. Will they ever be happy for me?

Welcome to the
Hotel Psychiatric

Kurt Sass

Day 12

I've been such a good boy so far. Not by choice, actually. I've been so overly medicated with Thorazine and Mellaril that I don't have the strength to act out, even if I wanted to.

But since I've been such a good boy, I've actually earned a chance at partial freedom; in other words, a day pass. This is all contingent, however, on getting approval from the therapist I will be seeing today. I sure hope it's the same therapist I saw on day 2 (or was it day 3?) or the therapist I saw around day 8. Maybe they'll see some improvement, or at least that I haven't gotten any worse.

I'm supposed to see the therapist at 11, but of course I'm kept waiting, which only builds up my anxiety, which is the last thing I want him or her to see. Finally, at 12:43, the therapist arrives. Of course it's a completely different therapist, one who has never seen me or my records before. Third therapist, third face.

He motions me into a small room, and we sit. As I sit there, doing my best to erase all the nervousness and fear that has built up in the last hour and one-half of waiting, he begins to ask me all the obligatory questions, just as therapists #1 and #2 had: "Do you know why you are in here? Do you feel like you may do harm to yourself or others? How are you feeling now?"

After giving him the answers I think will benefit me the most, "I was admitted for depression and suicidal thoughts. I have no feelings of hurting myself or others. I'm feeling good, very good." He begins to go through my life history, just as #1 and #2 had done before. (Don't these guys ever write things down and share their notes so they don't have to repeat everything?) I go on to tell him everything I can remember. I start with my childhood, growing up with my parents and two older brothers. I tell him that I actually had a very good childhood. The only two traumatic events I can think of are my grandmother's (on my father's side) suicide in an "asylum" when I was 5 years old, and my father's alcoholism. I emphasize to him that, although these were two extremely powerful and horrible things for a child to have to deal with, I had a terrific mother and two excellent role models for brothers, which in my opinion more than made up for the above-mentioned trials and tribulations.

At this point, I fully expected the therapist to stop me. After all, the other two therapists both stopped me at this juncture, as they both felt they had enough information to come up with their theory of the cause for my depression and suicidal thoughts. The only problem was that each theory was different. Therapist #1 came to the conclusion that the one and only reason for my problems was an overriding guilt and shame from having an alcoholic father. He made no mention at all that there was any possibility whatsoever that my depression could be genetic, despite what I told him about my father and his mother. I was told simply to concentrate more on myself and less on my father.

Therapist #2 came to a different conclusion. According to him, the one and only reason for my depression and suicidal thoughts was that I was the youngest of three sons and had an inferiority complex when it came to them. Once again, no talk of genetics playing any role in this. He basically told me to live my own life and not try to live up to my brothers. In other words, to concentrate more on myself. I must admit one thing, however. Even though both of their theories were miles apart, their conclusions were the same: simply concentrate more on myself. My God, this was so easy! Why didn't I ever think of that? Just concentrate more on myself than others and I won't feel bad anymore. Funny thing, though. As much as I tried doing so, it didn't help one goddamn bit!

Let me digress back to Therapist #3. He actually wanted to hear more. Perhaps he, unlike the others, didn't think it was simply a case of mind over matter, that all I needed to do was just change my thinking. I proceeded to tell him the rest of my story, including the near present, the time right before I was hospitalized 12 days earlier. I explained to the therapist that I honestly had no idea at all why I was so depressed and suicidal. After all, everything in my life at the time had seemed to be going along so well. I was a Senior at Hunter College, majoring in Business Economics, with minors in both English and Theatre. I was living with my parents and had a part time job, so money was no problem whatsoever. I also had a girlfriend for the last 6 months, someone whom I had known for over 5 years, and the relationship was not causing any stress at all. I also told him about the other two therapists' theories. He told me that he did not concur with the other two therapists and thought it was something "completely different."

At this point I must tell you that for the first time since my admission to the hospital I felt that someone who worked there really cared about me and understood me. This feeling lasted about 5 seconds, until the therapist continued speaking. He told me that he was positive that the reason I felt so depressed and suicidal was because everything was going so good in my life, and if I could only learn how to accept it when good things happen to me, rather than feel guilty about it, I would be better. Once again, no talk about genetic, biological, or chemical causes. It was all in my mind. If only I could change the way I was thinking about things.

I honestly had to fight the impulse at that moment to attack this third of three incompetent, ridiculous, professionals. (I'd slap you silly, but you're already there). Fortunately I remembered the ultimate goal was to "earn" my day pass, so I told this "idiot" that he was probably right, and that was enough for him. He signed my day pass and said I could leave immediately.

"Not so fast, Chris!" I should have known better by now. Attendant Borges, who was by now probably the tenth person who forgot that my name was, is, and always will be Kurt, said that I wasn't going anywhere until a psychiatrist signed off on the day pass. He asked me what I was trying to pull. I told him it was the therapist who said I could leave immediately, but of course he was long gone by now to back up my story.

After another anxiety-riddled 45 minutes or so, a psychiatrist happened to appear on the ward. He was handed the day pass, and stared at me for about 5 seconds. I gave him my best "everything's calm and peaceful" look. He then signed the day pass, telling Attendant Borges "A doctor doesn't have to sign this. The therapist's signature is enough." Once again, I had to control my anger for the sake of the day pass.

Attendant Borges motioned to me, and he and I started walking toward the locked door of the ward and toward my first taste of freedom in almost two weeks. At that time I remembered that I had heard on the radio that the temperature was barely in double digits (11 degrees, to be exact), and that all I was wearing, in addition to my pants, sneakers, socks, and underwear was a short-sleeved tee shirt. I made the mistake of asking Attendant Borges if I could get my jacket. This "major" request angered Borges, who said: "Can't do it. They're all in the basement and we got nobody free to go down and get it."

I then made the bigger mistake of telling Borges "I know the coats are kept in the closet by the bathroom. Can't you just unlock the closet and get it for me?" Borges then pushed me against the wall and whispered "You don't want me to tell anyone you're acting up, now do you?" I got the point, and for the third time in the last hour resisted the use of justified violence.

Borges then walked me to the door, unlocked it, and told me "You better be back by five!" This of course added to my anxiety, since I had no watch and knew I would constantly have to look for places with a clock so I would make it back on time.

I started walking toward the elevator, fully expecting someone to call me back in the ward, that there was some sort of paperwork or procedural problem. Fortunately, this was not the case. I pushed the button for the elevator, feeling elated at my new-found freedom, figuring this must be what prisoners feel like when they are released. It was not the first, nor last time I'd be feeling like a prisoner during my stay.

I got on the elevator. There were about six other people in the car, and all were peeking glances at me, while trying to make sure I didn't see them looking. This was not paranoia on my part. In fact, I don't blame them for being concerned and scared. All you had to do was see me. I had no coat on, pants that were wrinkled beyond belief, and a 12-day growth of un-combed facial hair. Hey, I'd be scared and apprehensive, too! I don't think I smelled, but to be honest, I don't remember. When we got to the ground floor and the elevators opened, the other six passengers got off first and walked very fast to the front door. Maybe I did have an odor. Anyway, I then got off the elevator and walked through the front doors of the hospital.

I have to admit, my very first thought once outside was to take off my hat and fling it like Mary Tyler Moore did in the opening credits to her show. But alas, no hat, no coat. A coat is very, very important in 11 degree weather. I remember other times in my life in this predicament, but it was always while I was participating in a football game, where I was constantly moving. I decided to start walking, and walking fast.

About two blocks away from the hospital was a coffee shop. Perfect! I'll just get a booth, get some coffee, warm up, keep an eye on the clock, and enjoy my little vacation until it was time to return. Then I remembered that I had no money. And with the way I looked, I was way too self-conscious to ask them to let me stay there. So I kept walking.

I was walking for about 45 minutes (I know this for a fact, because I looked in every window to see if they had a clock so I wouldn't lose track of time) when all of a sudden I heard a loud megaphone. I didn't pay attention to it at first, at least not until a huge, bright light shone on me. It was the police. They motioned me over to the car. "Don't you know its cold outside?" this extremely perceptive policeman asked me. "Yes," I told him, while feeling another case of justified anxiety coming on. "It's crazy to be dressed like that in this weather," he added, thus giving me another fact I would have never known if he had not advised me. I wanted to tell him that, yes, I indeed know that I should be wearing a coat, but the minute I mentioned that I came from the hospital, he interrupted. "Oh, you're one of those," he said, with, (How can I put this?) not the greatest amount of pride in his voice, and drove away. Thanks for the caring, officer!

Within the next hour I got stopped twice more by the cops. I guess I should have been grateful. The police were the only people who spoke to me the entire time I was out. Anyhow, when the police did stop me these two other times, I was ready. I didn't want to get into another useless question and answer period with them, so each time they called me over, I simply pointed to the hospital, and they drove off. I guess this sort of thing happens all the time.

While walking, I made it a point never to venture the more than four blocks away from the hospital. The last thing I wanted to do was get lost and not make it back on time. Who knew what repercussions this major crime of coming back late would cause? Would they not give me any more day passes? Would my eventual (hopefully) full release be delayed indefinitely? I certainly didn't want to find out, so at precisely 4:30 I walked back to the hospital lobby, where I arrived at 4:35.

Funny thing about old hospitals, things break a lot. When I got to the elevators, there was a big crowd of people. None of the lights showing what floor the elevators were on, or what direction they were going were lit. I waited about 5 minutes and nothing changed. Still no elevators. I walked over to the policeman in the lobby and explained that I had to get back to the ward, or else I'd be in trouble. "Nothing I can do. You just have to wait." Thanks for the caring, Officer!

A few minutes later, the officer opened a door to the stairway and said that people could use it if they liked. What he meant to say was that anyone except the person who needs to get back to the psych ward so as not to endanger the chance of getting released sometime in the near future could use the stairway if they liked. For the second time today I was pushed against a wall. "Psych patients are not allowed to use the stairs. You'll just have to wait." Thanks for the caring, Officer!

Now, I feel I have to emphasize something at this point. As far as I know, one of the goals of treating a person in a psychiatric setting is to reduce their stress and anxiety. This day alone, in a little less than 6 hours, I've had to put up with the following situations which I believe would cause stress to the most cool, calm, collected, and emotionally stable person on the planet:

- Waiting an extra 2 hours for the therapist who might give me a day pass. Getting a third completely different diagnosis from a third therapist.
- Being told I'm depressed because things are going good.
- Thinking I can leave, only to be told that a psychiatrist also has to sign the day pass.
- Waiting 45 minutes for the psychiatrist.
- Hearing the psychiatrist say he didn't need to sign it, anyway.
- Being shoved against the wall for asking for a coat in

frigid weather. Being told I must be back by a certain
time, but without a watch. Being stopped three times by
the police.

• Being shoved against the wall again, and told that I'm
not allowed to use the stairway access to get back to the
ward by 5:00, although everyone else could use it.

And let's not forget the fact that I still am feeling depressed and suicidal.

As the time gets closer to 5:00, I get more and more nervous. I ask the policeman if I can use the phone to call the
ward, just to let them know that I am in the building. "No,
you can't." I ask the officer if he can call the ward and explain
the situation. "No, I can't." Thanks for the caring, Officer!

Sure enough, 5 o'clock passes, and I'm still in the lobby. At
precisely 5:23 (you bet I was watching the clock!) the elevators
finally start up again, and I jump into the first one and zoom
up to the 2nd floor ward. (That's right. All I needed to do was
to walk up one flight of stairs, but that f—-ing cop wouldn't
let me!) I get off the elevator and knock on the locked ward
door. Attendant Reca opens the door and promptly states,
"You're late, Sass! They told you to be back by five!" I start to
explain the situation, but Reca doesn't want to hear any of it.
"Tell the doctor next time you see him. See what he has to
say." Since I have no idea when I will next be seeing the psychiatrist (I've only seen him twice, so far) I'm relatively sure
that by the time I do, no one will remember that the elevators
broke down, only that I was late from my "privilege" and
"test" of having a day pass. This will undoubtedly have a negative impact on the chance of any future freedom, even
though I was actually back in the hospital 25 minutes early.
One more anxiety to add to my list.

Once back on the ward, a smiling Nurse Kelly goes out of
her way to tell me that because of my lateness, I missed out on
snack time. She seems to get some sort of strange satisfaction
out of this. I'm surprised she didn't just stick her thumbs in her

ears, wave her hands back and forth and say "Nuh, nuh, nuh, nuh, nuh!" I guess Nurse Kelly isn't one of the "caring, dedicated and professional nursing staff" the intake person told me about when I was admitted. I'd love to say this to Ms. Kelly personally, but after seeing the movie "One Flew Over the Cuckoo's Nest" I figure it's best not to get any of the staff upset.

After dinner, I eagerly await my favorite time of the day, visiting *hours*. (This is a misnomer, because visiting hours is only one hour.) I'm extremely anxious, but for a change it is not the hospital's fault. I'm very nervous because my girl-friend Marta has not seen me in three days. When I was first in the hospital she saw me at least every day or two at the most, but the visits are becoming less frequent. I don't know if it is because the visits are very difficult for her or if she is los-ing feelings for me. I'm really concerned because when she left after the last visit (on Sunday) she said she couldn't come Monday or Tuesday because her favorite movie was being shown on TV, in two parts, and she didn't want to miss it. At least I think that's what she said. To be honest, I have so much medication in me, a lot of things are fuzzy. When I told the psychiatrist about this constant mental confusion a few days earlier, he just told me to bear with it, that the sedative "qual-ities" would *probably* wear off. Probably is a very scary word. I tell you, if there is one thing I had learned so far from my "visit" here, it's that not a single doctor, or nurse, or therapist, or social worker, or attendant knows how important it is to care and to pay close attention to how one speaks to a patient, and, just as importantly, how to listen to a patient. I tell you, so far the only people that have shown me any kindness, car-ing, or concern whatsoever and have listened to my concerns have been a few of the other patients. And I guess that makes sense, if you think about it. What doctor, or nurse, or thera-pist, or social worker, or attendant knows what it is like to be so heavily medicated that you can't think straight, and how it feels to be so afraid you will always feel that way? Which one of these "professionals" has ever felt suicidal, or so extremely depressed without knowing why they had fallen into this abyss? I just wish there were some way that we could inject these people with severe depression, or schizophrenia, and throw in a dash of suicidal thoughts, just for a day or two. Perhaps after an experience like that, compassion would finally start to come to the surface. That's why the only kind and caring people I've met so far have all been patients.

One person I met was Martha. (Not to be confused with my girlfriend Marta.) Martha and I had a long talk one day. There was a song playing on the radio, a song by a group called Sister Sledge. The song was called "We are Family." Martha was telling me that she disliked the song. I asked her why, because it sounded good, and seemed to have a positive message, about the importance of families sticking together. She then started going over some of the lines in the song. She said that many of the lyrics emphasized the notion that as long as you have faith in yourself and all that you do, that you will never get depressed and that everything will be all right. She then began to give me many more examples from her own everyday life of how so many people, from priests to teachers to guidance counselors and even her own parents, would tell her that all she had to do was believe more and have more faith in herself, and that this would stop her depressive feelings. She explained that all these words would do, despite their good intentions, were to make her blame herself for her depression even more. According to what they were saying, she had the power to make herself feel better, so if she wasn't, it had to be a weakness on her part. When I heard this, it sank in for the first time that maybe my depression wasn't my fault, and maybe it wasn't a character flaw on my part. In my opinion, Martha gave me much more therapy than any of the "professional" therapists.

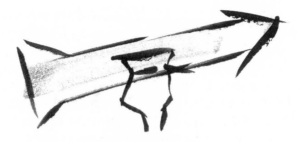

Interview 1

Steve Maxim

03/12/08 Operation Freedom PTSD

Steve Maxim is a veteran of Operation Freedom (the first Gulf War). He currently resides in an apartment in the same building as a homeless shelter. He qualifies for this housing because he is a vet. Mr. Maxim has been diagnosed as suffering from PTSD.

INTERVIEWER: Are your parents alive, Steve?

STEVE: Yes.

INTERVIEWER: Do you visit them?

STEVE: My mother owns a house here in Lansing. Same one I grew up in. I try to get to see her when I can.

INTERVIEWER: Do you have any brothers or sisters?

STEVE: Yeah, two brothers. They're twins.

INTERVIEWER: What are they doing?

STEVE: One's in sales, the other one works for the Veterans Housing Bureau. He was recently diagnosed as schizoaffective.

INTERVIEWER: That's my diagnosis.

STEVE: Yeah, what is it?

INTERVIEWER: Well, the diagnosis includes some characteristics of a mood disorder and some characteristics of schizophrenia. If you are medicated properly, you can sometimes do well. That's my understanding of schizoaffective disorder.

STEVE: My brother perseverates a lot.

INTERVIEWER: How so?

STEVE: He always sees and tells you over and over about the negative side of things. When you try to do something positive, he always tells you nothing good is going to come of it. He spends a lot of time alone.

INTERVIEWER: Let me tell you a little about my family. My father was an attorney. I had three brothers, Fred, Keith, and Denny. Keith recently passed away. He was a Vietnam veteran.

STEVE: Yeah.

INTERVIEWER: You were born where, Steve?

STEVE: Right here in Lansing. Just up the street at Sparrow Hospital.

INTERVIEWER: How old are you?

STEVE: I'm thirty now.

INTERVIEWER: Where did you go to grade school?

STEVE: I went to Catholic grade school and Catholic high school. For high school I went to Catholic Central. I spent my senior year in public school. There was a vast difference between Catholic school and public school. I took the easy way out by leaving private school my senior year. I was supposed to do a report for my senior year in Catholic school. I thought it was too hard so I went to public school.

INTERVIEWER: Did you get your high school diploma or not?

STEVE: I did. I got my high school diploma from public school. I graduated from high school in Dexter, Michigan.

INTERVIEWER: After you graduated from high school you went into the military?

STEVE: No. I really needed some guidance. I lived with my girlfriend and we lived with her mother for a while. That got to be too much. We got our own apartment. My girlfriend was pressuring me into marriage and for whatever reason, I don't know why, we had our differences and the differences took us apart and we split up. She went into the military and then soon after I did.

INTERVIEWER: What branch of service did she go into?

STEVE: She went into the Air Force.

INTERVIEWER: And you went into the Marines?

STEVE: Yeah.

INTERVIEWER: So how many years were you in the military?

STEVE: I was in the military for six years.

INTERVIEWER: You served in Operation Freedom. How long were you there?

STEVE: From February 03 to October of 03.

INTERVIEWER: You were in active duty for six years?

STEVE: No, I was in the reserves for a while. I tried to get some money for school. I lived in Ann Arbor [Michigan], after being discharged. I went to Washtenaw Junior College.

INTERVIEWER: What were you educated in?

STEVE: Criminal Justice is what I studied.

INTERVIEWER: You wanted to be a police officer?

STEVE: Yeah, that's what I thought. I thought I wanted to be a police officer.

INTERVIEWER: What happened?

STEVE: After I returned I took advantage of the G.I. Bill, which I'm thankful for. After a while I realized there was a side to the Military Police I didn't like. So, I decided not to be a police officer.

INTERVIEWER: Sure, you are surrounded by the seedier side of life.

STEVE: Yeah. I didn't want to deal with the criminal element. You're dealing with people who are routine law-breakers. I've heard stories about police officers becoming corrupted. It's a difficult, high stress job.

INTERVIEWER: When were you diagnosed as mentally ill?

STEVE: In 2007.

INTERVIEWER: What was your diagnosis?

STEVE: Post traumatic stress disorder.

INTERVIEWER: What do you believe brought on your illness?

STEVE: I'll do my best to try and explain what I think happened to me. What I think was the trigger was an unstable environment. I was always on my toes. I think the stress I went through in Operation Freedom solidified the diagnosis. When we first got to the base in Kuwait at Camp Fox, the area I was in had all the ammunition for the whole conflict. The explosives went on for miles. We were around the parameter of Camp Fox.

I was supposed to guard the bombs. We were keeping everything secure and here comes this guy driving a Hummer with his horn sounding and signaling with his arm. He was speeding wildly and honking his horn. You don't do what he was doing around a base unless there's trouble. I thought, there's something not right about this. Usually everything was so orderly. I didn't realize he was signaling a chemical attack with his arm. I didn't know at the time what his arm signaling meant. [Steve obviously seemed uncomfortable about relaying these events.]

INTERVIEWER: Can you talk a little more about this?

STEVE: Yeah, that's part of the treatment actually. He was signaling for a gas attack. The commanding officers realized it was a gas attack and they ordered us to take out our chemical suits for a chemical attack. We had to carry these suits wherever we went. I got my suit out and I thought, shit, I don't know how to do it. [Put the suit on.]

I have to backtrack here. Two weeks prior to leaving the country, I was supposed to be learning to put the chemical suit on and my wife was nine months pregnant. [Steve got married in the same house his family lived in by a Chaplin on February 26, 2003. She was the first girl he'd met upon returning from infantry school in December of 1999. They had two children.] I was with my wife while the other Marines were being trained in putting these suits on in an expedient manner. I remember my wife was having labor pains. My First Sergeant told me, "Get to the hospital." You were supposed to know how to put these suits on in 14 seconds. So I missed out on the training. In Kuwait these sirens kept going off. We had two different suits. One was for gas, the other was for explosives. Nobody knew what to do. Everyone was scrambling. We didn't have bunkers yet. The base was new. We were sitting ducks basically. Everyone was putting their suits on and I didn't know how.

INTERVIEWER: So did the gas attack ever occur?

STEVE: No, it didn't. The sirens indicating attack went on from twenty-two to twenty-eight times a day every day thereafter. You had to be in a chemical protectiveness mode. We were in Military Preparedness and we were on High Alert. A lot of times we had to walk around in our suits. It was over 100 degrees at the time, sometimes 120 degrees.

INTERVIEWER: And you were under the threat of chemical attack at any moment. Did you wake up to the sirens?

STEVE: Oh yeah. That's the thing. It was scary. The preparation for chemical attack happened at all times of the day. Just as soon as I thought, "I came out of the good side of this one," there was another one.

Saddam was shooting these Scud missiles. When the Scud missiles were coming they activated the sirens for the whole region. I didn't know how close we were to these Scuds. This went on for a couple of weeks. After a while you thought it was just another siren and you got used to it. But at our base there were sirens throughout the night.

The first couple of weeks we couldn't use the showers. They didn't want somebody to be in the shower. They locked the showers down.

INTERVIEWER: So, do you think your mental illness was caused by your war experiences?

STEVE: Yeah, I would say so. You have a fight or flight response they say. The medical people say it changes brain chemicals and you can develop mental illness from constantly being in a fight or flight response. I'm not able to focus and I lose my train of thought. It happens all the time.

INTERVIEWER: If you had to do all over again would you have gone into the service?

STEVE: Yeah, I think I would have.

INTERVIEWER: You think it's a worthwhile endeavor.

STEVE: Exactly.

INTERVIEWER: The Marines need dedicated people to do what you did.

STEVE: That's it. If it wouldn't have been for soldiers in America, we wouldn't enjoy the freedoms we have today. My father was in Vietnam.

INTERVIEWER: You said he's still alive?

STEVE: Yeah, he's still alive. He's in Grand Rapids [Michigan]. He was recently divorced.

INTERVIEWER: How old is he?

STEVE: I don't know exactly. I think he's fifty-seven. He drives a truck.

INTERVIEWER: When you were a kid you wanted to be a soldier?

STEVE: I thought about it, yeah, in the back of my mind.

INTERVIEWER: So it was always with you, the wanting to be a soldier?

STEVE: Yeah, definitely. I don't know, maybe I was daydreaming at the time.

INTERVIEWER: Do you take medicine that helps with your train of thought?

STEVE: Yeah, back in 05–06 the doctors prescribed Adderall, for me.

INTERVIEWER: Do you know what kind of drug Adderall is?

STEVE: It's an amphetamine.

INTERVIEWER: Does it help?

STEVE: Yeah, some.

INTERVIEWER: Do you drink coffee on top of the amphetamine?

STEVE: Yeah.

INTERVIEWER: Does it make you edgy?

STEVE: Well.

INTERVIEWER: I believe one of the problems with amphetamines is that they can make you edgy. Have you experienced this?

STEVE: I imagine so. Yeah, they do make you edgy.

INTERVIEWER: But if you do take them you're better off?

STEVE: I don't know. I think they have a motivating effect for some people.

INTERVIEWER: Do you see a psychiatrist regularly?

STEVE: No. I see a psychologist through the VA every week.

INTERVIEWER: Are you sometimes afraid to tell the psychologist everything because the doctor might recommend different medication?

STEVE: Yes, you could say that. I see a psychologist at the Veteran Affairs building here in Lansing. They have a contract with the military. Also I'm in a Veterans' housing program. The psychologist I see specializes in PTSD. The vet housing program has been convenient but the caseworker is overworked. She delegates case management to the intern who I feel is unqualified and who has not been helpful.

INTERVIEWER: So, you're not a heavy drinker.

STEVE: No. I used to drink after I came back from overseas but not at this time.

INTERVIEWER: You don't drink at all?

STEVE: When I go out I'll have an occasional beer.

INTERVIEWER: But it's not a problem?

STEVE: I don't think so.

INTERVIEWER: Do you feel like a hero?

STEVE: Ahh.

INTERVIEWER: Or is that a problem? You did all of this for your country and now you're in a homeless shelter.

STEVE: When we came back from Operation Freedom they treated us warmly at the airport. It was just the opposite of Vietnam. I think we didn't do as much as we should have over there. I think we should have taken Saddam out. I didn't see a whole lot of action. The sirens and Scuds spooked us.

INTERVIEWER: Do you feel like it was dangerous?

STEVE: Yeah, well, we were always on High Alert. It never ended. It was day and night.

INTERVIEWER: In bed at night does it bother you?

STEVE: Yeah.

INTERVIEWER: Do you feel like the American government has been fair with you?

STEVE: In some respects, yeah. It's really bureaucratic and there's been a lot of red tape. For the most part they've been fair.

INTERVIEWER: You're receiving V.A. benefits?

STEVE: Not yet. I'm in the process.

INTERVIEWER: Are you on any form of Disability now?

STEVE: No. I'm working full time. I work as a custodial supervisor. We offer our services to companies that have large military contracts. The company [that we offer our services to] makes uniforms for the military. The company I work for hires a lot of refugees.

INTERVIEWER: Do the people you work with have disabilities?

STEVE: Yeah.

INTERVIEWER: Are you able to live on your salary?

STEVE: No, it's not enough.

INTERVIEWER: Do you think you had problems before you went to war?

STEVE: I think it is very possible. I don't know whether I did or not. I haven't given it much thought but I need to give it some thought. I don't know.

INTERVIEWER: Do you think the war you fought is justified?

STEVE: No.

INTERVIEWER: You think we should have allowed Saddam to run all over Kuwait?

STEVE: No, I don't think he was trying to do that. I think we should have taken Saddam out the first time around. I'd say before the Iraq War. It would have been justifiable then because he was trying to overrun this country [Kuwait]. I think the Iraq War is a smoke screen to get oil.

INTERVIEWER: You think so?

STEVE: I think so.

INTERVIEWER: Do you think we tried to stabilize the region?

STEVE: I think it was stable before [we went to war].

INTERVIEWER: Sometimes I think our country seems to have an unlimited amount of money for war but a very limited amount of money for mental health. What do you think?

STEVE: Definitely.

INTERVIEWER: Do you have any friends now?

STEVE: Not a whole lot. There's few people I'm really close with.

INTERVIEWER: You live an anonymous life?

STEVE: Yeah.

INTERVIEWER: You're making it the best way you can? Are you able to save any money?

STEVE: Yeah.

INTERVIEWER: You're one of the few people at the shelter saving money to get out?

STEVE: You could say that. There's another guy in his mid-thirties saving some money.

INTERVIEWER: Do you feel abandoned?

STEVE: Well, yeah. I can't say I feel that way all that much. My mom, she's still around. I try not to rely on her too much. In general, I tell you, if it weren't for her. . . .

INTERVIEWER: What do you think is going to happen to you, Steve?

STEVE: I want to believe that, well, ah, I've got to get back to school. Get a more promising job. The kids need to see me do that. I'm going to search for a better job but I have to get back to school.

INTERVIEWER: So, you have to support your kids.

STEVE: The older one is five and a half tomorrow. The other one is two and a half. They live on the south side of Lansing. Child support is taken out of my check. The child support would be taken out regardless of where I live. When I was at my mother's the court ordered at the time of the divorce to take so much money out of my check.

INTERVIEWER: Do you feel you have something to hide?

STEVE: Yeah, I feel that if my employer knew about my problems beforehand he wouldn't have hired me.

INTERVIEWER: Are you homicidal?

STEVE: No.

INTERVIEWER: Are you suicidal?

STEVE: Not at this point.

INTERVIEWER: Are you still a patriot?

STEVE: Yeah.

INTERVIEWER: Do you think America is the best country in the world?

STEVE: It depends on what you're talking about.

INTERVIEWER: I don't think there's a Marine alive that doesn't love his country.

STEVE: Yeah, well, in what other country do you have the freedoms we have but maybe they don't provide services for the mentally ill.

INTERVIEWER: A number of years ago when I was first on disability I realized that there was a change in the way you think of yourself and your illness after you enter a homeless shelter and can no longer provide for yourself. What do you think? What kind of feelings did you experience?

STEVE: It's discouraging. It really is. At the same time I'm thankful that it's there. You're not under a bridge.

INTERVIEWER: Exactly.

STEVE: They ask for random urine tests and they take breathalyzers and I pay some rent. [Homeless vets pay a reduced rent.]

INTERVIEWER: Would you say [in your experience], that most of the people who are in the shelter have drug and alcohol problems?

STEVE: Yeah, and they're mentally ill too. They're one or the other or both.

INTERVIEWER: Many people don't like to go to homeless shelters because they can't drink at night and have to get up early in the morning.

STEVE: That they do. The general population at the shelter has time restraints. Upstairs [in the vet area], where I am you can sleep as much as you want. As long as you're not disorderly they pretty much leave the guys upstairs alone.

INTERVIEWER: Has anyone ever stolen any of your belongings? [Theft is often a problem in some shelters.]

STEVE: No.

INTERVIEWER: The street people are not allowed up in the part of the shelter you live in?

STEVE: No, they're not allowed up there.

INTERVIEWER: Do you eat three meals a day?

STEVE: Yeah. You can buy your food upstairs.

INTERVIEWER: Do you dwell on your war experiences?

STEVE: Yeah, I think about it all the time.

INTERVIEWER: Do you ever discuss your condition with other soldiers?

STEVE: We have weekly groups at the shelter.

INTERVIEWER: Were you ever a patient at the V.A. hospital?

STEVE: Not for an extended period. A couple of weeks ago I went down to the V.A. hospital in Ann Arbor [Michigan].

INTERVIEWER: Do you think men go to war to exert their manhood?

STEVE: Definitely.

INTERVIEWER: Do you have trouble controlling your anger since you got back?

STEVE: I used to be angry when I first got back. I was impulsive and aggressive. I was angry at my wife about the things she would do. I think it was my anger when I got back that led to my divorce.

INTERVIEWER: Would you say your personality changed when you came back?

STEVE: I was on high alert when I came back.

INTERVIEWER: Do you ever think you'll get back together with your wife?

STEVE: I'd like too. I asked her that if she could see the amount of progress I've made would she give me a second chance.

INTERVIEWER: Has she dated other guys?

STEVE: She's dated various guys. It hurts. It makes you angry.

INTERVIEWER: Do you think she was faithful when you were in Kuwait?

STEVE: I do think she was faithful. I don't think many military wives are unfaithful. My wife gave me no reason to mistrust her.

INTERVIEWER: Have you been arrested for anything?

STEVE: No.

INTERVIEWER: Do you have nightmares?

STEVE: I used too. More than I do now.

INTERVIEWER: Are you ever afraid you might do something violent?

STEVE: It's not in my nature. But when I see Muslim extremists I get angry. Sometimes I feel like I wouldn't hesitate to kill them with my bare hands when I get agitated.

INTERVIEWER: Have you ever thought you might end up in prison?

STEVE: No.

INTERVIEWER: Do you feel like war damaged your mind?

STEVE: Yeah, I definitely do.

INTERVIEWER: Do you think war creates criminals?

STEVE: Yeah, I'd say so, in some people.

INTERVIEWER: Many people don't understand mental illness. Have you ever thought that if you lost a leg or an arm people would realize your sacrifice but as an ex-military man with mental illness that they don't understand your illness or empathize with the problems you have?

STEVE: Yeah, oh yeah, my dad thinks PTSD is a cop out. He thinks there is nothing wrong with me. He said there was nothing wrong with him when he came back from Nam.

INTERVIEWER: Have you ever tried to get temporary relief from drugs and alcohol?

STEVE: Yeah, I'm not as strong as I want to be.

INTERVIEWER: What happens? Does it work or not?

STEVE: I try to stay away from it now. Unfortunately, I have to admit that I'm not as strong as I want to be. Recently there's been cocaine use. It's not a regular thing. I don't crave it or anything.

INTERVIEWER: Did you drink and do drugs before you went to war?

STEVE: Yeah.

INTERVIEWER: But you weren't a drug addict or an alcoholic?

STEVE: No. Well, it depends on what you mean by addict or alcoholic.

INTERVIEWER: Did you have more than two drinks a day?

STEVE: I used to.

INTERVIEWER: Do you feel that war numbed your emotions?

STEVE: Oh yeah, definitely.

INTERVIEWER: Do you feel like war has made it difficult for you to love someone?

STEVE: Oh yeah, it made it harder to be compassionate. It definitely did. It's harder to let people in.

INTERVIEWER: Because you just don't feel those emotions?

STEVE: When you're at war you're close to your buddies but you're on alert and not allowing anybody to get too close to you.

INTERVIEWER: Do you have insomnia? Do you wake up three and four times per night?

STEVE: No, but I can't get to sleep.

INTERVIEWER: Did the overstimulation of war make civilian life seem dull?

STEVE: Yeah, definitely. I wanted to get a gun when I got back. I bought a forty-five, a pistol. I used to take target practice to hear the sound of a gun. I bought the pistol largely because I thought it was highly likely that some one would come to my house to threaten me or my family.

INTERVIEWER: It was a stimulus for you? A form of enjoyment?

STEVE: Yeah.

INTERVIEWER: Are there any jobs you qualify for based on your military experience?

STEVE: I didn't go into the service to get a job. No, I'm not employable but I'm not bitter about it. I think anyone who can work some kind of job should work.

INTERVIEWER: Have you had trouble holding down a job?

STEVE: Yeah, I've had some disciplinary write ups. They say I have a lack of focus. There's been a lack of follow through on my part. I don't make some employees do what they're supposed to do. I haven't gotten the work done. I seem to think in terms of immediate results rather than a plan. It's been a problem for me. My lack of focus is more than what most people have.

INTERVIEWER: You have a problem with planning and then executing the plan.

STEVE: Yeah. I have problems with preparation and planning.

INTERVIEWER: Do you ever feel like you were a pawn in the war? That they just used you?

STEVE: Yes, but willingly almost.

INTERVIEWER: I guess you didn't know what you were getting into.

STEVE: Yeah.

INTERVIEWER: Do you ever feel paranoid or like there's a death trap around every corner?

STEVE: Yeah, I'm always on high alert. When I got back I used to take a gun everywhere I went.

INTERVIEWER: Everywhere you went?

STEVE: At least in the car.

INTERVIEWER: You've lost your wife. You've lost your children.

STEVE: Yeah.

INTERVIEWER: Have you ever tried to use sex as a temporary relief?

STEVE: There's a problem with anger and intimacy. I had problems being romantic when I got back. I've always been a romantic person but not as much since I've been back.

INTERVIEWER: Do you act differently towards women than before you went to war?

STEVE: Not a whole lot. I'd say I don't care as much as I used to.

INTERVIEWER: Do you feel like civilians who've never been to war don't understand it?

STEVE: Yeah, but I can't blame them for not being able to. Maybe I had a lack of ability to describe it when I got back. I think a lot of people don't appreciate it, that's for sure.

INTERVIEWER: Some people who experience acts of violence in their lives have the problem that the violence is with them every hour of every day of their lives. Do you have that problem?

STEVE: No, I'd say no. I've been able to get over it. If the events were more traumatic I may have had that problem.

INTERVIEWER: Do you want to be alone a lot?

STEVE: Yeah.

INTERVIEWER: Have you seen any of your comrades since you've been back?

STEVE: You know, I haven't. I may be the exception to the rule but I sure haven't. I haven't had contact with these guys at all. One of the guys I was with lives in Canton [Michigan]. We were in reserve duty together. I saw him then.

INTERVIEWER: Do you feel that the story you tell about your war experiences has changed over time?

STEVE: No, for the most part I think I remember it [as it was].

INTERVIEWER: Do you ever feel like you're just holding on?

STEVE: Yeah, for the most part. It's frustrating.

INTERVIEWER: Do you feel guilty?

STEVE: No, and if I did, I don't think I'd want to talk about it.

INTERVIEWER: Are you jealous of people who have not experienced war? If you wouldn't have gone to war, do you think you would have been okay?

STEVE: If I wouldn't have gone to war I wouldn't have been in the situation I'm in now. I would have been on the right track now. People don't have enough respect for you [as a veteran]. They don't understand my thought processes have changed. Personally I've been treated with respect but I know many others who have not. They would really see that my life is not as easy as it seems.

INTERVIEWER: Did you have a traumatic childhood?

STEVE: It was mostly normal but my dad abused my brother. My dad was strict. I saw my father throw my brother around. When my mom and dad were going through a divorce my dad beat my brother.

INTERVIEWER: Do you think that what you saw as a child is partially responsible for your condition?

STEVE: Yeah, I'd say it did have an indirect affect. You're a product of your environment.

INTERVIEWER: Do you feel demoralized?

STEVE: Sometimes I wish I had more discipline and focus to get out of the rut I'm in.

INTERVIEWER: Do you lack self respect?

STEVE: Not so much.

INTERVIEWER: Do you like to fight physically?

STEVE: Sometimes I feel like I would just like to go off on somebody. Like these Muslim extremists. If there was a fight I wouldn't hold back.

INTERVIEWER: Do you believe mental illness is the main reason for your problems?

STEVE: I'd have more money now if it weren't for mental illness. I lost a period of my life but I've gained strength in character. I would have had a good job making more money. I've lost time that could have been productive.

INTERVIEWER: Do you have problems trusting people?

STEVE: Yeah, when someone says they're going to be around and they don't show.

INTERVIEWER: Do you feel like you were wrecked by war?

STEVE: Damaged, but not ruined. I'm not going to let them keep me down. That's what happens to you [they try to keep you down]. You can't let them keep you down.

INTERVIEWER: If your son wanted to go to war what would you say?

STEVE: That's something I've contemplated myself. My first reaction is to say that if he wanted to do it, I'd tell him it's honorable but bad things can happen to you. I'd be scared for my son. I'd probably tell him to go ahead but I wouldn't want to see him get hurt.

INTERVIEWER: You think it's honorable to serve.

STEVE: Yeah, I think it's honorable.

INTERVIEWER: Do you think every man should serve his country?

STEVE: Yeah, I think he should serve his country but combat's not for everybody.

INTERVIEWER: One thing therapists talk about is letting go. Terrible things happen to you. You talk about them and then it helps you let go of them. Other people may say you should never have talked about them in the first place because you push everything from the subconscious into the conscious and then you have even more problems. What do you think?

STEVE: Ah, boy, I'm at the point now of thinking what's the point of all the therapy? I'm trying to decide if it was better to talk about these things with a psychologist. I think PTSD is stronger in some than in others.

INTERVIEWER: Do you ever think that if you were with the right woman your life would be different?

STEVE: Yeah, Yeah.

INTERVIEWER: Have you ever thought that if you had been closer to other soldiers you'd be better off today?

STEVE: I had a couple, two, three close friends so I don't know about that. It would have helped now that I think about it. I would have been able to let off some of my frustrations, you know.

INTERVIEWER: Do you sometimes feel that if you had the right support person, such as a supportive spouse, that your life would be a lot different now? You're the Lone Ranger over there at the homeless shelter.

STEVE: I think so. I think that's true about people in general.

INTERVIEWER: In the United States there have already been movies made about the war in Iraq. Do you think this is a good way to help society to understand what the war was like? Or do you feel these movies are unpatriotic?

STEVE: The media seems to take sides. No, I don't think these movies are necessary.

INTERVIEWER: Do you think these movies are unpatriotic?

STEVE: No, I don't think that either. I think it's a money making thing.

INTERVIEWER: Do you think that most Americans believe there could be no peace without soldiers?

STEVE: No the vast majority of them [Americans], no. You've got to have a strong military. This hippie thing of peace, love and happiness is not going to happen. That's a fantasy.

Interview 2

Leo Lenaghan

March 17, 2008

Leo was recently discharged from the Army. He appeared well groomed and highly intelligent. His speech was clear and concise. His attributes made me wonder if Leo was indeed really incapable of working or if he had simply given up because of his difficulties. Leo seemed to have insight into his disease, which made me wonder if he had been in psychosis at the time of military service and now possessed clearer thought processes because of medication. On the other hand, intelligent schizophrenics can appear normal in an initial impression. The interview transpired at a restaurant. Upon ordering our lunch, Leo made it clear to me that he had no money. I assured him that I intended to pick up the tab. As the interview unfolded Leo seemed to be overly assertive and angry. My impression was that he was withholding something from me.

I started the interview by telling Leo a little about my own situation and my family background and then I requested that Leo tell me about his background.

LEO: I've suffered from depression most of my life. I've had alcoholism. Medication hasn't helped me. My brother and I recently had a falling out because I wanted to live with my mom. This was in February when I thought the Navy was going to accept me. I was living with my mom. I'm 32 years old. My brother said no [regarding living with my mom], you can't be a burden and nuisance to our mother. My brother has always been stiff.

INTERVIEWER: So can you tell me a little more about your family background?

LEO: My dad's a vascular surgeon. One night in late 1985 he attacked my mom. He tried to strangle her so there was a divorce. She is a religious fanatic and she's also mentally ill. My brother suffers from depression. I suffer from depression and paranoid schizophrenia. My sister seems to be doing okay for herself

INTERVIEWER: So, you were born where?

LEO: Pontiac, Michigan, 1975, August 12.

INTERVIEWER: And how old does that make you now?

LEO: 32

INTERVIEWER: Where did you go to grade school?

LEO: Horton.

INTERVIEWER: In what city?

LEO: Birmingham [Birmingham Michigan is an upper middle class city in suburban Detroit.]

INTERVIEWER: Where did you go to high school?

LEO: Seaholm.

INTERVIEWER: And you graduated [from high school].

LEO: Yes

INTERVIEWER: What branch of the armed services were you in?

LEO: Army.

INTERVIEWER: For how long?

LEO: Total six years off and on. In my twenties I was either in college or in the army. I went to college to study Criminal Justice. When I was younger I wanted to be a police officer, which was a very foolish mistake. It's against my personality. It's a bad job to have with bad coworkers. None of this occurred to me [at the time I was studying]. I thought, oh, how neat, I get to drive around a car with lights on it and work in Birmingham and that just goes to show you how naive I really was.

INTERVIEWER: How long were you in college?

LEO: (unintelligible _____) years and I wasn't allowed to graduate because I had ten credits left and this one professor, she taught statistics and she was in charge of my senior seminar. She made me do senior seminar twice. And she failed me for no reason and her stats class was impossible. So, eventually, I dropped out and the other professors were picking on me, so I just left.

INTERVIEWER: Did they tell you that you were sick?

LEO: No.

INTERVIEWER: So you were in active service for six years?

LEO: Yes.

INTERVIEWER: What was your rank?

LEO: The highest rank I ever made was E4 and that's what I was recently discharged at.

INTERVIEWER: What was the date of your discharge?

LEO: December 20th, 2006

INTERVIEWER: You were diagnosed as mentally ill when?

LEO: This was 2005.

INTERVIEWER: You were diagnosed when you were still in the service?

LEO: Yes.

INTERVIEWER: Do you think war contributed to your condition?

LEO: No I don't.

INTERVIEWER: You would have been mentally ill regardless of whether or not you went into the military?

LEO: Yes, in November of 2004 it occurred to me that people on television, like the news, could see me. I could wave at them and they could wave back. Then in July 2005 it occurred to me that people can hear my thoughts. It occurred to me that I was pretty sure that President Bush was going to kill me in Iraq because I'm a government experiment. So I went to the doctors. This was right before Iraq.

A week before deploying to Iraq, September 25, 2005, I went to the doctor. I told them everything that I told you and they said, "No, you're not going to Iraq." So then, someone, probably the Colonel, I forget his name, Colonel Gray, he overturned that [the decision to not send Leo to Iraq]. So, I went to Iraq anyway. I was like, well, whatever. I was worried about the Iraq war and the media people being able to see me and people being able to hear my thoughts. I was worried about some soldiers wanting to shoot and experiment for the fun of it. There was mischief going on. There were unruly things happening and I was just going crazy.

INTERVIEWER: If you had to do it over again would you have gone into the service?

LEO: Well, I had to because I had no other place to go, but I would have done something differently. I would have joined the Navy, not the Army.

INTERVIEWER: Did you want to be a soldier when you were a kid?

LEO: Yeah, off and on. I went through a lot of things [phases]. I wanted to be a carpenter. I wanted to be a construction worker, a policeman, a soldier and I wanted to be a doctor. I had no direction in my life. I needed the guidance of a father who would have said, "Look, son, get a skill."

INTERVIEWER: So, you weren't close to your father?

LEO: No, I haven't seen him since 1986.

INTERVIEWER: How old were you then?

LEO: Eleven years old.

INTERVIEWER: That's a long time.

LEO: Well, I saw him once in November 2004. I looked him up on the Internet. My brother and I went to see him. He didn't seem to be interested in our visit with him.

INTERVIEWER: What does he do?

LEO: Kentucky. He helps people with a clinic that he owns called Figure Eight Loss.

INTERVIEWER: He still practices medicine?

LEO: Yes.

INTERVIEWER: And he helps people with weight loss?

LEO: Yes.

INTERVIEWER: You think he suffers from mental illness?

LEO: There's something wrong with him. I'm not sure what he has, but he's not normal.

INTERVIEWER: Unemployment was not a reason you joined the armed services?

LEO: Yes it was. I dropped out of college because they wouldn't let me graduate. So, I was carpet cleaning. I was losing weight to join the Army. The army was inhospitable to me because I'm a government experiment. I should have joined the Navy or the Air Force.

INTERVIEWER: You were injured?

LEO: Just mentally.

INTERVIEWER: Can you describe how combat contributed to your illness?

LEO: I wasn't in combat. I mean they would take pop shots at us. They would lob explosives at the unit. I was more worried about my own soldiers and the fact that my thoughts were broadcasted and that I was a citizen of a very hostile country.

INTERVIEWER: What else were you worried about?

LEO: I was more concerned about the fact that I am unique and the country was basically bashing me and trying to kill me.

INTERVIEWER: But you weren't in combat?

LEO: I was in a combat zone. I left the camp a few times and did patrols and things.

INTERVIEWER: Do you feel the war contributed to your illness?

LEO: Yes.

INTERVIEWER: Would you like to expand on that?

LEO: I was scared. I didn't let it get the best of me until it occurred to me that the President was going to kill me. So, I spoke to the doctors but they never told me the truth. They said, "You're schizophrenic, we're going to fly you back to Fort Camble and medical board you out of the Army." I was medically separated but they never gave me my medical board because they said my disability occurred prior to service.

INTERVIEWER: I see. Did you have to readjust when you got out of the service?

LEO: I was on unemployment and when unemployment ran out I was in and out of hospitals. I was at Marquette Hospital in 2007, Petoskey Hospital, Lansing Hospital, and Battle Creek Hospital [all hospitals in Michigan]. Other people can hear my thoughts. I'm the only unique person in the world. The idea was to embarrass the President into leaving me alone.

INTERVIEWER: Other symptoms?

LEO: Thought broadcasting, persecution, thinking I'm unique. Thinking I'm a government experiment. I was paranoid, very paranoid. Always thinking people are trying to frame me of mischief.

INTERVIEWER: Do you think the government's been fair with you?

LEO: Not at all. Another symptom of mine, which I think proves my case, is that for a year now wherever I go people will go around whistling. I don't know why. I just know they're whistling. I just know it's inappropriate. People will walk by me or in the hallway or in line and they'll just whistle. They do it to annoy me.

INTERVIEWER: Do you think you can work?

LEO: I don't think so.

INTERVIEWER: Do you think you had problems before you went to war?

LEO: I was unique before I went to war but it didn't occur to me before July of 2005 that people can hear my thoughts.

INTERVIEWER: Were you involved with drugs and alcohol?

LEO: Yes, I drank a lot and I used to smoke a lot of marijuana.

INTERVIEWER: You did that while you were in the service?

LEO: No, I just drank on weekends [while in the service].

INTERVIEWER: Do you think the war in Iraq is justified?

LEO: No, I think it's ridiculous. There were no weapons of mass destruction, number one. It's also been proven that Saddam Hussein was not affiliated with Bin Laden or Al Qaeda and those were the two reasons we went charging in there. Come to find out there were no weapons of mass destruction and he [Saddam] had nothing to do with September 11. So, it's just a big mistake and a quagmire. I read in the news today that we've been in it for five years now and we're about halfway through it. That's what military experts are saying.

INTERVIEWER: So, they think we're going to be there another five years.

LEO: [It will be] another six or seven years until we can hand over the government back to the Iraqis.

INTERVIEWER: What did you think about war before you went to war?

LEO: Well in 2001 I thought we've got a new President and we've got a threat [to our country]. In a way it's complicated because I don't know if they were a threat. As bad as Saddam was he kept the country [Iraq] in line.

INTERVIEWER: He didn't have weapons of mass destruction.

LEO: I guess the CIA director told Bush and Dick Cheney it's a slam dunk. They said there were weapons of mass destruction there and there actually were none.

INTERVIEWER: Vietnam vets always say it was difficult coming home because there was no one to welcome them home. Do you feel the same way?

LEO: No, over the years I've become increasingly paranoid. So, I just want to be left alone. I lived with my mom for twenty days and she was behaving strangely and really, really bothering me.

INTERVIEWER: You lived with your mother for twenty days after coming back from Iraq?

LEO: Yes, she has mental illness herself. I don't know what [she has] but she's a religious fanatic.

INTERVIEWER: What religion?

LEO: Christian.

INTERVIEWER: She's protestant?

LEO: Just nondenominational.

INTERVIEWER: She spends a lot of time reading the Bible?

LEO: Yes.

INTERVIEWER: Do you think the war was a waste of taxpayers' money?

LEO: Absolutely, no doubt about that. It's a waste of money, period.

INTERVIEWER: Do you think it's odd that they have so much money to contribute to war but they have no money for mental health?

LEO: A lot of things bother me. There's homelessness, disease, crime. I mean we're trying to bring democracy to Iraq and show them the way and our own country is messed up. Our economy is going through tough times and gas is about four dollars a gallon.

INTERVIEWER: What was a typical day at war like for you?

LEO: I did PMCS

INTERVIEWER: What's PMCS?

LEO: Preventative Maintenance Checks and Service. I just tinkered with the trucks.

INTERVIEWER: Do you feel abandoned?

LEO: Yes.

INTERVIEWER: What do you think is going to happen to you?

LEO: I'm hoping that I'll get my disability and go to Sioux Saint Marie [Michigan], and live and get a job. If not, I'm going to the White House to see the President and tell the President to leave me alone.

INTERVIEWER: Do you think you had some form of mental illness before you went to war?

LEO: Yes.

INTERVIEWER: Do you think you have something to hide because of your war experience?

LEO: No.

INTERVIEWER: Are you homicidal?

LEO: No, not at this time.

INTERVIEWER: Are you suicidal?

LEO: Well, that's a good question. I'm depressed but I won't take my own life.

INTERVIEWER: Is there anything you'd like to say about being in the military?

LEO: It sucks.

INTERVIEWER: Anything else?

LEO: The Army is a gamble. It all depends on what company you're assigned to and your sergeant.

INTERVIEWER: If you don't have the right commanding officer then your life is hell?

LEO: Yes, I've seen it happen and also if someone doesn't like you and you're an average soldier they can micromanage you out of the Army. I've seen it happen. It's a crap shoot.

INTERVIEWER: Do you consider yourself a patriot?

LEO: Yes.

INTERVIEWER: What's it like in the homeless shelter?

LEO: Abysmal. Very long days, very boring, very painful because people can hear my thoughts. There's a great big TV screen that I don't want there because the actors on television can see me. It's very painful and very awkward.

INTERVIEWER: Do you think that a person goes through a psychological barrier when they go into a homeless shelter because they can no longer support themselves?

LEO: I think it's a lot of things. I think it's very depressing and discouraging. You spend a lot of time thinking, "Well if I had done this or that I wouldn't be here."

INTERVIEWER: Sometimes people don't like to go to homeless shelters because they can't drink at night. Do you feel that way?

LEO: No.

INTERVIEWER: People in homeless shelters have to get up early in the morning because of the shelter's rules and some don't like to do this because they're hung over. They'd rather drink alcohol then go into a shelter.

LEO: If someone likes alcohol, if they don't like the structure of the shelter, I can see why they'd do that.

INTERVIEWER: Do you get up early in the homeless shelter?

LEO: At about eight. The biggest thing about me and the war in Iraq is that they don't want us there in the first place. So, we're giving them all this money and they don't want us there. So the idea is they are going to be oil business partners. Well, if someone doesn't like you you're not going to be able to be good business partners. If someone doesn't like you you're not going to be able to be their friend and if you keep trying they're going to dislike you even more.

INTERVIEWER: I think I understand what you mean. Has anyone stolen any of your belongings while in the homeless shelter?

LEO: No.

INTERVIEWER: Do you have a psychiatrist?

LEO: Yes I do.

INTERVIEWER: How often do you see him?

LEO: I see him every two weeks at the VA center in Lansing.

INTERVIEWER: And there is a social worker at the homeless shelter?

LEO: Yes.

INTERVIEWER: Are they helpful?

LEO: Yes, very.

INTERVIEWER: Do you trust them?

LEO: Yes I do.

INTERVIEWER: Do you think the medical treatment at the VA Center is good?

LEO: Yes, I do. It could be better but it's pretty good.

INTERVIEWER: Do you know other mentally ill soldiers?

LEO: No, I don't.

INTERVIEWER: There's no group therapy?

LEO: There's group therapy for PTSD but there's no group therapy for schizophrenia. I probably have PTSD too, but I don't know.

INTERVIEWER: Do you discuss your condition with other soldiers at the shelter?

LEO: No, not really. I keep to myself. My thinking is they can hear my thoughts and they know who I am so there's no need to tell them I'm a paranoid schizophrenic, I'm unique and that television bothers me.

INTERVIEWER: What is your medical treatment like?

LEO: I just take Risperdol [an antipsychotic medication].

INTERVIEWER: Does it work?

LEO: No, it doesn't. I take Lazapram (an anti-anxiety medication) and Benzodine (a tranquilizer or sleeping medication).

INTERVIEWER: What's the Lazapram for?

LEO: That's for nerves.

INTERVIEWER: What's the Benzodine for?

LEO: I don't know. I think it's an antipsychotic.

INTERVIEWER: Do you dwell on your military service?

LEO: Yes, I do.

INTERVIEWER: Tell me about that.

LEO: I thought I was going to get a check for being a government experiment. If I would have stayed in Iraq President Bush would have given me a check because I'm pretty sure my own troops were shooting at me. I don't know, everything is kind of coulda, woulda, shoulda. Being at a homeless shelter gives me all the time in the world to think about how this happened to me.

INTERVIEWER: It's with you every hour of every day.

LEO: Yes.

INTERVIEWER: Do you have nightmares?

LEO: Yes, nightmares that I'm not skilled and that I'm hopeless or nightmares with themes of death like a coffin or something.

INTERVIEWER: If money were no object where would you go to get treated?

LEO: Alaska.

INTERVIEWER: Why Alaska?

LEO: Well, marijuana is legal there.

INTERVIEWER: Do you smoke pot now?

LEO: I haven't smoked pot in over four years.

INTERVIEWER: But if you moved to Alaska you would smoke pot?

LEO: Yes I would.

INTERVIEWER: Do you think it would help your condition?

LEO: Probably.

INTERVIEWER: What would you say about the present condition of your health, good, not so good?

LEO: Good condition. I could be better. I'm working on quitting smoking. I want to get a membership to a gym. I need to lose about thirty pounds.

INTERVIEWER: Do you smoke cigarettes?

LEO: I've smoked. I've been at two packs a day for seventeen years and I'm thirty-two. So I started when I was fifteen. It's time for me to quit.

INTERVIEWER: Do you eat regularly?

LEO: I've only been eating one meal a day to lose weight.

INTERVIEWER: How about your clothes?

LEO: I just took my clothes with me. I only have a few pair of clothes.

INTERVIEWER: How do you feel when politicians say we should pull out of Iraq?

LEO: I agree one hundred percent.

INTERVIEWER: You think the war is unjustified?

LEO: Yes I do. I think it's stupid. I don't know why we're there.

INTERVIEWER: Is there anything you think can help you?

LEO: A check, having my head deactivated. Have it so television can't see me and have a normal life.

INTERVIEWER: So you qualify for Veteran Benefits and Social Security Disability?

LEO: I don't know.

INTERVIEWER: I think you might qualify.

LEO: I did apply for service and nonservice disability and they told me I would get whatever one is higher.

INTERVIEWER: You don't feel like we must win the war or everything will be lost?

LEO: I think it would be nice if we won the war. I don't think everything will be lost and the country will go down the tubes and there will be anarchy or something [if we lose the war]. I do think it would be very positive for both the Americans and Iraqis if we won the war. Losing the war is not a good option and that's what we've been doing.

INTERVIEWER: Do you have second thoughts about signing up for military service?

LEO: No.

INTERVIEWER: You'd do it all over again?

LEO: Yes.

INTERVIEWER: Do you feel like you're filled with hate? Do you have a problem with anger and hate?

LEO: No. I have a problem with bitterness and service related depression.

INTERVIEWER: How long have you suffered from depression?

LEO: Off and on most of my life. I've never been overly happy. I don't smile much.

INTERVIEWER: When were you first given antidepressants?

LEO: I guess Walter Reed in 2006.

INTERVIEWER: That was after you came back from Iraq?

LEO: Yes.

INTERVIEWER: Do you think your experiences in Iraq made you more depressed?

LEO: Absolutely.

INTERVIEWER: Has war changed your personality?

LEO: I'm probably more depressed and it's depressing to see the state of the country. The economy is in bad shape. Ever since Bin Laden knocked down two of our buildings, Americans have been freaking out. Ever since September 11, 2001, Americans have just been hyper, jumpy, anxious, depressed. It's just a different country than it was.

INTERVIEWER: So you think the Iraq War has affected the psyche of the country?

LEO: Absolutely. It seems the terrorists hit us or if you want to use slang they bitch-slapped us and got away with it.

INTERVIEWER: It seems to me that when a country fears the enemy that no amount of money is too much for war, but when it comes to your disability benefits people think you're greedy. Do you feel that way?

LEO: Yes, some people do, I'm sure. There are always people who have negative thoughts. There are many people who are opinionated. Some people just don't empathize so they come to the wrong conclusion.

INTERVIEWER: Based upon your service experience are there any jobs you qualify for?

LEO: Not except fast food. That's why I'm spending a lot of time with I coulda, woulda, shoulda. Out of high school I could have learned welding and I wouldn't be in the situation I'm in now.

INTERVIEWER: You said you do have nightmares.

LEO: Yes.

INTERVIEWER: Do you dwell on your war experiences?

LEO: No, not really. I just have unpleasant dreams [about] death or being trapped.

INTERVIEWER: Do you ever have the urge to kill?

LEO: No, never. Not people. Not animals.

INTERVIEWER: Have you ever committed a felony?

LEO: No.

INTERVIEWER: You're sure that you won't do something violent?

LEO: I'm sure I won't.

INTERVIEWER: So, you self treated your condition with alcohol for a period of time.

LEO: Yes, but that's ingrained as part of my personality. I just like to drink. If I have a night off I'll spend it alone drinking, watching movies.

INTERVIEWER: What movies do you watch?

LEO: Action adventures, comedy, wrestling, concerts.

INTERVIEWER: How much do you drink?

LEO: A twelve-pack of beer and shots of Captain Morgan and a pack and a half of cigarettes.

INTERVIEWER: Do you crave violence?

LEO: No.

INTERVIEWER: Have you ever thought you might end up in prison?

LEO: No.

INTERVIEWER: Do you feel like the war damaged your mind?

LEO: Yes.

INTERVIEWER: How did that happen?

LEO: It made me more paranoid, made me more uncomfortable, more depressed.

INTERVIEWER: Do you think war breeds criminals?

LEO: No, I think people make their own choices.

INTERVIEWER: So you think when soldiers come back and become criminals that they would be criminals anyway?

LEO: Possibly.

INTERVIEWER: Many people, maybe most, don't understand mental illness. Have you ever thought that if you had a limb missing that people would realize the sacrifice you made but as an ex-military man they don't understand your mental illness?

LEO: No, they don't. I read in *Army Times* an interview by a colonel and he basically said that people who have PTSD and seek treatment for it are losers. That's basically what he said.

INTERVIEWER: Drug and alcohol abuse is common among many with PTSD but you don't have PTSD.

LEO: I've never been diagnosed as [having] PTSD.

INTERVIEWER: Are you an alcoholic?

LEO: Yes, I'd say so.

INTERVIEWER: Do you go to Alcoholic Anonymous meetings?

LEO: No, I don't want to live long anyway.

INTERVIEWER: Do you suffer from insomnia?

LEO: I've always had trouble getting to sleep.

INTERVIEWER: Your whole life?

LEO: Yes.

INTERVIEWER: Do you ever engage in risky behavior?

LEO: No, I'm very square.

INTERVIEWER: Did civilian life seem dull after you returned from Iraq?

LEO: No, Iraq for me was a scary place to be. People knew my thoughts and television could see me.

INTERVIEWER: Have you found it difficult to deal with the Veterans Administration?

LEO: No.

INTERVIEWER: Do you feel like they [the V.A.] are trying to help you out as much as they can?

LEO: Yes, but all I do every hour of every day is wish my disability will go through and I wish it wasn't months away.

INTERVIEWER: Have you talked to a social worker about vocational training?

LEO: No, I should do that. I do have the GI bill.

INTERVIEWER: When you were in Iraq did you ever fantasize about being a hero?

LEO: No.

INTERVIEWER: Do you think you'd have trouble holding down a job if you were hired?

LEO: No, because I'm desperate.

INTERVIEWER: You think you could work if you could just find where?

LEO: Yes.

INTERVIEWER: And you think you'd be a good employee?

LEO: Yes.

INTERVIEWER: Do you have a hard time getting along with other people?

LEO: No. I'm a solitary person. I like to be by myself.

INTERVIEWER: When you start talking to people about being a government experiment do they believe you?

LEO: I think they just blow me off.

INTERVIEWER: Does the psychiatrist believe you?

LEO: I don't know.

INTERVIEWER: Have you told him about it?

LEO: Yes.

INTERVIEWER: What were your commanding officers like in the military?

LEO: They were pretty good.

INTERVIEWER: They kept everyone in line?

LEO: There was a lot of mischief and they [the commanding officers] never seemed to do anything about it and the reason I left Iraq was a few days before I left I was in the dining facility, which I avoided because the television could see me, and I saw a live interview of the President. He went like this, [Leo waves his hand].

INTERVIEWER: He gestured with his hand?

LEO: Yes, he was telling me he was going to throw me away. I took that as he was going to shoot me which was probably right.

INTERVIEWER: Did the commanding officers keep control of everyone?

LEO: Yeah, more or less.

INTERVIEWER: Did you abuse alcohol and drugs while you were at war?

LEO: Not drugs and I couldn't drink.

INTERVIEWER: They didn't have anything for you to drink?

LEO: They were trafficking cocaine through the civilian gate.

INTERVIEWER: Oh, really.

LEO: But I had nothing to do with that.

INTERVIEWER: Do you feel like a pawn?

LEO: Yes I do.

INTERVIEWER: Could you expand on that?

LEO: I made a very big mistake in life. I putzed around with the Army and Criminal Justice when I should have gotten a degree I could use. I should have learned a skill. I should have gone into a more reputable branch of the service. If you're a grunt you're basically screwed. Which is where I'm at right now.

INTERVIEWER: Do you think that the Army was not a very good place for military service because you didn't learn anything?

LEO: Yes.

INTERVIEWER: You were a grunt?

LEO: I was a truck driver.

INTERVIEWER: Are you afraid something is going to happen to you?

LEO: I don't know but I don't want to live very long. So, I've reached the point that I really don't care anymore.

INTERVIEWER: Why do you think you're not going to live very long?

LEO: I'm very depressed. I drink and smoke heavy and I just don't have that spark of life in me anymore.

INTERVIEWER: So you don't care what happens to you?

LEO: I care very much. I want to be comfortable and have money.

INTERVIEWER: But you don't think it's going to happen?

LEO: I don't know. First and foremost I have to wait for disability.

INTERVIEWER: How much money can you earn and still receive V.A. benefits?

LEO: I don't know but as soon as I get my disability I'm going to call and say "Hey, look, I get this amount of money. I'm this amount disabled, how much can I work?" because I want to work five days a week because I don't want to become an alcoholic.

INTERVIEWER: You think you need disability?

LEO: Yes I do.

INTERVIEWER: Do you have any idea what kind of job you can get?

LEO: I could work at a casino, for the Sioux locks. Work at a restaurant, K Mart.

INTERVIEWER: Did your attitude toward women change when you returned from Iraq?

LEO: No.

INTERVIEWER: Do you trust women?

LEO: I'm gay, so. But yeah, I trust them.

INTERVIEWER: Is there anyone you're close to?

LEO: No.

INTERVIEWER: Have you had intimate relations with any men since returning from Iraq?

LEO: No.

INTERVIEWER: Do you think your military experiences made it more difficult for you to be intimate?

LEO: No, just the overall wear and tear to my brain didn't help.

INTERVIEWER: Do you think war contributed to your problems?

LEO: Well, it didn't help.

INTERVIEWER: But it's not the root cause?

LEO: No.

INTERVIEWER: Do you want to be left alone?

LEO: I always want to be alone.

INTERVIEWER: Did the doctor say that it's not good to be alone?

LEO: No, they never said that. But I don't think it's good to be alone all the time.

INTERVIEWER: Have you ever thought you should do some type of employment that you can do alone?

LEO: No.

INTERVIEWER: What about art work or creative writing?

LEO: I don't have the skills

INTERVIEWER: You don't think you could learn to be an artist?

LEO: I can't draw or paint.

INTERVIEWER: Have you ever tried?

LEO: No, but that would be a nice way to earn a living.

INTERVIEWER: Do you blame yourself for what happened to you?

LEO: Yes and no. I wish I hadn't joined the Army. I wish I didn't leave the Army but it's not my fault. I'm a government experiment so, it was inevitable. There's too many disadvantages [in military service].

INTERVIEWER: Would you like to get into a relationship with a man that was stable?

LEO: Sure, that would be nice.

INTERVIEWER: Do you feel like you live on the edge or like you are about to go off at any time?

LEO: No.

INTERVIEWER: You just drink to numb yourself?

LEO: Yes.

INTERVIEWER: Have you spoken to any of your fellow soldiers since returning from Iraq?

LEO: No.

INTERVIEWER: You said you're depressed but not suicidal.

LEO: Yes, I'd like to be dead. I think I'd be happier in the here-after. Which is presumptuous I know. There's only so long you can go.

INTERVIEWER: You believe in life after death?

LEO: Yes.

INTERVIEWER: What do you think it is?

LEO: There's no sin, perfect love, harmony, peace.

INTERVIEWER: So, you believe you are paranoid. Did the doctor say you were paranoid?

LEO: Yes.

INTERVIEWER: Do you have insight into your disease? Do you realize you're paranoid?

LEO: Yes I do.

INTERVIEWER: Is there anything that can be done to take you out of your paranoia?

LEO: Yes, deactivate my head and explain to me I'm a government experiment. Sorry about what we did to you. Here's your check. Have a nice day.

INTERVIEWER: Do you think the military caused your paranoia?

LEO: I think it exacerbated it.

INTERVIEWER: You believe it made your illness, your paranoia worse?

LEO: Yes.

INTERVIEWER: Do you feel like you're just barely holding on to life?

LEO: Yes, if I don't get my disability, I'll be a bum.

INTERVIEWER: Have you ever held down a job?

LEO: No. I have no money. I have no skills. I have no savings. So, I'm pretty grim.

INTERVIEWER: Do you feel your poverty is unfair?

LEO: Yes, if I would have been left alone there'd be no problems.

INTERVIEWER: Left alone by whom?

LEO: By the country, government. Eventually I had to go to the doctors and say, "Hey, look what is happening to me." As a result I was separated from the Army.

INTERVIEWER: Have you applied for work since your return?

LEO: Yes, I went to a McDonalds. They said, okay, we'll call. Then it occurred to me that if I work I could screw up my disability."

INTERVIEWER: So, McDonalds is the only place you applied for work?

LEO: Yes.

INTERVIEWER: Do you feel undervalued?

LEO: Very much so.

INTERVIEWER: You seem to be a really intelligent guy.

LEO: Yes.

INTERVIEWER: Have you ever had an IQ test?

LEO: I did and mine was 120.

INTERVIEWER: Do you trust anyone now?

LEO: Not really. Like I said, my mom won't let me live with her. My brother's a dick. My sister, she's in California and doing her own thing. Like I told you, my mom's weird and my dad attacked my mom and maybe tried to kill her. I don't know but more or less I grew up well fed in front of a television and my dad was a doctor so, until 1986 I was rich in a big house.

INTERVIEWER: Did your family have a lot of money?

LEO: Yes, but then my dad didn't pay child support either.

INTERVIEWER: I see. So you lived with your mother and your father wasn't paying child support.

LEO: Yes.

INTERVIEWER: Do you feel like you haven't been given the honor and recognition due to you?

LEO: Yes I do, very much so. Well, I'm getting an opportunity with disability because I'm a Vet. So, that's good.

INTERVIEWER: Do you think military service can breed character?

LEO: Yes, I definitely do.

INTERVIEWER: Did it do that to you? Did it change who you are?

LEO: I would say no. There's the old adage that the Marine Corp brainwashes you and I think that's wrong.

INTERVIEWER: You don't believe the Marine Corp brainwashes you?

LEO: No I don't.

INTERVIEWER: Do you think it makes you a better person?

LEO: It does, yes.

INTERVIEWER: How do you think military service makes you a better person?

LEO: They're swift with justice. You can't use drugs. It gets you in better shape.

INTERVIEWER: What about thinking? Does the military help you be more organized with your thinking?

LEO: Yes, if people hound you, you take care of your appointments. Make sure your barracks is in order and make sure you don't fall behind in bills.

INTERVIEWER: So it teaches people responsibility?

LEO: Yes.

INTERVIEWER: Have you ever thought the American people think only about their own families?

LEO: I think that's first and foremost in their minds, yes, some of the time but I don't know, I don't know what everyone thinks all the time.

INTERVIEWER: Do you think if they knew about your medical condition they'd be more understanding?

LEO: Yes, I do. Instead people just think I'm crazy.

INTERVIEWER: Do you think the Iraq war was just a result of 9/11?

LEO: I think there was anger involved, yes.

INTERVIEWER: But they went after the wrong people?

LEO: Yes, I think that's what happened.

INTERVIEWER: The American people demanded that something be done.

LEO: Yes.

INTERVIEWER: And so we went after the wrong people.

LEO: Americans have become very paranoid and they want to see tangible change. They want a white knight to slay the dragon.

INTERVIEWER: They are vindictive?

LEO: Yes they are.

INTERVIEWER: So what are your plans? You're going to go up to the Sioux and your going to take your disability and . . .

LEO: Yes, get a job.

INTERVIEWER: You're going to get a psychiatrist up there?

LEO: No.

INTERVIEWER: You're not going to take medication anymore?

LEO: No. Medication doesn't help me and it's too expensive.

INTERVIEWER: Let's talk about that for a second. You said that medication doesn't help you because you're suffering from a personality disorder?

LEO: Schizoid personality disorder and paranoid schizophrenia.

INTERVIEWER: Could you explain to me what schizoid personality disorder entails?

LEO: Spending a lot of time on yourself (and) mystical thinking. Those are the two big things. It's a light form of schizophrenia.

INTERVIEWER: Do you believe in mysticism?

LEO: I believe in a higher power.

INTERVIEWER: Mysticism has been interpreted differently around the world. The Buddhists have one concept of mysticism, Christians another and Islam another. Is there any mystical philosophy you adhere to?

LEO: No, I'm just spiritual and religious.

INTERVIEWER: What do you do that's spiritual?

LEO: I try to be a good person. I pray.

INTERVIEWER: What kind of prayer do you engage in?

LEO: Lord my God in Jesus's name forgive me of my sins.

Grant me the Holy Spirit and cleanse my soul. Be good to those who've been good to me.

INTERVIEWER: So that's a prayer you say over and over?

LEO: Yes, usually.

INTERVIEWER: Where did the prayer come from?

LEO: Over the years, Bible school and being in church, I was taught that was how you pray over and over again.

INTERVIEWER: Do you feel any self hate?

LEO: No.

INTERVIEWER: Do you lack self respect?

LEO: How so?

INTERVIEWER: It seems that sometimes what happens after people are diagnosed as mentally ill is they think it's the kiss of death and from that point onward they just hate themselves. They look upon life as no longer worth living.

LEO: Well, like I said, I'm very depressed and I don't want to live long but I wouldn't say I lack self respect.

INTERVIEWER: Have you withdrawn from society almost completely?

LEO: Yes.

INTERVIEWER: Do you like to fight when you drink?

LEO: I'm not a rowdy drunk. I'm mellow.

INTERVIEWER: Do small things make you angry?

LEO: Some things can be annoying like snoring.

INTERVIEWER: If guys in the homeless shelter snore you get upset?

LEO: It irritates me but I wear ear plugs.

INTERVIEWER: Do you feel like you've lost your ambition?

LEO: Yes.

INTERVIEWER: Are you sad because ambitions you once had never materialized?

LEO: Yes, very much so.

INTERVIEWER: Do you ever think your lack of ambition could be from alcohol and drug abuse?

LEO: No.

INTERVIEWER: At one time you had high hopes for yourself.

LEO: Yes.

INTERVIEWER: Could you tell a story about what happened there?

LEO: I made bad decisions. Instead of learning to be an electrician or a lawyer I wasted my twenties in Criminal Justice at some hillbilly college or just fooling around in the Army. Instead of digging one forty-foot well I dug forty-one foot wells.

INTERVIEWER: Do you vote?

LEO: I will in the coming election.

INTERVIEWER: Have you voted in the past few years?

LEO: No.

INTERVIEWER: Did you vote in the last presidential election?

LEO: I would have voted in 2000 but I was in Belgium and they didn't have an overseas ballot.

INTERVIEWER: Why were you in Belgium?

LEO: I was in the Army.

INTERVIEWER: The Army has a base in Belgium?

LEO: Yes.

INTERVIEWER: Do you think that health care professionals take too much credit in treating mental illness?

LEO: No.

INTERVIEWER: Therapists talk about letting go but you didn't have to let go of anything that happened to you.

LEO: No, I didn't.

INTERVIEWER: Do you feel like the American government is wasting your life?

LEO: Yes, very much so. They used me as a government experiment. I think the last person who was used as a government experiment was killed by the police.

INTERVIEWER: Can you explain that?

LEO: Well, I'm a government experiment and there was one before me. I think he was born around 1960. He died in '79. The Sioux Saint Marie police I think framed him and killed him.

INTERVIEWER: This reminds me about what they said about LSD

being used as a government experiment. LSD was given to members of the military as a government experiment.

LEO: The government is experimenting on me, yeah.

INTERVIEWER: Were you close to your commander when you were in the military?

LEO: Not really, no. I was almost arrested by a police narc in 2002 for marijuana possession. So, ever since then I've been paranoid.

INTERVIEWER: You were afraid of getting busted for using drugs?

LEO: Not only that but just paranoid, period.

INTERVIEWER: So, you first became paranoid when you were almost busted for marijuana?

LEO: Yes.

INTERVIEWER: What happened?

LEO: I came back from Belgium to go to college and my friend turned out to be a police narc and I was buying small quantities of marijuana. I was lucky enough to get away and ever since then I've been paranoid.

INTERVIEWER: I see. Do you think you'd be better off if you had the right support person or a significant other?

LEO: Yes I do.

INTERVIEWER: Are you actively trying to find someone?

LEO: No.

INTERVIEWER: You're not.

LEO: I tried living with my mom and she said no.

INTERVIEWER: You and your mother had a falling out? Did you have a big argument?

LEO: No, she was just being weird and I didn't want to live with her.

INTERVIEWER: Has she ever been diagnosed?

LEO: No, she's crazy though. There's a lot of things wrong with her.

INTERVIEWER: Is she paranoid?

LEO: I think so. She's real big into conspiracy theories.

INTERVIEWER: Did you feel at home when you returned home?

LEO: No.

INTERVIEWER: Do you ever think that you and your buddies at the homeless shelter could get together? Hang tight?

LEO: No, I'm too depressed, too old.

INTERVIEWER: Are you disturbed about your inability to own a home?

LEO: Yes.

INTERVIEWER: All these people have gotten on track and you just lost your twenties.

LEO: Yep.

INTERVIEWER: So, what's your plan? Are you going to try to reverse what happened to you in your twenties? Are you going to get into the mainstream of American life? Own a home?

LEO: No, I'm just gonna get my disability and move back to the Sioux and get an apartment, get a job and just live there until I die.

INTERVIEWER: Do you feel like you're being discarded by American society?

LEO: No.

INTERVIEWER: They just don't want to deal with you.

LEO: Yes.

INTERVIEWER: This is the last question I'm going to ask you. Do you think that many Americans realize that there can be no peace without soldiers?

LEO: No, I don't. I think we need more security and why? Because some countries aren't as good as we are. There's different cultures, different societies. If we didn't have soldiers then we'd be sitting ducks for terrorists.

Interview 3

David Bean

On a Sunday afternoon, I took David to dinner at a restaurant in Ypsilanti, Michigan. David was living at a homeless Salvation Army center in Ann Arbor, Michigan. He seemed very willing to tell his story, as apparently it was his wish to prevent what happened to him from happening to someone else.

INTERVIEWER: Your name is Dave?

DAVID: Yes, my last name is Bean.

INTERVIEWER: You said you were in the Army for four years. How long were you in Iraq?

DAVID: Seven Months. Two months in Kuwait and five months combat in Iraq. I was in combat at the start of the invasion. We were one of the first groups across the Iraqi border. My company was actually the one that took the airport.

INTERVIEWER: Oh, really.

DAVID: We were one of the first groups that actually went up into Baghdad.

INTERVIEWER: And now you are homeless?

DAVID: Basically, without my VA benefits I'd be homeless. I was drinking. I turned myself into a mental ward in Ann Arbor.

INTERVIEWER: You committed yourself?

DAVID: Yeah, I turned myself in. Basically, I stayed in the hospital for two weeks and they put me in a program. They

didn't just want to send me back home. So, they put me in
a substance abuse center in Ann Arbor. I did one week
there. Then they sent me out to Battle Creek into another
substance abuse program and they diagnosed me with
PTSD (post traumatic stress disorder). Then they turned
around and put me in a PTSD program in Battle Creek and
set me up with a doctor.

INTERVIEWER: I had a brother who was in the Navy and he spent
thirteen months aboard a hospital ship in Vietnam. I feel
guilty that I didn't try and help him more. He died of cir-
rhosis a few years ago. Our organization, Outsider Press, is
a not-for-profit publishing house. We sponsored a national writing contest and we worked with the National
Alliance on Mental Illness (NAMI), which is a an organization dedicated to advocating for rights for persons with a
mental illness.

DAVID: I've heard of them before.

INTERVIEWER: We worked with the NAMI affiliates, which are
local chapters throughout the country. We contacted
them and advertised our writing contest through them.
Then we put on writing workshops at Community Mental
Health outlets and we worked with clubhouses, which are
meeting places for persons with a mental illness. Some
people are able to find employment through the Clubhouses. So, that's a place to think about if you're going to
look for work.

DAVID: Do they have a Clubhouse in Ann Arbor?

INTERVIEWER: Oh, I'm sure they do. All you have to do is look
up Clubhouses on the Internet. The first Clubhouse that
was formed was in New York, some years ago. It was called
Fountain House and many chapters have been formed
throughout the world since that time. So, I'm almost certain that there's one in Ann Arbor. I can also give you
some information that I gave to a guy that was in Kuwait.
I found a lot of information that would help him as a vet.
There's a lot of people that will try to help a vet. I mean

there are organizations for disabled vets. Maybe I can get that information to you.

DAVID: Okay.

INTERVIEWER: Our belief at Outsider Press is that if the American people knew about how the mentally ill are treated they would do something about it. Where were you born?

DAVID: Monroe, Michigan.

INTERVIEWER: In what year were you born?

DAVID: 1978.

INTERVIEWER: Where did you go to grade school?

DAVID: I went to Airport Community school, initially.

INTERVIEWER: And that was. . . .

DAVID: I ended up graduating out of Monroe High School.

INTERVIEWER: And what about your family?

DAVID: I have a father and mother and two sisters. I'm the oldest. My sisters are both younger than I am.

INTERVIEWER: And you were in the Army for four years and you served in Iraq for how long?

DAVID: Seven months. Two months in Kuwait. Five months total in Iraq.

INTERVIEWER: You were in Operation . . . ?

DAVID: Operation Iraqi Freedom.

INTERVIEWER: And how long were you deployed in active service?

DAVID: One month shy of four years.

INTERVIEWER: What was your highest rank?

DAVID: E-4 Specialist.

INTERVIEWER: That's a petty officer?

DAVID: No, Specialist.

INTERVIEWER: When were you discharged?

DAVID: January, 2005.

INTERVIEWER: And when were you diagnosed with a mental illness?

DAVID: A few months prior to discharge.

INTERVIEWER: Your diagnosis?

DAVID: Basically they diagnosed me with depression from

combat service. They paid me severance pay when I got out. My depression was service-connected.

INTERVIEWER: Do you think that your experiences in the military caused you to be mentally ill?

DAVID: Yes, definitely.

INTERVIEWER: If you had to do it all over again would you have joined the service?

DAVID: It's a yes and a no for me. I got benefits that I wanted for college. They're going to help me pay for school. I got that wish but I also got a lot of extra baggage. It caused my divorce. It caused different problems with my mental disorder. As far as sleep, I have nightmares, flash-backs. I isolate a lot. I've had a couple of bouts with suicide afterwards.

INTERVIEWER: You tried to commit suicide? How did you try to commit suicide?

DAVID: Overdose on pills.

INTERVIEWER: Did you want to be a soldier when you were a kid?

DAVID: No, actually I didn't

INTERVIEWER: Some men grow up seeing their father in the military and then want to be like him. Military families.

DAVID: Yeah, that's true. My family wasn't really a military family.

INTERVIEWER: Was unemployment a reason that you enlisted in the armed services?

DAVID: It was mainly to pay for college. I've gone to school off and on.

INTERVIEWER: Were you injured in Iraq?

DAVID: I hurt my back prior to going to Iraq but I was never injured, never actually injured in Iraq. I aggravated my back. I was never shot.

INTERVIEWER: Do you feel like a hero?

DAVID: That's another yes and no. I mean I thought we should have taken Saddam out. Ninety percent of the people of Iraq were glad that we liberated their country.

INTERVIEWER: But nobody knew it was going to drag on as long as it did. I think most Americans thought it was going to be in and out.

DAVID: Exactly. Now I basically feel like we are sitting ducks. I'm proud of what I did but now I have personal problems and now it's something I have to deal with the rest of my life. It's been hard on me. It's really taken its toll.

INTERVIEWER: Was it hard for you to readjust when you came back?

DAVID: Extremely. Basically, it caused my divorce, nightmares, I started having problems. I was an excellent soldier. I was getting rank extremely quickly. There were different schools. I moved to the head of my platoon. I was a right-hand man. I was top-of-the-line everything, and when I came back from Iraq it just went all down hill from there. I got busted with a DUI. I didn't care.

INTERVIEWER: So, you developed an attitude?

DAVID: Towards everybody. It wasn't just towards the military. It was life in general.

INTERVIEWER: You thought it wasn't fair?

DAVID: I really didn't know what I was dealing with at the time. It was something I thought I was going to get over in a week or so, or a month or even a year.

INTERVIEWER: And then you didn't get better.

DAVID: I didn't want to get help. There's a stigma. I mean I thought: there's nothing wrong with me. I thought it was going to pass. I really wasn't remembering my nightmares. When I was married my wife heard me talking in my sleep. She would see me wake up and it scared her.

INTERVIEWER: When you were in Iraq did you try to stay awake at night?

DAVID: Yeah.

INTERVIEWER: I have heard other guys talk about that. They were afraid that if they fell asleep they'd be killed.

DAVID: I would have. The very first week I didn't sleep at all, and then I'd go for days without sleep, and when I came back I went for days without sleep.

INTERVIEWER: So, can you describe your symptoms a little bit more?

DAVID: Basically I have nightmares. I wake up startled. I get cold sweats. I don't sleep well. I isolate really bad. I have outbursts of anger for no reason. I've been extremely depressed and anxious. I really worry about everything. I have daytime flashbacks and problems with guilt.

INTERVIEWER: What are your daytime flashbacks like?

DAVID: Basically, it's just like you are back there at the time. I have flashbacks about incidents in the past. It's difficult and that's why I isolate.

INTERVIEWER: Do you feel like the government has been fair with you?

DAVID: Initially no, I didn't think I was getting a fair deal. When I got in the military I liked it and I wanted to make a career out of it.

INTERVIEWER: So you did want to make a career out of it?

DAVID: Once I got in it, I wanted it. I think the career was taken away from me but I also have a lot of guilt. I do feel like the military didn't care.

INTERVIEWER: I have read stories about how soldiers go into the military and make a career out of it and then they are demoted just before they're discharged so the military doesn't have to pay as much money in benefits.

DAVID: Yeah, they basically black-balled me. They don't want to hear it if you have a problem. I didn't face my problem and then I was in a mental ward at Fort Benning for two weeks.

INTERVIEWER: What was that like?

DAVID: To be honest, I really don't remember a lot of it. A lot of it is a blur. I just really don't remember much of it. I remember my outpatient stuff.

INTERVIEWER: What was your diagnosis when you were there?

DAVID: They diagnosed me with major depression.

INTERVIEWER: Do you think you can work now?

DAVID: I haven't been able to hold a steady job. I bounced around. I moved because of my isolation problems. I stayed in Georgia for a few months, where I got help. I moved back to Michigan, to the down river area in Michigan. I went back to Monroe. I stayed there a couple of months. I went to Florida for a year. Then back to Monroe.

INTERVIEWER: How many hospitalizations have you had?

DAVID: Two times.

INTERVIEWER: Where?

DAVID: Ann Arbor, and Fort Benning.

INTERVIEWER: You were at the VA hospital in Ann Arbor?

DAVID: Yes, that's where they diagnosed the PTSD. They sent me to Battle Creek to deal with the substance abuse.

INTERVIEWER: Do you feel like you received good medical care from the doctors at the VA hospital?

DAVID: Yeah. This time I feel more comfortable at the VA. I feel the staff actually cares and are actually trying to help me get on with my life.

INTERVIEWER: The University of Michigan has some good doctors.

DAVID: Yeah, I mean I basically look at it like they saved my life.

INTERVIEWER: Do you think you had problems before you went to war?

DAVID: No, I was an excellent soldier. I had a great track record.

INTERVIEWER: Was there a lot of booze and drugs in the war?

DAVID: Actually no. There was a little bit of alcohol. People were buying alcohol on the black market because Iraq is a dry country.

INTERVIEWER: In the Arab world, pharmaceuticals are commonly abused because alcohol and recreational drugs are illegal. Did you see any of that?

DAVID: No, I didn't know that.

INTERVIEWER: Do you think the war you fought in was justified?

DAVID: Like I said, I guess initially I agree with removing Saddam but now I feel bad. I don't like hearing stories about other soldiers dying over there. I don't like pictures of the war on TV.

INTERVIEWER: If you see it on television it bothers you?

DAVID: It bothers me bad. I get pretty emotional.

INTERVIEWER: What did you think about war before you went to war?

DAVID: Initially, I was gung ho. I kind of felt that being a soldier was the thing to be. I thought we were going to kick the bad guys' butts. All that hoopla. Once you're actually there and have gone through it—I would never like to go back there again.

INTERVIEWER: Vietnam soldiers sometimes say that coming home was difficult because there was no welcome home. Do you feel the same way?

DAVID: I had a welcome home but I hid a lot of my issues. I hid my problems from my ex-wife and from my family. I didn't talk to anybody about it. I thought it was a phase. I thought it would pass.

INTERVIEWER: Do you think that the war was a waste of money?

DAVID: Now I do. What did it cost? Ten billion a month or whatever it is. We could be funneling that money into the American economy.

INTERVIEWER: They say we will have spent a trillion dollars on the war.

DAVID: And that could have been spent here.

INTERVIEWER: Sometimes I think that the country has lots of money for war but no money for the mentally ill. Do you feel that way?

DAVID: Yeah, because even the VA doctors admit that they are understaffed. They're just now getting the support money. They're understaffed and underfunded.

INTERVIEWER: What was a typical day like for you at war?

DAVID: I was infantry. Basically, we were the front lines. We had targets. We were moving pretty quick, at a high rate of speed, once we crossed the border. They were trying to rush us to get to the airport as quick as possible. Basically, we were in the outskirts of a lot of cities. They didn't want us getting too deep in the cities. They didn't want us tied down in urban combat. We encountered enemy vehicles and stuff like that.

INTERVIEWER: Did you knock people's doors down?

DAVID: Not at first.

INTERVIEWER: I don't mean to offend you but it seems knocking down doors would be a horrific thing to do, to just go in there and intrude on those people's lives like that. Those people must have been really scared.

(pause)

INTERVIEWER: Do you feel like nobody cares?

DAVID: I don't think nobody cares. I just think they don't understand.

INTERVIEWER: They don't understand mental illness.

DAVID: Yeah. It's easier if I talk to other combat vets. For me to talk to one of my buddies is easier.

INTERVIEWER: Do you go through group therapy with other soldiers?

DAVID: Yeah.

INTERVIEWER: Does it help?

DAVID: Extremely. The one on one with the doctors and the group therapy is helpful to me.

INTERVIEWER: What do you think is going to happen to you now?

DAVID: I don't know.

INTERVIEWER: Are you scared?

DAVID: Yeah. My whole future life is up in the air right now. I signed back up for school. I only signed up for one class.

INTERVIEWER: Where?

DAVID: Washtenaw Community College.

INTERVIEWER: And what class are you taking?

DAVID: Just keyboarding. I didn't want to overwhelm myself. I just kind of wanted to get my feet in the water and to take things slow.

INTERVIEWER: So, do you feel like you have something to hide because of your war experience?

DAVID: I do. I can't have a normal conversation about my personal issues with the majority of other people. I mean they're talking about how they got a bad grade in school and I'm thinking about this.

INTERVIEWER: There's no comparison between what they've gone through and what you've gone through.

DAVID: My situation is I've only had an hour of sleep because I was up with nightmares.

INTERVIEWER: Are you homicidal?

DAVID: No, I never was homicidal.

INTERVIEWER: Suicidal?

DAVID: Now, no. Previously, yes.

INTERVIEWER: You're currently taking Seroquel?

DAVID: I'm off Seroquel. They switched me to Abilify. I take Effexor and Abilify.

INTERVIEWER: Well, I've been told that Abilify is supposed to be an energizer and so is the Effexor for some people. You don't feel tired all the time like you do on other major tranquilizers and some other antidepressants.

DAVID: I do feel more energetic now.

INTERVIEWER: Is there anything you'd like to say about being in the military? Do you have any feelings about it?

DAVID: Like I said, I still have guilt.

INTERVIEWER: Are you still a patriot?

DAVID: Yeah. I'm a patriot but I'd like to see some changes. That's why I've considered going into Social Work. I know what some of the people are going through. I just wish that for me personally I would have gotten help sooner. I think my last three years would have been a lot different if I would have gotten help three years ago.

INTERVIEWER: What's life like in the homeless shelter where you are?

DAVID: I don't know, it's okay. We share meals. They cook three meals a day. I mean it's not the greatest spot to be in. I feel uncomfortable about my life because I have no place that's a permanent roof over my head.

INTERVIEWER: When I was faced with homelessness I tried to stay out of the shelters. The reason I tried to stay out is because I was always afraid I'd never get out if I went into a homeless shelter. It seems it would be easy to get down on yourself.

DAVID: Yeah, but I understand its purpose. It's there to help you.

INTERVIEWER: Some homeless people don't like to go into shelters because they can't drink at night. A lot of people don't understand that. In California, you have to go into the shelter early at night and if you stay out all night and drink you can't go back to the shelter. They won't let you in. That's why those guys are under the bridges. Is it the same way where you are?

DAVID: Yeah, well, we have an eleven o'clock curfew. You can't leave until six in the morning. You can't stay somewhere else. If you do you're out.

INTERVIEWER: I guess the same people that don't want to stop drinking at night don't want to wake up early in the morning because they're hung over.

DAVID: We have chores in the morning we have to do.

INTERVIEWER: Has anyone stolen any of your belongings?

DAVID: No, this shelter is supposed to be one of the best in the city. It's supposed to be the cleanest and nicest. They let people in that they think are going to get on their feet quicker. Most of the people who live in this shelter are only allowed to stay for ninety days. Except for veterans, who can stay for two years.

INTERVIEWER: How long have you been there?

DAVID: Two weeks.

INTERVIEWER: Do you have a social worker?

DAVID: Yes.

INTERVIEWER: Is she helping you?

DAVID: Yes. She's helping me with clothing and stuff. She helps me get interviews for jobs.

INTERVIEWER: Do you trust her?

DAVID: The whole trust thing is a big issue. I don't trust anybody.

INTERVIEWER: But you said the medical treatment at the VA hospital is good.

DAVID: There's always areas they can improve on but I think that with what they have right now it's good.

INTERVIEWER: Are you friends with other mentally ill soldiers?

DAVID: No. I'm just getting myself set right now so I can get into outreach. I don't want to go back to what I was. I'm trying to do my best.

INTERVIEWER: Did you kill anybody in combat?

DAVID: I had vehicle kills. I mean I didn't actually see myself shoot anybody when I fired shots. I destroyed probably fifteen vehicles.

INTERVIEWER: Do you have a hard time dealing with that?

DAVID: Yeah. I mean if you have any moral standards at all. . . .

INTERVIEWER: When you take somebody's life it's not something you take lightly.

DAVID: It's the kill or get killed philosophy.

INTERVIEWER: Is it with you all the time? Do you dwell on it?

DAVID: Yeah, a lot.

INTERVIEWER: If money were no object where would you go for treatment?

DAVID: I don't know, because I really don't know what's out there. This stuff is all new to me. I've heard that Chicago has a really good PTSD program. It's supposed to be one of the top-notch programs in the country. I did enjoy Battle Creek. I had one excellent doctor there. No matter what I said or did he knew exactly what I was talking about. He would just come right back and he would know what to say. It was as if he was living right in your shoes, period. No matter what you said or how you were feeling.

INTERVIEWER: I guess you hear the same stories over and over again. How do you feel when politicians say we should pull out?

DAVID: I agree. I mean I don't want these soldiers going through this.

INTERVIEWER: At this point what do you think can help you?

DAVID: I don't know. I just don't know. I don't think there's any one person whose going to help me. They say it's a chronic problem. Get used to it. It's something you're going to have to deal with for a long time.

INTERVIEWER: Maybe the rest of your life? Some medical people say that some patients are so into their own drama that they can't help them. Do you feel like that sometimes?

DAVID: Sometimes I do live in my own little world. As far as drama is concerned, I wouldn't use the word drama.

INTERVIEWER: Do you want to be a hero?

DAVID: Yes and no. I mean I do and I don't. I just don't like the idea of me having to live with this the rest of my life.

INTERVIEWER: Do you have trouble controlling your anger?

DAVID: I used to have a really bad problem with that. That's one of the things that is on my list of things I want to work on. I mean, I've tried to overcome it for the most part.

INTERVIEWER: We now know that Saddam Hussein had no weapons of mass destruction and that the Bush administration skewed the facts. Do you feel that the sacrifice you made was in vain?

DAVID: Yeah. When you look at it in that light, yeah. It pisses me off. I sometimes think Bush did it as a payback.

INTERVIEWER: Saddam tried to kill George Bush's father and the country wanted revenge for 9/11. Do you feel like we must win the war or all will be lost?

DAVID: I don't think we can win.

INTERVIEWER: You don't think it's winnable. You think as soon as we pull out there's going to be consequences?

DAVID: Yeah.

INTERVIEWER: Do you have second thoughts about signing up for military service?

DAVID: Yeah, I mean it's what I deal with now. I mean, if I wouldn't have signed up and taken a different avenue I'd be working or going to school. Now I'd be living a normal life.

INTERVIEWER: Do you feel like you're full of hate?

DAVID: I'd say I have a lot of hate.

INTERVIEWER: How would you say war has changed your personality?

DAVID: I used to tell my therapist and the people in my group that I can never be that person I was before I went to Iraq. No matter what I do, I'll never get that person back.

INTERVIEWER: Do you think you remained in combat mode when you returned?

DAVID: Yeah, oh yeah. Definitely. One night I ran out in the streets and started stopping cars. I thought I was at a check point.

INTERVIEWER: The war never wore off.

DAVID: No. I'm jumpy if I hear noises. I don't like people behind me. I don't like it one bit. I get paranoid in huge crowds. I become a nervous wreck.

INTERVIEWER: Because of your military service, which jobs do you think you qualify for? Is there anything they prepared you to do?

DAVID: (laughter) No!

INTERVIEWER: Are you bitter about being unemployable after risking your life?

DAVID: I mean, I served in the military for four years and I have some college behind me and I have leadership skills and. . . .

INTERVIEWER: Were you ever involved with senseless risk-taking, either when you were in the military or when you got out?

DAVID: Yeah, well, that's kind of what it's all about, especially being in the military, that's what it's all about.

INTERVIEWER: Do you ever feel the urge to kill?

DAVID: I had thoughts of going out in a blaze of glory in the battle-field.

INTERVIEWER: Are you afraid you might commit a felony?

DAVID: No.

INTERVIEWER: Have you ever wondered why you lived while others died?

DAVID: Yeah. I wonder why God allowed me to live while others died.

INTERVIEWER: Do you crave violence? Do you get an adrenaline rush from violence?

DAVID: I used to. Now, I don't know if I do or not but—, yeah, sometimes I would fight to get that adrenaline going.

INTERVIEWER: Do you think war damaged your mind?

DAVID: Yeah.

INTERVIEWER: Do you think war breeds criminals?

DAVID: I would say, yeah, because I got a DUI when I came back. I got in bar fights. I got in trouble with the law.

INTERVIEWER: Some say you need innocence and forgiveness when you return from war. Do you agree?

DAVID: It's a good way of putting it. I don't know.

INTERVIEWER: Sometimes male soldiers look for a woman who will give them innocence in trying to leave the war behind.

DAVID: That's why I moved a lot. Trying to get away from it.

INTERVIEWER: But it follows you no matter where you go. Many, maybe most people, do not understand mental illness. Have you ever thought that if you'd lost a leg or an arm, people would understand your sacrifice, but they don't understand your mental illness?

DAVID: That's true.

INTERVIEWER: Some people think that some soldiers were ill before they entered combat and that combat just aggravated their condition. What do you think?

DAVID: No. I didn't have this problem before. I didn't have flashbacks and rage and outbursts. I didn't have any of that before.

INTERVIEWER: How long have you been sober?

DAVID: Four months.

INTERVIEWER: You're in AA?

DAVID: I'm in AA and different groups.

INTERVIEWER: Do you feel like your problems are bigger than you?

DAVID: I just can't control my rage.

INTERVIEWER: Would you rather have the temporary relief drugs and alcohol offer?

DAVID: Yeah. I think about that a lot. When I drank I used to forget about a lot of it. It would kind of take it away.

INTERVIEWER: It would numb your senses.

DAVID: Exactly. Now, without alcohol and drugs, I have to deal with it on my own.

INTERVIEWER: If I told you that the combination of drugs and alcohol abuse coupled with mental illness is a recipe for violent behavior, what would you say?

DAVID: I used to get in bar fights all the time. I started a reputation around town when I started drinking.

INTERVIEWER: Do you think war numbed your emotions?

DAVID: Yeah, in some ways it did. It numbed some emotions and made others more intense.

INTERVIEWER: Did you feel like you were the iceman when you came back?

DAVID: Yeah.

INTERVIEWER: Do you have a hard time expressing your emotions?

DAVID: Yeah.

INTERVIEWER: You suffer from insomnia?

DAVID: Yeah.

INTERVIEWER: Do you try to get back to sleep by drinking?

DAVID: Yeah.

INTERVIEWER: After the overstimulation of war, does civilian life seem dull?

DAVID: Yeah. I have a very short attention span. Very short. I get bored very easy. In my relationships, I would get bored with a girl.

INTERVIEWER: Do you have any vocational training?

DAVID: As far as . . . ?

INTERVIEWER: Are there any vocational programs you can get into?

DAVID: They do have them but I haven't gotten into that yet. That's what I'm trying to research now.

INTERVIEWER: Do you feel like you have spoiled golden opportunities that were given to you in the work-place?

DAVID: Yeah. Employers would see I have potential but then they'd find out more about me.

INTERVIEWER: Did you have a hard time getting along with other employees?

DAVID: It's been a problem.

INTERVIEWER: What were your commanding officers like?

DAVID: I would look up to them when I was in war with them but I had problems when I came back. They didn't want to hear about my problems. They were like, "Suck it up and get over it." They were redeploying and going back to war.

INTERVIEWER: Do you feel like a pawn?

DAVID: Yeah, I mean definitely like a number. I'm just a number. I mean if I would have died over there, only my family would have cared.

INTERVIEWER: When you first came back, were you paranoid that there was a death trap around every corner?

DAVID: Yeah, oh yeah. I thought that especially when I was drinking.

INTERVIEWER: Are you afraid of being sniped?

DAVID: Yeah, I watch overhead.

INTERVIEWER: Did you react to women differently after being in combat?

DAVID: I would distance myself from everyone. I haven't dated since returning.

INTERVIEWER: Do you trust women?

DAVID: No.

INTERVIEWER: And you lost your wife. How did that happen?

DAVID: Mainly because I think that I can't deal with my rage. My life was literally spinning out of control. My wife couldn't help me.

INTERVIEWER: You said you have one child.

DAVID: A son, ten years old.

INTERVIEWER: And you've lost him?

DAVID: No, I still see him, but it's difficult. He's my son and I love him, but well . . . my isolation caused a lot of problems. He wants me to be with him and I have gone through entire months when I didn't want to leave the house.

INTERVIEWER: In Vietnam, the male soldiers always came back with stories about what happened between them and the Asian women but in the Middle East this didn't seem to happen because the Middle Eastern women were guarded. Were there any romantic relationships between American male soldiers and Middle Eastern women that you know of?

DAVID: There were soldiers who got proposals for marriage. They were trying to marry off their fifteen-year-old daughters.

INTERVIEWER: Did you ever use sex as a temporary relief?

DAVID: Probably, yeah.

INTERVIEWER: Has intimacy been a problem?

DAVID: Yeah, I don't trust them.

INTERVIEWER: Have you often thought civilians who have never been to war don't understand the grief that's always with you?

DAVID: They don't have a clue, the majority of them, and then you get the really ignorant ones who the first thing out of their mouth is, "Did you kill anyone? You know, how is it, pretty cool?" It's like you look at them and bite your tongue.

INTERVIEWER: So you prefer to be alone.

DAVID: I feel safer when I'm alone.

INTERVIEWER: Do you think you'll ever get back together with your wife?

DAVID: No, she's dating someone else. I'm the one who left her. We were at each others' throats.

INTERVIEWER: Have you visited any of your comrades since you've been back?

DAVID: No.

INTERVIEWER: Did you ever think you weren't going to make it home alive?

DAVID: Yeah, a lot of times. I had a lot of close calls.

INTERVIEWER: Do you think there is such a thing as a beautiful death in war?

DAVID: (Smiles) I've heard other people say that and I've even thought that myself. Sometimes I wish that I did die so that I didn't have to go through what I'm going through. It's almost like I did die. It's just not a physical death.

INTERVIEWER: When you recollect your war experiences do you ever think they happened one way when in actuality they happened another way?

DAVID: No, I don't think so.

INTERVIEWER: You're on government assistance right now?

DAVID: Yeah.

INTERVIEWER: Disability benefits from the military?

DAVID: Yeah, from service-connected back injury, and I now have a claim in for PTSD.

INTERVIEWER: Is it enough to live on?

DAVID: I haven't seen the check yet.

INTERVIEWER: Are you paranoid? Sometimes this symptom can be resistant to medication.

DAVID: (No response.)

INTERVIEWER: As I've asked previously, if we pull out now will we lose the war? Then why did all these people die?

DAVID: No, because I'd rather see these guys home safe and then less people will have to go through this. It affects not only them but everyone around them.

INTERVIEWER: You feel like you're barely holding on to life?

DAVID: It's definitely my lowest point.

INTERVIEWER: Do you feel like your poverty is unfair?

DAVID: Yeah.

INTERVIEWER: Did your wife remain faithful when you were in combat?

DAVID: She said she did.

INTERVIEWER: Have you ever run into the situation where an employer refused to hire you because you were a vet?

DAVID: Not that I'm aware of.

INTERVIEWER: Are you jealous of others who have not experienced war because they have successful careers and good spouses?

DAVID: That could have been me if I wouldn't have chosen the military path. My life would be a whole 180 [degrees different].

INTERVIEWER: Do you trust anyone?

DAVID: I trust my parents to an extent. I mean I trust them like a normal person but I still have a problem talking about my experiences to them. They know I'm in a PTSD program. I don't know how to talk to them about it and I don't think they know how to talk about it either.

INTERVIEWER: Do you think you had a normal childhood?

DAVID: Yeah, very normal.

INTERVIEWER: So there's nothing in your childhood that could have caused the problems you have now?

DAVID: I grew up in a normal, middle class [family].

INTERVIEWER: Do you ever think people are afraid of you because you were in combat?

DAVID: Yeah, I've actually had people tell me that.

INTERVIEWER: Do you think that if they knew what you did at war they would be afraid of you?

DAVID: People told me when they found out I was in war and I killed people and stuff, they said they didn't know how I would react if I flew off the wall. This was essentially when I was in my heavy drinking stage.

INTERVIEWER: Do you think that Middle Eastern men you met in Iraq were appalled by what they might interpret as a lack of honor toward men in American society?

DAVID: I think the women are mistreated over there.

INTERVIEWER: Do you think that military service breeds character?

DAVID: Yeah. I think in some ways it helped me. Like I said, it made me a better person. More organized. I can't say everything was a negative. It's made me a better person in some ways.

INTERVIEWER: Have you ever thought that in America people only care about their own families? What do you think about that?

DAVID: They don't appreciate it. A lot of people don't appreciate it. They don't understand the sacrifice. It would be different if I was moving around in a wheel-chair versus being mentally ill.

INTERVIEWER: They think there's nothing wrong with you. You just have to get over it, snap out of it. Do you feel demoralized as a result of war?

DAVID: It took a lot out of my sails. No doubt about it.

INTERVIEWER: Are you able to take care of yourself?

DAVID: Physically, yeah.

INTERVIEWER: Do you feel self-hatred or a lack of self-esteem because of what you had to do in the war or what has happened to you since you've been back?

DAVID: I wouldn't say hate.

INTERVIEWER: You've gone through periods in which you've withdrawn from society. What did you do? Spend your time alone in a room?

DAVID: There were things I couldn't face.

INTERVIEWER: Do small things make you angry?

DAVID: Yeah. I've gotten irate over stupid things. I've got that pretty much under control now.

INTERVIEWER: Have you lost all your ambition?

DAVID: I'm hoping. I hope. I mean that's what I said about college. I signed up for one class. I'm just kind of touching the water. I'll get my feet wet and see what happens. I don't want to get in over my head and overwhelm myself.

INTERVIEWER: Are you sad because your ambitions are not materializing?

DAVID: I feel like my goals for college have taken far too long to materialize.

INTERVIEWER: You've described yourself as one person before you went to war and then you experienced all this violence and came back a different person. Did the violence ruin your life?

DAVID: Yeah, that type of violence.

INTERVIEWER: Do you feel like you're losing your youth to mental illness?

DAVID: I definitely feel that.

INTERVIEWER: When you go for an interview, people want to

know what you've been doing. In my case, I couldn't say I've just been released from Houston International Hospital. You've got to lie. One lie leads to another lie and it just goes on and on.

DAVID: You've got to lie on your application.

INTERVIEWER: You've said you have problems trusting people?

DAVID: Unless I've known them for years on end, I don't trust them.

INTERVIEWER: Do you vote?

DAVID: Yeah.

INTERVIEWER: Is that important to you?

DAVID: It is. I'm hoping that something will change in this country. Whether or not it will happen I don't know. I have my doubts.

INTERVIEWER: Do you feel like you were wrecked by war?

DAVID: Definitely. Like I said, I'd rather see the war end, even if it takes saying that we lost or whatever. Every day the war goes on it's another person that's going to have to go through what I've been through.

INTERVIEWER: Do you feel that some health care professionals take too much credit for helping veterans with PTSD?

DAVID: No, I think they are helpful. My group therapy helped me a million times more than taking classes where they educate you.

INTERVIEWER: So, you believe in therapy.

DAVID: Not only does it help with what's on my mind that day but it teaches me ways to cope. My sleep has been better. Things like that. It hasn't been working miracles, but I'm making gains, and that's the only thing I have to hold onto. It gives me hope when I see some slight improvement.

INTERVIEWER: People try to create meaning with their lives. Do you ever think that some vets hold on to their memories because their lives after war seemed uneventful?

DAVID: Yeah. I see that in Vietnam vets. I don't want to be like that forty years from now.

INTERVIEWER: Some say you just have to let go.

DAVID: Yeah.

INTERVIEWER: The experiences were too gruesome. It's as if the violence has caused an indelible mark on your brain.

DAVID: I can't control it. I mean how do you let go of it?

INTERVIEWER: Do you feel like the American government ruined your life?

DAVID: Yeah.

INTERVIEWER: Do you think PTSD is stronger in some than in others?

DAVID: You see that in groups.

INTERVIEWER: How would you rank yourself?

DAVID: I think mine is pretty high compared to most because I was actually on the front lines. The way that I feel is that I was confronted with violence on a daily basis. We were firing rounds everyday.

INTERVIEWER: If you had been closer to the other soldiers when you were in combat, do you think you could have had less fear?

DAVID: No.

INTERVIEWER: You were close to them?

DAVID: Yeah, I thought I was close to them.

INTERVIEWER: Everybody was looking out for the other guy?

DAVID: You have to. If you don't, you're a dead person. I think it's just a natural instinct, what they call fight or flight. You have to have fear. The fear makes you want to live. Stay alert. Stay alive.

INTERVIEWER: Do you think if you had the right support person you could put your whole life back together again?

DAVID: Eventually.

INTERVIEWER: This is key in your life that you've got to find a spouse.

DAVID: I wouldn't say a spouse but maybe someone that I could talk to on a daily basis, that would understand what I'm going through.

INTERVIEWER: And would care enough to help you.

DAVID: Yeah. I think that would help but it's a double-edged sword. You've got to get past the trust factor, too. I don't know. Sometimes I think that it would be nice, but is it going to happen? I don't know.

INTERVIEWER: Did you ever feel at home when you returned?

DAVID: No, like I said, I didn't feel like the same person when I came back. I felt that my old self had died there.

INTERVIEWER: When you returned did anyone recognize you for who you were?

DAVID: I know myself better.

INTERVIEWER: Do you feel undervalued for your heroic efforts?

DAVID: No. I don't know if I still look at myself as a hero or not. I feel undervalued, yes.

INTERVIEWER: How about being able to own a home?

DAVID: I would like to have my own place. I mean, even an apartment. How nice it would be to be living a normal American life.

INTERVIEWER: And have the ability to support a family. Do you feel discarded?

DAVID: Yeah.

INTERVIEWER: Do you feel that violence in American warfare is tyrannical?

DAVID: A little bit. Like you said, it was revenge for Bush.

INTERVIEWER: Do you think that many Americans realize that there can be no peace without soldiers?

DAVID: We actually discuss this in the PTSD program. A lot of Americans do not realize that.

Cruel To Be Kind

Kurt Douglas Sass

This is the true story of what I had to do to get my son the help he so desperately needed.

Let's begin about 20 years ago—1982, to be exact. My wife Valerie was pregnant with our first (and only) child. She was extremely concerned during the pregnancy, partially because my brother's baby, who had been born just six months earlier, was delivered with the umbilical cord wrapped around her neck, and her face was extremely bluish. Everyone was gravely concerned at that time about the possibility of brain damage, but I can gladly report that my niece is currently a junior in college and is even the editor of the school's newspaper.

My wife took excellent care of herself during the entire pregnancy. She had never smoked or drunk alcohol to begin with, so these were never issues in the first place. She also avoided all medications. In fact, the only pill that crossed her lips during the entire nine months was one Tylenol. Nevertheless, we still prayed each and every day, up to and including the day of delivery, that everything would be fine. I guess all expectant parents do that.

We took pre-natal classes, and I remember one session in particular, in which the instructor spoke of what is called the

"APGAR score." This stands for: Activity (muscle tone), Pulse, Grimace (reflex), Appearance (skin color), and Respiration.

The APGAR is a two-part evaluation of the baby. The evaluation is done twice, once immediately after birth and again just a few minutes later, and is supposedly a strong indicator as to the overall health of the newborn. The APGAR score is based on the five factors listed above. Each of these factors is given a score of 0, 1, or 2, so the total score could range from 0 to 10. We were told during the pre-natal class that a score of 6 or higher for the first evaluation and 8 or higher for the second evaluation is usually a good sign of a healthy baby. With this in mind, the minute Kurt Junior entered the outside world I immediately focused on "6 & 8," "6 & 8." After a few minutes I asked one of the nurses what the APGAR scores were. She seemed surprised by my asking, but her reply was music to my ears; "9–10," she said, "can't get much better than that." At that moment, everything was right with the universe, and my world seemed totally secure.

Kurt seemed to be perfect. With a birth weight of 9 pounds, 10-1/2 ounces, he had a head start on most babies. He turned over, crawled, and walked much earlier than expected. Everything seemed to be going along just fine.

It was somewhere around his first birthday that we started to think that things just weren't quite right. It seemed that Kurt wasn't listening to us, and he was making fewer and fewer sounds. Even if we said something like "Kurt, if you come here you can have some ice cream," (which was his favorite) he failed to respond. Frightful that Kurt had a possible hearing loss, we scheduled a hearing test for him at Lenox Hill Hospital.

The hearing test was a disaster. Kurt would not sit still at all and wouldn't even let the audiologist put headphones on him. The most disturbing part, however, was that I could tell immediately from the audiologist's facial expressions that he thought there was some other problem. He told us after the aborted test that he didn't think Kurt had a hearing problem, because although Kurt wouldn't allow the test to be done he seemed to respond to all the sounds he had heard. He also recommended that we see a neurologist, but refused to elaborate on a reason why.

When we finally got to see the neurologist a week later, our world started to crumble. He diagnosed Kurt with mental retardation. Valerie and I were obviously devastated, but almost immediately turned our attention to getting Kurt whatever help he needed so he could lead as normal and productive a life as possible. After all, Valerie's brother is mentally retarded (the politically correct term today is "developmentally disabled") and he is living a full-life, complete with a wife and a full time job as a messenger. Valerie and I decided to turn our pain, hurt, and anger into action. As soon as we could, we got Kurt enrolled in a special education pre-school program, as well as an excellent recreation program on Saturdays.

However, as Kurt got older, his behavior changed drastically for the worse. He would become extremely agitated and angry, sometimes for no reason at all, other times if just one minor thing was changed. One example was the day we moved some furniture in the living room. When Kurt saw that the furniture was in a different place he got very upset and banged the table over and over with his fists. When we took Kurt to a specialist, he diagnosed Kurt with autism, in addition to the mental retardation. The autism explained why Kurt would get so upset over the slightest of changes.

As time passed, the aggressive behavior kept escalating. Kurt started throwing objects like chairs, and was becoming violent toward himself and us. He also began a pattern of only sleeping 2 or 3 hours a night, every night. Valerie and I actually had to take shifts sleeping because anything could happen when Kurt was awake. One minute he'd be laughing hysterically at nothing at all and the next do a complete 180 and start kicking and biting. It was around this time that a third diagnosis was added to the mix. In addition to everything else, we were now told that Kurt was also manic-depressive, or bipolar. This would explain Kurt's rapid mood swings. The doctor started Kurt on small doses of the medications Elavil and Lithium; and although he was only six years old at the time, when the small doses did not seem to have any effect, they raised the Elavil to 300 mg and added 400 mg of Mellaril. Even at these high doses, we saw not one change in Kurt. The behaviors were exactly the same, and he was still sleeping only 2 to 3 hours every night. Then the doctor, over the course of many months, proceeded to try another six or so different medications, such as Ritalin and Tegretol, each also having no positive effects at all.

When Kurt was about seven years old, Valerie and I made the painful decision that the best thing we could do for Kurt was to find him a good group home, one where he could be monitored much more closely than it was humanly possible for just Valerie and me, because the ever-increasing violence he was exhibiting was becoming far too dangerous for us to handle alone.

We obtained a list of approximately 20 group homes and contacted them all. Over the course of the next two years only six of them responded that they might even have an opening. We visited all six of them, some hundreds of miles away and in different states, but not a single one would accept him. The answer we got was usually along the lines of: "Kurt is just too violent and aggressive for our program," or "We just don't have the adequate staff to meet Kurt's special needs." I would ask these programs if they knew of any others that might accept Kurt, since he was a child who definitely needed a group home setting, more so than just about anyone else, but they could not help me.

One visit to a potential group home stands out in my mind. This particular group home was upstate, about 300 miles away from our house. Needless to say, by the time we got there Kurt was extremely agitated, and proceeded to slap the face of the person interviewing us. So it ended up taking about 5 hours to drive there, 5 minutes to realize that Kurt wouldn't be accepted, and another 5 hours to drive back home.

By the time Kurt turned nine, his behavior was worse than ever, with no end in sight. It seemed like we were taking him every other week or so to The Children's Psychiatric Emergency Room.

It was during one of these visits to this ER that our world would start to change again. Kurt was having a horrible time of it at home that night, knocking over the TV set and a wall unit. When he started to bang his head on purpose against the wall we knew we had to take him in. While there, one of the ER docs motioned me over to him. He asked, "Have you thought about placing Kurt in a group home?" "Of course," I told him, then proceeded to tell him our two-year saga of unsuccessfully trying to place Kurt in a group home.

The doctor then brought me to a small room and closed the door behind us. "I want to tell you something, Mr. Sass, but you can never tell anyone that I told you this. Most group homes will never take on a child like Kurt, because it comes down to a matter of money, and Kurt requires so much additional attention that it is not cost effective for them to accept him. In other words, most group homes only want the kids that don't really need to be in group homes, because they are easier to take care of and require less staff."

"There is one thing we can do, Mr. Sass, but you have to promise not to tell anyone you heard this from me." He had my full attention. "The only way a group home will accept a child like Kurt would be on an emergency basis—in other words, if Child Welfare felt that he could not under any circumstances remain at home because his life would be in danger. What I can do is refer him overnight to the Bronx Children's Psychiatric Hospital for evaluation and to put on my report that it is for the child's safety."

"What you need to do, Mr. Sass, is to come to the hospital the next day, and then pretend you are the absolute worst parent on the face of the earth. You'll have to convince Child Welfare that you hate him and that if he is returned home you will harm him. And you'll have to be very convincing, because if they believe you're faking, they'll send him right back to your house. One other thing—come alone, don't bring your wife. If both parents come, the odds are much more likely that the child will not be considered in danger. Now remember, Mr. Sass, you did not hear this from me. But you must decide. To be honest with you, this is the only way to get him in a group home."

I discussed this with Valerie and, through tears, we decided to go ahead with it since it was truly our only option.

The next day I went to the Bronx Children's Psychiatric Hospital, alone, and was led to a room in which there were four people; Kurt, a member of the hospital staff, and two people I believe to be from the Department of Child Welfare. As soon as I spotted them, I went into my performance mode. I yelled at Kurt and called him every name in the book. I had never cursed at Kurt before and felt like the lowest scum on earth for doing so. I called him a "fucking retard" and told him I wished he had never been born. I still had no idea if they were buying it, so I proceeded to pick up a chair and throw it past Kurt, but close enough for the others in the room to think he was the intended target. I will never forget the look of fear on Kurt's face for as long as I live. I still have nightmares about it.

Well, whatever I did, it worked. They refused to let me take Kurt home, and "miraculously," just two days later he was placed in a group home just five minutes from our house, a place that we had been told many times in the past had no openings.

Was it worth it? Of course, it was. Kurt has flourished in the highly structured environment of the group home.

I can never thank the doctor enough for his courage—he put himself at risk to help my son. However, I am still appalled that I had to be so cruel to my son to get him the help he needed.

Too Little, Too Late

Cynthia S. Rayne

For My Brother Adam

Where does one begin to tell a story but at the beginning of past recollections and memories? Although this is a true but painful thing to write, hopefully previous good times will act as a catalyst, and perhaps I may be able to save the life of one person, change the attitude of one mental health worker, evoke the empathy and undivided attention of one social worker, elicit the consideration of one physician, change the vote of one politician, alter the policy of one administrator, enable the understanding of a student, or arouse the devotion of a relative or friend who is able to find a distraught person immediate life-saving aid. Then the guilt, agony, and grief that I and the people who loved my brother live with will have some semblance of purpose after all.

Sandy was our oldest sister. Adam was two years younger than her, followed by me, who was five years his junior, and last was Amy, who was seven years younger and the baby. My first recollections of Adam are of the photographs taken by our Uncle Albert of him (and all the family members) each time there was a family gathering. In addition, our father was also a shutter-bug, taking photographs with different cameras he purchased shortly after they had been released for sale, as well as with his movie camera, which at that time produced no sound. Looking at those things brings back warm memories of previous good times.

I also remember my brother and older sister walking to primary school as I watched out our front door, as well as anxiously awaiting their return. I felt lonely when they left and glad when they finally came into view once again. Then we would all sit in the dining room at our child-size table and chairs, eat cold cereal and milk, and watch children's shows on our small black and white T.V.

Since Adam was the only boy, he got special attention from my parents and other family members as he "would carry on the family name." We were Jewish, and in the fifties, it seemed that boys were valued over girls—at least that's how I saw it.

Before I was able to ride my own bike, Adam would ride his two-wheeler with me on the handlebars. It was so much fun riding instead of walking! At other times, he would go ice skating with his friends and take me along—probably not because he wanted to, but because my mother had requested it of him. He would skate away with his friends, but always return to check on me and eventually escort me home.

He was always doing something—riding his go-cart or bicycle up and down the streets, going to friends' homes. I remember when he taught me to ride my two-wheel bike down a hill near our primary school. Unfortunately, he forgot to tell me to turn the handlebars when I got to the bottom, and I careened into a fire hydrant and sustained a badly injured, bloody right knee. He told me to stay on the side of the road while he pedaled my bike with lightning speed to notify my parents of what had transpired. They returned shortly, placed me in the back seat of the car, and drove me to our pediatrician, who assessed the damage and worked his magic on my right knee.

When I was in grade school and Adam was in junior high,

he would teach me how to do math, and I in turn would help him with spelling. I would read him lists of words and he would repeat each one, spelling it back to me in preparation for his weekly spelling tests.

I remember practicing songs that were popular at the time, such as, "Find a Ring," sung by Perry Como. We rehearsed the songs constantly. Adam was more than a brother. He was a friend and confidante. He collected *Mad* magazines, which he kept in his bedroom closet. I would sneak in his room when he wasn't around and look at the funny cartoons and then return them to their proper place.

As we got older, he would ask me to clean his room, telling me he would pay me if I did. I always would do so and put the money he gave me in the right front corner of my top bureau drawer. I noticed that shortly afterwards, when I checked my drawer, some of the money had gone missing. When I confronted him about it, he would look at me and laugh the way he characteristically did and ante up. How I miss the sound of his laughter! It was so endearing.

I remember summers that we spent at our parents' cottage, which was about twenty miles away from our home. We had a summer camp with a huge, screened porch at the front of the house. There were also several enormous pine trees there under which we played Monopoly and various card games. My father's parents and sister and brother-in-law and their two children and relatives of in-laws also resided there. Our relatives from New York visited us there often: mother's parents, three sisters and brother, and their respective families. We even had a swimming hole replete with infamous bloodsuckers!

Those times were grand—the softness of pine needles under our bare feet, the smell of the evergreens. The hours spent amusing ourselves with child's play. During card games, the younger children had to keep their "hands" easier to hold with the use of wooden springed clothespins.

I remember the parties Sandy and Adam used to give at our house. They would frequently co-host get-togethers in our knotty-pine paneled, cellar room. They would play 33-rpm records and do the popular dance crazes such as the stroll and the twist. They would also dance to be-bop and slow dance cheek to cheek. They munched on potato chips and pretzels and drank gallons of soda as they danced and laughed the night away. I was envious of the fun times they had while they were in the party mode.

My father had a small fishing boat, a Pen-Yan. Adam helped him launch and remove the boat from the water as well as steer it. He loved the boat and was a good captain and co-captain. They would also go fishing together. How we loved the wind blowing against our faces when we were all treated to a ride!

We never expressed our emotions in our house. While growing up, our mother was busy shopping, cooking, cleaning, doing laundry, etc. She was never a big believer in hugs, kisses, coddling, and telling us she loved us. If she gave us a compliment, we questioned if she actually meant it. Her expression did not show genuine happiness for us. It was as though she answered by rote. Her mind always seemed to be elsewhere.

Father went to work every day when he was able. He didn't talk to us much. He was a manic-depressive. Dad had few friends and seemed troubled and introverted. His mental illness reared its ugly head shortly after our parents got married and he exhibited mood swings. His condition got increasingly worse as he grew older. It was also more pronounced after he drank alcohol. Father would either be giddy and silly, or vicious and violent. When he was on medication, he seemed to be quiet and withdrawn. Dad was diagnosed with colon cancer while in his fifties. I was not told that our father was diagnosed with manic-depression until I was in my mid-forties and I had received a slew of medications which didn't seem to be relieving me from my deep depression at that time. My brother finally told me the "family secret."

Before then, at the age of twenty-eight, I had suffered a major depressive episode. I was incorrectly diagnosed as "schizoaffective," and was prescribed a large number of different drugs, including stelazine, cogentin, imipramine, and others I have since forgotten the names of. I was overmedicated and almost catatonic. I was admitted to the hospital for approximately six weeks, and was kept pretty much under lock and key. My freedom was returned to me in small increments. I felt that I was sinking deeper and deeper into a drug-induced depression, and pleaded with a different doctor than the one who was treating me to give me shock treatments. I explained my situation and he finally agreed. I was given two series of shock treatments. The first set was given to my brain on the opposite side of my dominant right hand, and initially did not yield the desired results. Even though I was right-handed, I was born with a dominant left hand that was changed in first grade for the ease of my teacher. It seems that the teaching of writing and printing would be less burdensome if all of her students were right-handed. The first series of shock treatments weren't effective because of this and I got a very bad short-term period of amnesia. Luckily, the second set of shock treatments worked as they were supposed to after being administered to the right side of my brain, and I felt almost immediately better after having received them. I feel that they and the physician who ordered them saved my life. I was released and then attended a day program at the hospital. About six months later, I was once again admitted for a relapse, and haven't been hospitalized since, although I've gone to about seven psychiatrists up to now—some much more in tune to me as an individual, while others, at a comfortable point in their careers, appeared to be pacing themselves, coasting, marking time. Maybe their case loads were mind boggling, or they detached themselves for self-preservation. Each one certainly had his or her own style. That is merely this author's observation.

In the 90's, after Adam's revelation about our father, I immediately notified the psychiatrist that I was seeing at the time, who had been prescribing his own choice of medications, which I had been taking in hopes of finding the correct combination. Afterward, I was immediately placed on lithium, which seemed to alleviate the symptoms at the time, as I, too, was manic-depressive or bipolar. My sister Sandy is also bipolar and a rapid cycler.

Adam was good-natured and could always make us laugh. I never remember him complaining or refusing to do anything that was asked of him. He had many friends and girlfriends while growing up. I really can't remember anyone who didn't like him. He had a winning personality, while I always considered myself to be more introverted and reserved.

When I was about seven, I noticed that my father seemed sad. He would sit in his wing chair at the back left corner of the living room and listen to his favorite records over and over again. While he sat in the chair, I would ask him if I could comb his hair and he would allow me to do so. One of his favorite records was "Porgy and Bess." To me it sounded so sad. He would also allow me to cut his nails with a nail clipper. During that time period, he went to the doctor about once a week. I thought he was physically sick, but saw no evidence of bandages upon his return. I repeatedly asked my parents what kind of doctor he was going to. They responded it was a "talking doctor." Someone he could talk to. I still couldn't comprehend the type of physician my father was visiting. I was always the curious child. Eventually, probably at the doctor's recommendation, they took me to one of his appointments. I used to call it "Little New York" because the tall buildings reminded me of the ones I had seen on trips there.

The doctor was an older fellow. He had nice blue eyes, was soft spoken, and smiled at me. I don't exactly recall what he said and did to Dad at their sessions, but I felt comforted, relieved, and satisfied by what he told me. I also felt hopeful. I was always very sensitive to the feelings of other people. It's possible that he reassured me that he was going to help my father get better. None of us received counseling except our father.

Adam enjoyed trying many things. He taught himself to

play the bongo drums, and even did a stint of playing music at night on a live radio show. One night he even brought me along. I thought there were no limitations on what he could accomplish. I looked up to and admired him.

One time when I was in my early teens, at overnight summer camp, Adam and one of his friends took a trip on Adam's motorcycle to visit me. I don't remember if he came to visit me because I was homesick or to bring me something I needed, but I was happy that he had taken the time to see me.

When my parents moved from one town to another nearby, Adam helped our parents pack and move all our belongings to the new house. He was always the devoted and helpful son.

As the years passed, our father became verbally and physically abusive to Sandy and me. When mother called out to him to tell him that we had done something she was displeased about, he would chase us around the house with a leather strap. In later years, he would substitute a knife for the strap. Having two children in college and a new house to make mortgage payments on probably contributed to our parents' stress levels. Drinking alcohol would also cause the abuse to escalate. I would either run and hide beneath our camel back sofa or lock myself in the bathroom. He usually was worse around holidays, during which I would leave the dinner table and retreat to my bedroom. I also found comfort in my room reading the Old Testament. I spent as little time at home as possible by going to girlfriends' houses, where I felt more comfortable and less afraid.

I remember returning home from junior high after the school bus had dropped me off, getting into an argument with our father, and locking myself in the bathroom to avoid an altercation, sometimes for three hours at a time. This was a frequent occurrence. Things seemed to be getting increasingly worse.

One year, my brother and father set out to take a road trip to Florida by themselves. Adam was nineteen and our father was in his early sixties. They were to be gone for one week. They did not stay away for that long. Adam said dad "was acting crazy." Adam had to drive home from Florida, as our father was incapable of doing so.

A few days later, I was alone in the house with my father. My mother and Amy had gone out in the afternoon to do errands. Adam had not yet returned from prep school. I was in my room taking a nap. I awoke to the flash of red lights through my bedroom window. My father had gone into the basement and had drunk a caustic solution that was used to clean the chimney. The local fire department and Adam lifted the stretcher and carried him to the waiting ambulance. He was taken to the hospital, where he lingered, after being hooked up to various medical equipment. Mother, Adam, and Sandy visited him there. Amy and I did not. Shortly thereafter he died from the severe, irreversible damage he caused to his internal organs. Once again, none of us received counseling. My mother told us to tell anyone who asked that our father had colon cancer but he had actually died of a heart attack. She feared the stigma that was attached to mental illness and suicide at the time. Nobody was to know the longstanding abuse that had taken place in our house.

Adam would never talk specifically about what exactly happened on the trip. I don't know if our father told him he was contemplating suicide and Adam didn't believe him. Perhaps Father told him not to tell anyone and to give his solemn word that he would look after our mother and us. I have always been in a quandary about that. I guess that some things in life are meant to remain a mystery.

I recall Adam having a bout of mononucleosis. He was holed up at home regaining his strength for quite some time. Finally, when he had had enough, he escaped from home and took off with his motorcycle. I can remember Mother calling after him not to leave. She depended upon him so much, she didn't want anything to happen to him.

Adam dutifully took on the role of "father substitute." He

assisted Mother in whatever way she asked. When he was home from college, he became the "chief disciplinarian," patterning his behavior after that of our father, and stepping into his shoes whenever Mother was dissatisfied with my behavior. Once again I was the target of abuse. Sandy was attending college in another state at the time and thereby escaped. She later married and moved to another state. I think Adam had mixed emotions about what he did, but it was obvious that his allegiance was to our mother. I think that because he was the only "man in the house," that role was his expected obligation.

Adam won a traveling fellowship when he was in college. He would be gone for almost one year, during which time he wrote letters to our mother and sisters, and me. He contracted malaria and was cared for by a family he had met during his travels. When he wrote home, he was sweating so profusely that his letters had puddled areas where his sweat had fallen on the blue air-mail stationery. He never complained, recovered, and then continued with his journey in spite of his life-threatening illness. He was even robbed as he slept during his year abroad. He had more courage than I could ever imagine myself possessing. We missed him terribly while he was gone, and anxiously awaited correspondence from him. In retrospect, accepting the traveling fellowship may have been necessary for him to remove himself physically and emotionally from the constraints placed upon him as a helpmate for Mother and the only surviving male in our household. Perhaps for his own sanity he needed to regain his independence, if only temporarily, and recapture what was left of his carefree, youthful experiences.

While I was in high school, my mother and brother told me that I had the choice of going to college to become a nurse or a teacher (the profession my mother would have chosen for herself if she was able). I didn't particularly prefer either, as I had always had the desire to become a writer. In high school, I especially enjoyed reading and writing poetry. I acquiesced reluctantly, applied to several nursing schools not too far from home, and was accepted to a three-year program several towns away. I struggled while in school, but eventually graduated in the top third of my class.

I got married to Tim, had two children, Lana and Steven, worked at a state school, and was promoted to head nurse. Eventually, through a series of industrial accidents, I became permanently disabled and could no longer work as a nurse.

In the meantime, Adam graduated from college. He met a girl, Celia, with whom he fell in love, and they married. He moved to New York permanently. They bought a brownstone and had a son, Kenny, who is a year younger than our daughter. They were both artists, and worked for other employers, eventually branching off into their own individual businesses. Adam became an entrepreneur, designing, printing, and selling T-shirts. After a while, difficulties arose between them, and they divorced, sharing custody of Kenny. Although they had the usual difficulties inherent in most divorces, they decided to get along amicably for the emotional well being of their son. Adam purchased a loft, which remained his primary residence while he lived in New York.

Sandy's marriage was also going through some rough times. She had two children, Sarah and Ella. One was emotionally delayed and the other was severely retarded. She attended college in an attempt to get her bachelor's degree as, she had not previously finished college. She also gave elaborate dinner parties, cooking and freezing various and sundry delicacies in preparation for these various functions. Her husband, George, had been a confirmed bachelor and was more than a decade older than her. He was a doctor, involved with his practice, and a well-known member of the community, in which he had lived for his entire life. He worked many long hours and spent his spare time playing golf. He pretty much left the responsibilities of running the household to Sandy. The stress of everything, along with the many doctors' appointments she took the children to, eventually got the best of her, and she began to exhibit bizarre behavior.

At Mother's insistence, my husband and I and our eldest child, Lana, who was a baby at the time, took a plane trip out of state to investigate the reality of Sandy's situation. Sandy was undergoing a major depression at the time. She was barely able to care for herself and the two children. There was a mountain of dirty clothes in the basement that almost reached the ceiling. She had ripped up the wall-to-wall carpeting, and the tacks and wooden strips were still attached to the flooring, causing a potential danger to anyone who stepped on them. Her husband had pretty much deserted her and the two children, although he remained in the area at the time. She was having yard sales and selling her personal possessions to get money to buy food.

Upon my return home, after reporting to Mother what we had witnessed, at her insistence I wrote a scathing letter to my brother-in-law, mailing it to the hospital where he worked. Shortly thereafter, Sandy was admitted to a psychiatric facility and the children were in the care of their father in the house they had previously lived in with Sandy.

Shortly after Sandy was committed, her husband and three rabbis paraded into the hospital with papers for Sandy to sign. According to George, they were divorce papers. I question the legality of what she signed, and how and where she signed the documents. Later on, her ex-husband married a woman he met at his workplace, who was even younger than Sandy.

Her life from then on was a nightmare. Mother and Amy visited her when she was hospitalized. She was transferred from the initial hospital to a state facility in the state where she lived. Eventually she was transferred to a state hospital where we lived, so at least we could visit her more frequently. She even lived with Mother for awhile, but she was too difficult for Mother to manage. Then she moved to New York, as was agreed upon by Adam and Mother. Mother would visit Adam and stay in his loft for weeks on end, visiting him, his son, and Sandy. By this time, Amy was attending college and also living in New York. Years later, she would marry Mike and reside in New York.

Sandy was in and out of various psychiatric facilities in New York. She was eventually able to live with Adam in his loft. He made a bed for her out of plywood and four-by-four posts and placed a mattress on it. The burden of primary care-taker for Sandy was now Adam's responsibility. In addition, he had the responsibility of calling Mother frequently and making repairs and doing odds and ends at her house when he visited. He also had his business, his ex-wife, his son, his other two sisters, and many short-term relationships with women to contend with. In addition, he would assist other of my mother's relatives when they asked him, never declining. He seemed to have a neverending supply of strength. He never complained.

Adam had kept in close contact with several friends he had known while growing up. People always seemed to gravitate toward him. He was nonjudgmental and always willing to listen and offered his assistance whenever necessary. One of his close friends had gotten married, had had two children, and ended up in a messy divorce. This was a childhood friend of Adam's. The other children in the neighborhood disliked him and called him taxi-cab ears because his ears stuck out. He always kept in touch with Adam and was grateful to him. Adam offered his emotional support. He then remarried, did well in the stock market, and turned his life around. One day Adam got a phone call from him that he had gotten a diagnosis of cancer of the blood. He had a prognosis of six months. He was calling to ask if Adam would be one of his pallbearers. He said that it would mean a great deal to him. Adam told him he would. A few months following their conversation, he died. Adam was so upset, he couldn't bring himself to attend the funeral. He told me he felt badly about it but just couldn't go. Obviously the old wounds of losing Father had never entirely healed. He had difficulty dealing with death after having experienced our father's attempted suicide, hospitalization, and eventual death. Adam rarely expressed any emotions. Everything was obviously repressed for many years. Always the strong one, he was the one we all leaned on over the years.

Another of his friends called him frequently. He had also gone through a divorce. Whenever he wanted to talk to Adam or visit him, Adam obliged. A true friend in the literal sense of the word, he was always available for the needs of others.

Adam rarely took a vacation. Mostly he worked, and fulfilled his many responsibilities and obligations. I observed him printing T-shirts one day. He had a contraption on which he would place each individual T-shirt. He would print one with a silk screen, then rotate the machine and work on the next one and so on and so forth. If he was going to use a second screen on that batch of T-shirts, he would wait for the paint to dry, then repeat the process. He worked nonstop, almost robotically. Because he worked so fast one of the shirts was put on the machine crooked. I made him stop the process and straightened it out for him. He didn't say anything, but seemed to appreciate the gesture. Most likely, his customers wouldn't have noticed the slight irregularity. He couldn't have taken the time with each T-shirt to ensure that it was perfectly printed. Economics would not have allowed it. In all the years he silk-screened, that was the only time I ever watched him. He was his own boss, set his own work schedule, and had the freedom to conduct his business without anyone standing over his shoulder. Perhaps he needed that freedom, as other areas in his life had been so constrained and restricted.

Boxes of T-shirts were delivered to him by UPS. He ordered the sizes that experience had showed him would sell the best. He would print them and put the various T-shirts in large plastic covered containers by design. He had to carry the individual boxes up and down three flights of stairs. He could only load and unload the boxes into his van during certain hours, as there was no parking on the street where he worked. That meant he had to park elsewhere, walk in the early morning to retrieve his van, load it, drive to the open air market where he sold his wares, unload the containers, park his truck, walk to the market, and then reverse the process when it was time for him to return. Eventually, an elevator was installed, which made at least part of his job easier. In good weather, he was also able to display his colorful samples of T-shirts on horizontal clotheslines with clothespins behind the table in his area.

He often joked with the customers and sometimes even took photos of them for his albums. He also had pictures taken of him and other vendors. He seemed most carefree when he was selling at the market. Being outside, being his own boss, controlling his own destiny, supporting himself and his son, kibitzing with the people, people-watching, and taking photographs gave him obvious enjoyment. He hired other people to sell his wares for him as well. He made more money in the warm weather than he did the cold. One of the bad things about being in business for oneself is the fact that the paychecks vary. Adam had no health insurance, so he rarely went to see a physician or dentist. Adam had to brave the elements at the market. Sometimes he had to sit in the sweltering heat, at other times, he had to brave the cold. He had an oversized leather jacket with sheep fur lining, under which he layered various clothing so he would stay reasonably warm in the bad weather. It is beyond me how he could sit in the elements for hours on end with hardly any breaks, food, or something to drink. It wasn't an easy task. Occasionally, he would get someone to fill in for him so he could stretch his legs or relieve himself, or he would ask someone to buy him food or beverages. He had the same routine for years and years.

Sandy was a rapid cycler. Before she was eventually stabilized on the correct medications for her, at times she would disappear. Once she ran away to Florida with our grandfather's car, telling no one where she was headed. Panic would set in, and all my mother's relatives would be contacted to see if they had either seen her or heard from her. Eventually, she would turn up after she had scared us all half to death. Her medications were changed continually. Many times she had to be hospitalized because of either suicidal thoughts or manic episodes. Adam was always there for her, visiting with her, advocating for her, speaking with the medical professionals, and making himself available for Sandy when she was finally released. He always seemed to take these episodes in stride.

More than once, she developed Stevens-Johnson syndrome due to being prescribed or given an incorrect combination of medications. This is a life-threatening rash. Luckily, she survived.

One time when we had all rented a cottage in Cape Cod for a week during the summer, a police car drove down the street and stopped in front of the house with its red roof light flashing. The door opened and Sandy exited. We laughed 'til we cried. We never knew quite what to expect from Sandy. She had what in Yiddish is called "chutzpah," and could also be very entertaining. She seemed to be fearless and outgoing throughout her life. That's probably what has kept her going all these years.

Adam found a new girlfriend after his son was about twenty-five and had moved to a different part of the country for a job. Millie was a number of years younger than Adam, and from what she told him she had had a difficult life. Most of Adam's girlfriends had some sort of drama as part of their past. He most always seemed to be attracted to that type of woman. Adam's new girlfriend had her own apartment and took college classes and visited with friends during the day, while Adam was either printing T-shirts or at the market selling them. In the evening, they would meet and go out for dinner. They seemed to have an open relationship, and I believe she helped to partially fill the void that Adam felt when Kenny moved away. I think I only met her twice in the many years that they were involved in a relationship.

Our mother had had a couple of health problems. One was a fall and the other was surgery. Adam came to visit while she was in the hospital and stayed at her home for a week after she had the surgery. She had a drug reaction and was hallucinating while he was with her. Adam was really affected by it. It occurred in Dad's and her bedroom in the house where Dad had drunk the poison. He was panic-stricken and hysterical, telling Mother, "You're not going to die on me, too!" She improved, thankfully, and Amy and I also stayed with her during her recovery.

The years passed and we saw Adam less and less. We figured that he was busy working, and he had a girlfriend, so at least he was not alone. He continued to speak with us on the phone and seemed okay. By that time, Sandy was stabilized on medication and seemed to be making progress, despite the occasional hospitalization. Once again, Adam was there for her.

One day, Adam had been summoned to appear in court as a juror. As he was walking in the vicinity of the courthouse, he saw a man looking up at the sky. Adam approached him and said, "Excuse me, sir, what are you looking at?" The man looked at him with a worried expression and replied, "The World Trade Center's been hit." It was September 11, 2001.

At that moment, Adam became obsessed with purchasing a camera and with taking pictures of the newsworthy story. He went from store to store, finally finding one where he could purchase a camera that would enable him to document the horrific events of terrorism unfolding before his eyes. He began to snap pictures of the blackened smoke emitting from the building and clouding the skies. One of the pictures was of a man in a suit hanging from the ledge on the side of one of the buildings. Upon photographing that, Adam was violently sick, and knew he had to run for his life as fast as he could toward his home. That was before the second building was struck. The phones were down. Eventually we were able to contact Adam, Sandy, Amy, and Mike. Although they were all traumatized by what had happened; fortunately, they were all alive and we were extremely thankful for that. He later told me that people looked like feathers floating down from the buildings toward their ultimate death.

Several months afterwards, he developed a lung condition

that he believed was a result of what he inhaled on that fateful day. After that, he didn't seem to take photographs as he once did. That didn't seem important to him anymore. He didn't have the quick wit that was so much a part of his personality prior to 9-11. He grew more somber and sullen, but nothing that was particularly disconcerting. We thought it was the reaction most people had following the attacks. That experience altered his life. It is possible that he was suffering from post-traumatic stress disorder, as I'm sure many others did, and still do. Once again, he never received counseling.

Around this time, Adam became irritable. Mother mentioned that he would get upset with her. She was set in her ways and could be difficult to deal with at times, so I didn't think much of it. In one conversation she had with Adam's girlfriend Millie, after a brief trip Adam had made to visit her, Mother said, "I'm worried about Adam."

Once again, Mother didn't really substantiate her feelings or give examples proving why she felt that way. I attributed it to the fact that Adam was overworked and tired.

Over the past several years, my husband's brother had gotten seriously ill. He didn't believe in preventive medicine. He had congestive heart failure, was diabetic, and broke his leg in a fall, after which he was unconscious for about two days. He was examined, treated, and it was eventually discovered that he had a tumor on his kidney, which eventually had to be removed. He was transferred from one hospital to another and then to a rehabilitation center. We made trips to two different states to spend as much time with him as possible. In the middle of this, Adam called and said, "I need to ask you something."

Without even asking him what it was, I started telling him about my brother-in-law and what we were going through with him at the time. Adam's response to me after a short pause was, "Sounds like you have enough on your plate right now." That's all he said.

As time went on, I often talked to Adam on the phone. He

told me then that he owed fifteen thousand dollars in legal expenses. He was not going to be able to print and sell T-shirts at the outdoor market because the space was valuable and they were going to put a high-rise there instead. He never told me what the lawsuit was about. When I offered to give him the money, he hesitated, thought it over, and said no. He said he would be out of work soon and nobody would hire him, as he felt he had no skills and would be undesirable as an employee.

I spent countless hours with him on the phone. The conversations were pretty much all the same. He would tell me that no one would hire him at sixty years old. I responded by saying there were programs available to retrain people for new jobs. He said he was going to be homeless and living on the streets. He said he didn't want to end up in a state hospital as Sandy had done many times. Adam also didn't want to spend the little bit of money that he had left. He was petrified he would be locked up in a state hospital. He was beginning to become anxious, paranoid, and delusional. He also told me he had lost weight and his appetite was down. I asked him the three things psychiatrists always ask: how are your sleep patterns; how has your mood been; and how is your appetite. Obviously he badly needed some psychiatric intervention. He had similar conversations with Kenny, Amy, Tim, Mike, and Celia, as well as one of his childhood friends. Everyone tried to console him, offer suggestions, and listen to what he had to say, to no avail. This continued for about a year. His ex-wife Celia and his girlfriend Millie had even begun helping him fill out the paperwork to see if he was eligible for Social Security Disability. He had seen too much of the mental health consortium in New York. He also said he hadn't slept in four months and was so tired he couldn't even get out of bed. He basically stayed in his darkened loft all day and night and didn't go out. I found out later he ate chocolate and drank caffeinated soft drinks and hardly ate anything. No wonder he was unable to sleep. Previously, he had been health-conscious. His diet was so totally wrong for a person who couldn't sleep and he would have been well aware of that if he had had all his faculties at the time.

He asked if he could come to live with me so I could "observe" him. Somehow I didn't like his choice of words, and I became alarmed. I asked him on many occasions to take the bus to visit us, and told him that we would pick him up at the bus stop. I told him he could stay for a couple of weeks to see if he liked it here. Several times we expected him and he didn't show up. He didn't have the strength to make the trip. Sometimes I would talk to him on the phone and he would want to end the calls abruptly; this was so out of character for him. I encouraged him to go to a doctor and at least get a prescription to help him sleep. Finally he went with his girlfriend. Clonazepam was prescribed. It was a thirty-day script. Adam told me he was taking it more often than he was supposed to and he was running out of it. I explained that it was highly addictive if not taken as prescribed. Once he called me, after I had already spoken with him a short time earlier, to ask if I had just called. I told him no. This was not the Adam we all knew and loved. He rapidly seemed to be slipping away from us.

After some research, I called Adam and told him to go to the doctor and have a series of preliminary tests done, including getting his thyroid checked, as mother, her sister, my cousin, and I all have hypothyroidism and have to take medication for the condition. He eventually went and was told that his thyroid was practically non-functioning. He was given a prescription and was taking it, but did not want to take it every day. I told him that if he wanted to feel better, it was necessary for him to take it daily. I even read him the paperwork that came from the manufacturer. Unfortunately, the initial strength prescribed was less than the correct dosage, which made his recovery even slower.

He eventually saw no way out for himself other than attempting suicide. Fortunately, his girlfriend had the wherewithal to call an ambulance so he could immediately get to the local hospital. He was admitted to their psychiatric unit

for thirty days which is all his insurance (which Kenny had finally talked him into getting) would allow. He did not want to
ever be admitted to a psychiatric ward, but he had no choice.
He felt that once he was locked up, he would never be released. That was the first time he had ever been admitted to a
hospital in his sixty years of life.

His girlfriend called to tell me what had happened. Amy
was away with Mike at the time. I think that was the first time
I ever spoke to Millie in all the years (about ten) that they had
been a couple. She gave me the phone number so I could call
Adam. I told him that Tim and I were coming to visit him as
soon as we could. He kept the conversation brief, and said
goodbye.

We took a cab to the hospital, went to the desk and got
passes before we were allowed to visit Adam. We took the elevator to the floor he was on and told one of the employees
who we were and who we wanted to visit. A few minutes later,
we saw Adam. We were shocked by what we saw. His brown
hair was long, his eyes were sunken, and he had dark semi-
circles under his eyes. His color was pale. He was wearing
long-sleeved cotton pajamas. His face was expressionless. We
hugged him and tried to maintain poker faces so he would not
know what we were thinking. After we hugged him, we sat
down at a table in a room that had two doors. The door closest to us was ajar and a mental health staff member was sitting
on a bench outside the room to the left side of the door.

Adam kept looking around the room as he spoke. His voice
was soft and he told me they were watching and listening to
everything he did and said. I tried to reassure him that that was
their job and was what they were supposed to be doing. We
talked for a while. He was apologetic that his attempt at suicide
was unsuccessful. He felt that along with everything else, he
had failed at that as well. I tried once more to reason with him
that he could start over. He said they had done some psychological testing on him, which he did not like. He said they
would retest him once more before they released him. They

also took blood from him. He said that Millie and he were having problems and he was considering breaking up with her. I told him this wasn't the time to make hasty decisions—that he should first concentrate on getting well. I recommended that he be honest with his psychiatrist and the people who were caring for him, because they had heard it all before, and would know when he wasn't telling the truth. I also told him that it would be helpful for him to participate in group therapy. People would talk about their problems, as would he, and everyone could offer suggestions to one another. He said some of the medications weren't working for him. At one point, he thought he was having a heart attack. When he explained his symptoms, I suggested that it may have been a panic attack. He also told me he suffered a major lapse of his memory, remembering only Millie's face, not her name. He was so frightened by those two experiences. He was sleeping slightly better and was getting his appetite back but was still depressed and sounding hopeless about his future.

During one of the visits, his doctor came over to his table and introduced himself. Adam left the table to speak with him and returned about ten minutes later. I asked him if I could set up a meeting with his doctor and social worker while I was there. He said, "That's not the way it's done here."

Apparently, to meet with the staff, I would have to make an appointment weeks in advance. I met the social worker, but other than introducing herself she had no time for me.

Adam told me that one of the mental health workers had told him that attempting suicide was a crime against the state. Perhaps he thought he was going to have to go to prison for attempting suicide. What sadistic mental health worker would say that untrue and threatening thing to my sick, sleep-deprived, anxious, panic-stricken brother, whose thyroid had not been functioning in months and who had never been in the hospital before? Obviously, someone who has no empathy, or likes to prey on vulnerable people.

I would like to meet with that inhumane person and tell

him or her that no one is immune from mental illness, and that they should seek a different line of employment. I told Adam that the state has a lot of other people they would rather put in prison.

I remember that during my hospitalizations, my family was allowed to speak with my psychiatrist. Adam and Sandy even came to visit me while I was there. The atmosphere was much different where Adam was. I thought that interactions between the patient, family, and the staff would have been conducive to the well-being and recovery of the patient, but I felt unwelcome.

Adam attended groups, played ping-pong, met with his psychiatrist (who was a student), and slept a little better some nights but not others.

After staying a week and visiting Adam every day, we had to return home. I told him he could live with Tim and me, and that we had plenty of things that he could help us with at our house. There was gardening that needed to be done, and we could make birdhouses and set them up in the yard. He could sit in the backyard and listen to the babbling brook. I told him he would like it there out in the country with the trees, birds, and flowers. It was spring at the time. He said, "Don't talk to me about birds and trees and flowers."

I knew then that he was determined to kill himself and that he had given up all hope.

He thanked me for making that "special trip." He remained in the hospital for another three weeks. At first he was somewhat optimistic because he was told while he was in the hospital that they would help him re-train for a different job or learn new skills. That never materialized. Once again he became despondent. There was no day program for him. The psychiatrist he had seen on an outpatient basis was retiring. That meant he probably would have to re-explain his past history, which he had previously repressed for so long. Everything he had shut himself off from emotionally was being dredged up. It was almost like the floodgates had been opened, and no amount of sandbags could slow the force of the unrestrained water.

Each time he talked about his past he probably remembered more, which to him might have been a double-edged sword. I think that may have been the final blow. He would be starting over with a new psychiatrist, and there was the question of what his insurance would cover. The monthly premiums were too high for him to continue paying, because he was not working and his money supply was dwindling.

One day after he returned from the psychiatrist's office, he went into his loft by himself for the final time. When he was alone, he succeeded in taking his life, and was found a short time later.

We were all distraught over the loss of Adam. We wondered how we had let this happen, what we could have done differently, how we could have learned something from the deaths of our father and uncle so we could have stopped the cycle of suicide in our family. We wondered if we had read the signals he was sending to each of us individually and had put them together sooner, if he had received counseling after our father's death, if he had learned to say "no" more often, if he had asked for help from us earlier; then perhaps things would have been different.

I feel that more and better options should have been made available to him, as a third-generation tax-paying American who deserved to be treated with dignity and respect. He more than paid his dues to society. He worked hard all of his life and asked for very little. He was compassionate and unselfish. He was never incarcerated for anything. I don't think he ever got so much as a speeding citation. When he needed help the most, the door was slammed in his face. All he wanted to do was to have a job and be a contributing member of society.

What can Americans do to prevent this tragedy from occurring again and again? Why do we prevent the mentally ill from receiving the assistance they so deserve, too little, too late? Where is the conscience of America? Whatever happened to "life, liberty, and the pursuit of happiness"? Is that merely a dream, not reality? Why aren't small businesspeople able to purchase less costly health insurance? Why can't the mentally ill receive longer and more individualized inpatient care, day programs, better nutritional programs, and vocational retraining, if necessary? Why is there a time limit on the treatment of the mentally ill? I believe these are discriminatory practices. Are we less deserving because we are mentally ill? I think not.

An Epilogue

John Laue

I am a widely published writer. Although I have won awards for my work in both poetry and prose most of my writings which honestly set forth experiences as a mentally ill person have been and are consistently rejected. I believe this is not the result of the manuscripts' quality but because I write about subjects which are beyond "normal" experiences. Yet some of these writings have value and perhaps wisdom that can be found nowhere else, especially for others who are suffering.

A few years ago there used to be a magazine of the California Alliance for the Mentally Ill, *The Journal,* which published some of my own and others' autobiographical prose and poetry, but the funding was cut and it went out of business, apparently because the opinions expressed were deemed too controversial. That magazine was the closest medium I know of to provide an appropriate and relatively unbiased outlet for our works.

As of this writing there is one woman, Psychology Professor Gail A. Hornstein, a teacher at Mount Holyoke College, who seems to be the only academic in this country to study writings about mental illness by people who have experienced it. She maintains lists of first person accounts, but I believe that not to be her main subject of concern. She is the only professor I know about who bothers with our literature unless it's written by someone already famous.

Two or three literary magazines state they are interested in, and in one case, restricted to mentally ill writers (this is out of thousands of literary journals). There are also one or two others that concentrate on disabilities of all kinds; however, outlets for our type of writing are few and far between. To remedy the problem I propose we find a way to fund a full-time chair in our literature at a U.S. university.

The chosen faculty member, who would be shared by language arts and psychology departments, would collect, study, catalogue and perhaps edit and publish writings by mentally ill authors and other writings related to that topic. In poetry, for instance, the span would be from authors like Sylvia Plath and Anne Sexton to unknown and hitherto unpublished poets. It might also take in some of the writings of psychiatrists and other authorities on the subject.

Is there enough material to justify a full-time professorship? I would suggest that there is much more than you, the reader, might be aware of. At any one time the mentally ill and their families comprise up to twenty percent of our population. A significant proportion of these people do write about their experiences. In my own limited circle and those of others I know there are people who write copiously in journals and compose reams of poetry.

You might think that if writings show any literary merit at all they would be published anyway. However, the stigma that surrounds us and our products implies that what we have to say is irrelevant and valueless to ordinary citizens. No one would deny that there should be specialists in works by minority authors; Asian-American Literature, Chicano Literature; Black Literature all exist as separate entities. We too, consumers and survivors alike, are a distinct minority group although most of us cannot be identified by outward characteristics.

A chair in *The Literature of Madness* would reduce stigma by legitimizing and "normalizing" the field; expand people's consciousness about mental health problems; aid in the training of those who work with the mentally ill and in discovering methods of healing; have a therapeutic effect on the writers by giving them a voice, perhaps reducing the suicide rate; possibly even reduce violence committed by "disturbed" people, e.g. what if Ted Kaczynski had been able to publish some of his diatribes without doing what he did to get the world's attention?

I believe people who become mentally ill are functioning like the proverbial canaries in coal mines. If we are to be a truly compassionate culture, more needs to be said and written about these illnesses which are life-changing for affected individuals and indications of the relative health of the larger society. The material is already there and waiting for us. All that we lack are appropriate funding and attention.

ORDER FORM

To order by fax, complete and fax form to 616-863-9515.

To order by telephone, call 616-863-6522.

To order online, go to outsiderpress.org and submit online order form.

To order by mail, complete this form with your check made out to Outsider Press in the amount of $28.95 plus U.S. $3.00 for shipping for the first book and $1.00 for each additional book and mail to Outsider Press, 400 E. Division, Ste #6, PMB 202, Rockford, MI 49341.

Please send _____ copies of *Different People, Different Voices* to:

Name: _____

Address: _____

City: _____ State: _____ Zip _____

Telephone: _____

Email address: _____

ORDER FORM

To order by fax, complete and fax form to 616-863-9515.

To order by telephone, call 616-863-6522.

To order online, go to outsiderpress.org and submit online order form.

To order by mail, complete this form with your check made out to Outsider Press in the amount of $28.95 plus U.S. $3.00 for shipping for the first book and $1.00 for each additional book and mail to Outsider Press, 400 E. Division, Ste #6, PMB 202, Rockford, MI 49341.

Please send _____ copies of *Different People, Different Voices* to:

Name: _____

Address: _____

City: _____ State: _____ Zip _____

Telephone: _____

Email address: _____

ORDER FORM

To order by fax, complete and fax form to 616-863-9515.

To order by telephone, call 616-863-6522.

To order online, go to outsiderpress.org and submit online order form.

To order by mail, complete this form with your check made out to Outsider Press in the amount of $28.95 plus U.S. $3.00 for shipping for the first book and $1.00 for each additional book and mail to Outsider Press, 400 E. Division, Ste #6, PMB 202, Rockford, MI 49341.

Please send _____ copies of *Different People, Different Voices* to:

Name: _____

Address: _____

City: _____ State: _____ Zip _____

Telephone: _____

Email address: _____